Get Your
Published
Katherine Lapworth

For UK order enquiries: please contact Bookpoint Ltd,
130 Milton Park, Abingdon, Oxon OX14 4SB.
Telephone: +44 (0) 1235 827720. Fax: +44 (0) 1235 400454.
Lines are open 09.00–17.00, Monday to Saturday, with a 24-hour
message answering service. Details about our titles and how to
order are available at www.teachyourself.com

For USA order enquiries: please contact McGraw-Hill Customer
Services, PO Box 545, Blacklick, OH 43004-0545, USA.
Telephone: 1-800-722-4726. Fax: 1-614-755-5645.

For Canada order enquiries: please contact McGraw-Hill
Ryerson Ltd, 300 Water St, Whitby, Ontario L1N 9B6, Canada.
Telephone: 905 430 5000. Fax: 905 430 5020.

Long renowned as the authoritative source for self-guided
learning – with more than 50 million copies sold worldwide –
the **Teach Yourself** series includes over 500 titles in the fields of
languages, crafts, hobbies, business, computing and education.

British Library Cataloguing in Publication Data: a catalogue record
for this title is available from the British Library.

Library of Congress Catalog Card Number: on file.

First published in UK 2010 by Hodder Education, part of
Hachette UK, 338 Euston Road, London NW1 3BH.

First published in US 2010 by The McGraw-Hill Companies, Inc.

This edition published 2010.

The **Teach Yourself** name is a registered trade mark of
Hodder Headline.

Copyright © 2010 Katherine Lapworth

In UK: All rights reserved. Apart from any permitted use under UK
copyright law, no part of this publication may be reproduced or
transmitted in any form or by any means, electronic or mechanical,
including photocopy, recording, or any information, storage and
retrieval system, without permission in writing from the publisher
or under licence from the Copyright Licensing Agency Limited.
Further details of such licences (for reprographic reproduction)
may be obtained from the Copyright Licensing Agency Limited,
of Saffron House, 6–10 Kirby Street, London EC1N 8TS.

In US: All rights reserved. Except as permitted under the United States
Copyright Act of 1976, no part of this publication may be reproduced
or distributed in any form or by any means, or stored in a database or
retrieval system, without the prior written permission of the publisher.

Typeset by MPS Limited, A Macmillan Company.

Printed in Great Britain for Hodder Education, an Hachette UK
Company, 338 Euston Road, London NW1 3BH, by CPI Group
(UK) Ltd, Croydon, CR0 4YY.

The publisher has used its best endeavours to ensure that the URLs
for external websites referred to in this book are correct and active
at the time of going to press. However, the publisher and the
author have no responsibility for the websites and can make no
guarantee that a site will remain live or that the content will remain
relevant, decent or appropriate.

Hachette UK's policy is to use papers that are natural, renewable
and recyclable products and made from wood grown in sustainable
forests. The logging and manufacturing processes are expected to
conform to the environmental regulations of the country of origin.

Impression number	10 9 8 7 6 5 4 3
Year	2014 2013 2012

Acknowledgements

There is a long tradition of authors thanking their agents and editors at the start of their latest work and this is no exception. The thanks, on this occasion, go to Victoria Roddam, my editor and publisher of the **Teach Yourself** lifestyle series of books.

A good editor is a great judge not only of the merits of a book but of character as well and able to dispense praise and criticism in just the right amounts to the individual writer to be effective. If I have been 'managed' at all, it never felt like it. Victoria has guided me and this book with a calm, efficient and extremely pleasant hand. I thank her for that and for having faith in me to write it in the first place.

Image credits

Front cover: © Vladimir Melnikov – Fotolia.com

Back cover: © Jakub Semeniuk/iStockphoto.com, © Royalty-Free/Corbis, © agencyby/iStockphoto.com, © Andy Cook/iStockphoto.com, © Christopher Ewing/iStockphoto.com, © zebicho – Fotolia.com, © Geoffrey Holman/iStockphoto.com, © Photodisc/Getty Images, © James C. Pruitt/iStockphoto.com, © Mohamed Saber – Fotolia.com

Contents

	Meet the author	ix
	Only got a minute?	x
	Only got five minutes?	xii
	Only got ten minutes?	xiv
1	**The publishing world**	**1**
	How it is set up	1
	Agent or publisher?	4
	Learn about the market	16
	Large versus small	22
	Timing	24
2	**What are they looking for?**	**31**
	What makes a publisher publish a book?	32
	Who to approach	33
	What to send	35
3	**Persistence**	**59**
	Be prepared for rejection	61
	Know your craft	66
	Being your own editor	67
	Networking	68
	Feedback	69
	Literary consultants	71
	The first meeting with the agent	74
	The first contact with the editor	77
	Accepting a publishing house	78
4	**Legalities and practicalities**	**87**
	Rights	88
	Contracts	92
	Other legalities	100
	Other practicalities	108
5	**In production**	**115**
	Preparing your manuscript	117
	Meeting deadlines	118

	What happens when the manuscript arrives at the publishing house?	119
	What happens if your editor moves on	129
6	**Self-publishing**	**136**
	Being self-published	139
	Being a publisher	143
	Vanity publishing	157
	Print on demand (POD)	158
	Marketing and promotion	161
	Other information	163
7	**Ebooks and epublishing**	**170**
	Epublishers	174
	Self-epublishing	176
	Digital Rights Management (DRM)	178
	Pricing	179
8	**Promotion and publicity**	**182**
	Publishing house marketing department	184
	Publishing house publicity department	185
	What makes you interesting?	186
	Promotional material	187
	Publicity in the media	189
	Publicity in bookshops	204
	Literary festivals	208
	Giving readings and talks	210
9	**Selling the book**	**220**
	Sales	223
	The price of a book – where the money goes	226
	Timing	227
	Getting your book stocked in a bookshop chain or supermarket	228
	Getting your book stocked in an independent bookshop	230
	Distribution and wholesalers	232
	Selling to libraries	240
	Selling online	240
	Independent Publishers Guild (UK)	242
	Left-over books	243

10 Being a writer	**252**
Income and expenditure records	254
Royalty statements	255
ALCS (UK)/Authors Registry (US)	256
Writers' unions	257
Be versatile	258
Discipline	258
Writer's block	259
Tools of the trade	260
Support network	261
Age	262
Conclusion	263
Appendix	**268**
Index	**285**

Meet the author

The number of people who claim to 'have a book in them' runs to hundreds of thousands; the people who actually do something about it and produce a book – considerably fewer. If you are reading this, it is because you have written or are writing something that you feel is worth getting published. That is the first successful step to publishing your book.

The second step is to start thinking like a publisher rather than a writer. Publishing is a curious mix of creativity, literary appreciation and hard-nosed financial decisions. Books that people want to buy tend to get published. You need to look at your work in the same way an editor or literary agent would: is there a market for it and will people buy it in sufficient quantities to cover the costs of getting it into print?

Whether you are writing what you hope will be a blockbuster novel or you want to see your poetry or memoirs in print so that your friends and family can have your books on their shelves, there are some definitive do's and don'ts to observe on the road to being published.

Along with practical information and guidance, this book features insider advice from literary agents and publishers and talks to writers who have successfully been published themselves – everything that you need to know to see your book in print.

Katherine Lapworth

1 *Only got a minute?*

A budding author should make sure that their work, whether fiction or non-fiction, is in the best possible shape before they send it out to literary agents or publishers in the hope of getting it published. Learning to be your own editor is as important as being a good writer.

When you are ready, take the time to target your work effectively. There are still a large number of aspiring authors sending their submissions to the wrong people.

If you write fiction, you will need to be represented by an agent; very few publishing houses take on unsolicited fiction work. Whether approaching an agent or a publishing house, follow their submission guidelines *to the letter*. They do not all want the same and one-size submissions do not fit all.

Submissions generally consist of a covering letter, a brief synopsis of the book, a few sample chapters and a description of where the book would sit in the marketplace. Agents and publishers want to see not only a great idea and good writing but also someone who is serious about the craft of writing and committed to working at that craft and producing more work. Alternatively, you can bypass the agents and publishers and self-publish your own book.

If the author drives their own marketing and promotion, the publicity can be as effective as – if not more effective than – a publisher's publicity. Shy authors do not sell as many books.

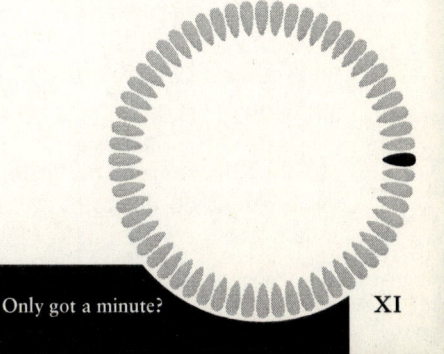

5 Only got five minutes?

There are several useful resources to help aspiring authors: the *Writers' & Artists' Yearbook* and the *Writer's Handbook* in the UK and *Writer's Market* in the US are published annually. These give information on publishers and agents, their contact details and favoured genres.

Draw up a shortlist of suitable agents and/or publishing houses. Include a mix of large and small agencies – and don't necessarily base it on just the big names. Younger agencies are often incredibly driven and hard-working; a newer agent may be just starting to build a list and be more open to new clients.

Go to the website of each company to double check contact details and submission guidelines. Avoid sending submissions around Christmas and book fairs when the slush pile – unsolicited submissions sent in by aspiring authors – has the lowest priority.

Once you have written, rewritten and polished your work, put it in an envelope and start thinking about it as a product, not a work of art. Send out several submissions at a time, otherwise you may have a long wait.

A submission represents you. It needs to be set out neatly and clearly with accurate spelling, grammar and punctuation. Submission requirements will vary from company to company. In general, they will consist of a covering letter, the first few chapters and a synopsis.

Your covering letter is effectively page one of your submission and should include:

- ▶ the title, subject and angle you will take
- ▶ a rough word count

- why people will want to read the book
- why you are the right person to write it: do you have the relevant background, qualifications or experience?
- whether it is the first in a series
- whether the subject matter is topical.

Remember that writing comes with a price – rejection. *Every* writer gets rejected at some point. Rejections are not pleasant but they will not kill you and you can learn from them.

When you do find an agent, you will sign an agreement. Some agents will offer editorial feedback – work with them. They will then submit your work to a commissioning editor at a publishing house. Agents know what individual editors are looking for; they can target your submission effectively.

Another way to get published is to do it yourself. In the past, self-publishing was seen as a last attempt for authors who could not get published, but that has changed and publishers and retailers – and the book-buying public – take self-publishing more seriously now.

Promoting your book is another important part of being an author. Shy authors do not sell as many books. The reward is that the more you promote your book, the more copies you will sell.

Writing is a solitary process; getting your manuscript accepted demands persistence; promoting your book is crucial – you have to be able to sell it. Someone said writing was a quiet business but promoting was a loud business.

You are a writer because you write, not because you have been published. Write for yourself first and foremost; write because you have to. Only when you do that, can you think about getting your book published.

10 Only got ten minutes?

Over 200,000 new titles are published each year in the US (that is 4,000 new books a week). The UK produces over 100,000 new titles a year. Those numbers would suggest that it is easy to get your book published. Sadly, they are a fraction of the books that their authors hoped would be published. To help your chances of getting your book into print, you need to study the publishing world and you need to think like an agent or editor.

Publishers are the link between the writer and the reader. A publishing house relies on its editors to keep a constant flow of publishable books coming in. Editors are under pressure to acquire titles that will be successful, bringing profit to the company. A lot of people have to be convinced of a book's suitability for a publishing house. But it is not just about finding and promoting new authors. Remember, too, that agents and publishing houses have existing authors whom they already know and represent. They will not just drop an existing author in order to take on somebody new. A new author is a high risk for a publisher.

Literary or authors' agents earn money only when their clients do; in other words, when they sell a book or rights to a publishing house. That means that they will take on only those authors who they feel are marketable. Agents put in a lot of unpaid time and effort on behalf of their clients – they need to feel confident that all that work is worthwhile. In *Get Started in Creative Writing*, Stephen May said that having a good agent was like having a native guide through hostile territory. They know the editors in the various publishing houses; they know what they are looking for, where the gaps in the lists are and whether they are looking to expand their list, move into new genres and so on.

A good writer is a good reader. Read widely so you know your market. Look at different categories, series, genres and publishers' imprints. Do you know what genre your work belongs to? The best way to categorize what you are writing is to think where it would be put if it were being sold in a bookshop. If you struggle to find the right shelf, imagine how difficult it would be for an agent/publisher to sell it.

An eye-catching title is a major part of a book's success. People spend around eight seconds looking at the cover of a book before they make a decision whether to buy it or not. If you are lucky, they might spend 12 seconds reading through the blurb and the opening page.

The aim of your submission is to give the key idea of your book. To do this, think of the 30-second rule. Sales reps have, at most, 30 seconds to sell a book into the shops. Having a constraint in your writing can force your creativity. Try to encapsulate your book in one or two sentences.

Submission guidelines will vary slightly from company to company. In general, they will consist of a covering letter, the first few chapters and a synopsis.

Your covering letter should give a sense of who you are, what genre you are aiming at and a brief pitch for your book. Nowadays, the writer is very much part of the package of a published book so you do need to give a sense of yourself in the letter.

Writing a synopsis is a skill that can be learned. If you are writing fiction, have a look at the *Oxford Companion to Literature* where you will find summaries of well-known works. Make writing a synopsis a positive experience. Show that you really know your work. Use it as an opportunity to go back, study what you have written and improve it if necessary.

You need to present a good argument that your book will sell. Give agents and, therefore, editors all the information they need to make a positive decision. Who is going to buy this book and why? You will have mentioned this briefly in your covering letter; now you need to expand on this.

The opening chapters will show the quality of your writing. The reader, in this instance the agent or the publisher, will want the interest that they felt on reading your covering letter and synopsis to be underlined in these chapters.

On average, the wait for a response from an agent is around two to three months; some companies will take longer. Don't expect to be given reasons for rejection. If there are any compliments (or criticisms) about your work, take them at face value and as a good sign. Good writers of great books get rejected – many times. Even when they are published, they will get their fair share of bad reviews. Rejection goes hand in hand with success.

A literary consultant will assess and give feedback on a writer's manuscript for a fee. There is a range of literary consultancies in the UK. Choose yours carefully. Literary consultancies should, like an agent, be there to help you make money (i.e. sell your work) rather than just take your money. Writers' forums, word of mouth and agent referrals are a good way of finding a good literary consultancy.

When your agent is happy with the manuscript, they will submit your work to a commissioning editor at a publishing house. If the book is accepted, the publisher will make an offer directly to the author or via their agent. If that offer is accepted, a contract will be issued and a deadline for delivery of manuscript will be set. Publishers always want the manuscript as soon as possible; authors always want more time than they get.

If there is something you do not understand, just ask. The intention is not to confuse you or hide things but a contract is a legal document and the language is not always the easiest to understand. A good editor will explain the details.

Once a contract is signed with a publishing house, the editor will be working backwards from a proposed publishing date. Keep your editor informed of how you are progressing. If you look like you will be late, let your editor know *as soon as possible* in order to avoid serious repercussions.

Self-publishing can seem an attractive alternative for authors. But you should be aware that selling goes hand in hand with marketing and publicity. If you don't like the thought of marketing and selling your own book, then self-publishing is probably not for you.

Whichever route you decide to take, remember that publishing houses will not be buying the kinds of book that are currently in the bestseller lists; they will be looking for something different. You have to be original and write from your heart.

Nigel Watts, author of *Write a Novel And Get it Published*, talks about the importance of writing for love, not money: 'If your first goal is to be published, such ambition will likely taint what you are writing and, ironically, reduce your chances of a sale.'

Mastering the techniques of the craft and improving their writing talent should be the goals of every writer. To see your book in print will require hard work, determination, perseverance and a dose of good luck. The only sensible thing you can do is to write because you love writing. Write the kind of book you would pay good money to read.

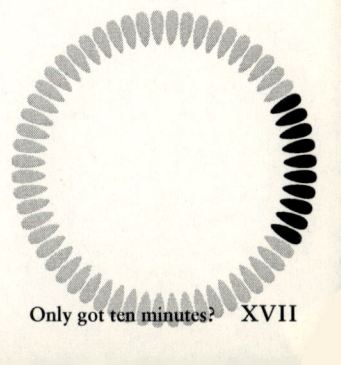

1

The publishing world

In this chapter you will learn about:
- *the publishing industry*
- *publishing houses and their imprints*
- *what they are looking for*
- *the pros and cons of large organizations versus small.*

Jules Renard, a French novelist and playwright, said, 'Writing is the only profession where no one considers you ridiculous if you earn no money.' That may be true of the act of writing but getting published is quite different. Then it becomes a matter of business.

Literary agents, editors and publishing houses do not exist to make writers feel good about themselves; they are there to make money – for themselves and the author. Of course, they love books in all their forms and they are always on the look-out for something exceptional but they cannot do this for love alone. And that is what you have to bear in mind, whether you are trying to get your manuscript accepted by an agent or publishing house or whether you have decided to self-publish. You have to stop thinking like a writer and start thinking like a publisher and, to do that, you need to understand the publishing world.

How it is set up

> *When I first came into publishing, it was a fairly gentlemanly profession. The agents were even more gentlemanly than*

> *the publishers. It was all about nurturing writing talent and sticking with authors over a long period of time; much less about getting them large amounts of money for their books and making sure that the marketing of the book was done properly. It's much more businesslike now.*
>
> Sue Fletcher, publisher, Hodder & Stoughton
> www.hodder.co.uk

Many of the famous imprints were founded in the nineteenth and early twentieth centuries: Andrew Chatto and W. E. Windus were business partners who published, among others, Mark Twain, Wilkie Collins and Aldous Huxley. Publishing houses were privately owned, usually by the family whose name was over the door. Editors decided what books to publish and worked with authors to that end.

In the 1960s and 1970s, literary agents came on the scene, representing authors and dealing with publishing houses on their behalf. As the 1970s turned into the 1980s, the family-run firms were being acquired by publishing and media businesses.

As bookshop chains expanded, the importance of publicity grew and a close relationship developed between the publishing industry and retailers. The importance of sales really began to influence which books were being published; now discussions at a publisher's acquisition meeting not only look at the relative artistic merits of a book but also focus on how well that book might do after publication. The world of the publisher is one driven by the marketplace.

Publishing houses are now made up of one or several imprints. Imprints are brands, the trade names under which books are published. Hodder & Stoughton have several imprints including Hodder Education (who publish the *Teach Yourself* series), Sceptre (literary fiction) and Saltyard Books (cookery, gardening, crafts,). Random House is made up of nearly 30 imprints, Lace, Chatto & Windus, Ebury Press, Fodor, Heinemann, Yellow Jersey and so on. Each imprint style and specialize in certain genres.

Following mergers and acquisitions, many of the imprints are now owned by four major multinationals in the UK:

Hachette Livre (Hodder Headline, Orion, Octopus, Watts, Chambers-Harrap, Time Warner, which includes Little, Brown) Bertelsmann (Random House, Transworld, BBC Books) Pearson (Penguin group) News Corporation (HarperCollins)

As well as the big four, there are major publishing houses such as Macmillan (owned by the German company Holtzbrinck Group), Oxford University Press, Quarto and Simon & Schuster (a division of the CBS Corporation).

> *You can't really publish by committee and therefore the federal construction of big groups, with individual imprints and individual editors with their own individual tastes, is essential because you need that variety and eclecticism to translate into a variety of published works. The big groups offer various economies of scale on things like paper buying, printing and warehousing – all the back office functions. But the creative functions still have to be managed in microcosm.*
>
> Sue Fletcher, publisher, Hodder & Stoughton
> www.hodder.co.uk

Despite the large groups, agents will still submit proposals to editors of particular imprints, rather than the larger group. That means that, when it comes to acquiring books, some imprints within a group may be in direct competition with each other.

The biggest domestic market for books is the US (well over 200,000 new titles are published a year; that is 4,000 new books coming out each week), followed by Germany, Japan, China and the UK. The UK produces over 100,000 new titles a year, well ahead of Russia, France, Italy and Spain.

Statistics like 200,000 titles in the US and 100,000 in the UK seem to suggest that getting a book published is quite easy. Sadly, the numbers that are being published are a fraction of the books that their authors hoped would get into print.

FRONT AND BACKLISTS

In publishing, you will hear references to 'backlist' and 'frontlist'. These are the lists of books that a particular publishing house or imprint produces.

> ▶ **Backlist** – *a publishing house's long-lasting titles which sell at a steady rate and therefore keep revenue coming in. A strong backlist is the backbone of many publishing houses.*
> ▶ **Frontlist** – *new books. Most of the publisher's marketing and promotion will go on frontlist books. Many books have a relatively short shelf life. Peak sales of most books occur in the first year of publication, often within the first three or four months. Some publishers have a greater reliance on their frontlist (for example, publishers who deal in TV tie-in books), while others rely on their backlist, constantly revising editions (as the* Teach Yourself *series does), rebranding or redesigning covers and so on.*

Did you know?
Almost ten per cent of Britons aspire to being an author, followed by sports personality, pilot, astronaut and event organizer on a list of most coveted jobs. (*The Guardian*, 21 August 2007)

Agent or publisher?

I'm sure the publishing industry is filled with absolutely lovely people who, if they had all the time in the world, would love to sit down with every aspiring author, go through their book and help them turn it into what they really want it to be. But these guys have hundreds of thousands of manuscripts to go through, so you should be grateful for any speck of kindness you receive from them.

Bryony Pearce, author, *Angel's Fury*
www.bryonypearce.co.uk

Very few large publishing houses will take unsolicited manuscripts nowadays. The more traditional route is for authors, certainly those writing fiction, to approach literary agents with their submission. If an agent likes their work, they will try to sell it on to a publishing house on behalf of that author. In effect, the agents are acting as a filter for the publishers.

> **Insight**
> Always be professional when you deal with agents, publishers, publicity people, bookshops (be polite, on time, etc.). Publishing is like any other business: if you act like a professional, you come across as reliable – that is a positive for anyone considering investing in you and your work.

Publishing houses, certainly the big ones and most of their imprints, won't accept unsolicited proposals, which is an aspiring writer's first obstacle. Some of the smaller publishers, like Atlantic and Profile, maybe even Canongate, will still look at unsolicited non-fiction projects but it is pretty rare for that to happen. I do and always have done; authors can submit to us and we will look at them. So, depending on what sort of fiction or non-fiction it is, you will still probably need an agent because a) that gives you an entrée and b) suggests that somebody who has a connection with the business has already said to themselves 'This is actually good and I can make some money out of it.' Sadly, it's a reflection on how busy publishers have to be these days to make sure the books they already have on their list sell as many as possible.

Trevor Dolby, publisher, Preface Publishing, an imprint of Random House
www.prefacepublishing.co.uk

Some publishers, like Preface, will look at unsolicited work; if they do, they will say so on their website. This can change from month to month if the publisher is over-subscribed; they will state if they are not currently taking submissions.

A few publishers are now taking a different approach to finding new authors and manuscripts: for example, Macmillan New Writing and HarperCollins authonomy.

Macmillan New Writing (www.macmillannewwriting.com)

An imprint dedicated to discovering new novelists in all genres. It welcomes unsolicited submissions from debut novelists. It pays its authors 20 per cent royalty on net receipts but does *not* pay an advance. The contract is standard and non-negotiable. Macmillan acquire world rights in all titles, with the rights revenue split 50–50. They reserve the option to publish a successful author's second novel on the same terms as the first; if they acquire the author's third and any subsequent novels, they will be published with an advance and under one of Macmillan's mainstream imprints. Over the first two years of the scheme running, 9,000 novels were submitted and 30 were published.

authonomy (www.authonomy.com)

This imprint invites unpublished and self-published authors to post their manuscripts online; they must make at least 10,000 words available for people to read. Visitors to the site can then comment on those submissions and recommend their favourites. The more recommendations a book receives, the higher its ranking on the site. It also ranks the visitors who consistently recommend the best books in its 'most influential trend spotters' listing. It costs nothing to upload your book or recommend books. Once a month, the top five books are read by the HarperCollins Editorial Board who will send their comments to the individual authors of those books.

PUBLISHERS

I still come across writers who turn their back on the fact that this is a commercial transaction and think that it's all about art. It isn't.

Doug Young, Publishing Director, Sport & Entertainment, Transworld
www.transworld-publishers.co.uk

Someone once described publishers as eternal optimists with short memories, constantly searching for and expecting success, believing that future rewards would surpass previous losses. They are certainly a curious mix of the business and the creative worlds. They have to be. Publishers are the link between the writer and the reader, looking for good books (creative) that sell (business).

I think there's a huge number of writers out there who believe it's an 'in' world, in which there's some mysterious literary cabal which gets published while other people don't and that simply isn't true.

Kate Parkin, publisher, John Murray Publishers
www.johnmurray.co.uk

What a publisher does
A publisher:

- ▶ *researches and understands the market*
- ▶ *looks for new authors and works to maintain a relationship with current authors*

- *adds the authority of their brand/imprint to a writer's work*
- *assesses the quality of a written work*
- *works out costs, schedules and potential sales*
- *finances the production and marketing of a book*
- *brings design and production values to the look of a book*
- *buys and oversees print production*
- *develops new technology*
- *works with wholesalers/retailers to promote and sell books*
- *fulfils orders and distributes books*
- *keeps stocks of books to meet demand*
- *collects royalties and distributes them.*

Judging whether to publish a manuscript involves a number of factors for an editor. Critical assessment is one – is it well written, involving, entertaining etc? – though inevitably personal taste comes into this. Personal passion too. You might admire a manuscript, but if it doesn't excite you in any way, you're not likely to get other people excited about it. You also have to consider it in the context of the list – do we already have something too similar, either in terms of the subject, the author, the audience or all three? And the market – is it unusual enough to stand out from the crowds of already published or forthcoming books? Can you envisage making people want to read it with just a brief description of it? Particularly in the case of non-fiction, is the subject one that enough people are going to want to read about, might be out of date by the time the book is published, has already been well covered in the press or would be better as an extended magazine article? Is the author well qualified to write on the subject? And if there is only a proposal to consider and it's the author's first book, what evidence is there that they will be able to deliver a finished script as good as the proposal promises. That's what an editor does: takes all such factors into account and judges whether to take something on.

The next stage can involve a lot of time and effort. In theory, if an editor likes something and wants to make an offer for it – whether there is an auction running or not – they will usually ask colleagues (in sales, marketing, publicity) to read it too. If it's a book to which you might be able to acquire world rights or, at least, serial rights, which can be particularly important with non-fiction, you would need to involve the rights department as well. What you want, ideally, is for them all to agree that the script or proposal is fantastic. Of course, you aren't always met by unanimous enthusiasm but that doesn't preclude you from taking the book on anyway. But you have to take into account other peoples' views; if, for example, a sales colleague is saying 'It's your call but, personally, I'm a bit lukewarm about it', they're going to do their best when it comes to selling the book but perhaps not with quite the heartfelt enthusiasm they would have for something they felt passionate about – and that kind of enthusiasm can make a crucial difference. If a rights colleague says they don't think they could sell the book in the US or to foreign publishers, or serial rights to a newspaper, that doesn't mean you shouldn't publish the book but does affect what you should be offering for it.

So the process of preparing to offer for a debut book (or deciding not to, after all) can take time. It involves researching the competition, gathering people's opinions, having discussions and calculating the advance based on projected sales figures and rights income. It can involve putting together a publishing plan with details of how your company would publish the book, from format to marketing to publicity, and presenting that plan in a meeting with the author and their agent. And sometimes, usually when it's a book other publishers are going after, you can go through all that and still not end up with the book.

Carole Welch, Publishing Director, Sceptre
www.hodder.co.uk

A publishing house relies on its editors to keep a constant flow of publishable books coming in. Editors are constantly under pressure to acquire titles that will be successful, bringing profit to the company.

A commissioning (or acquisitions) editor takes on a book and champions it in the company; senior commissioning editors are also responsible for developing the list in general (called 'list-building'). Editors sometimes commission books themselves, i.e. they have an idea and actively seek a suitable author to write the book (for example, in textbook publishing) or they will buy work from authors' agents.

At the editorial meeting, the commissioning editor pitches a book to other departments in the publishing house (including sales, marketing, publicity and rights). The manuscript is circulated to other departments for their input. To get approval for a new book, decisions have to be made on established sales figures, likely production costs, the author's track record and so on. The editor will prepare a costing to show the book's profitability because they have to balance the actual physical cost of producing the book (advance, production costs, etc.) against what the market is doing. As Carole Welch explains, it is not a straightforward process; a lot of people have to be convinced of a book's suitability for a publishing house.

Auctions
Auctions are a gift to an author. This is when several publishing houses enter into a bidding war to secure an author's book (generally a work of fiction). The auction takes place on the phone and can take a few days.

> *AA – There were the big advances for the celebrity autobiographies which put publishing in a bad place. The knock-on effect is that publishers have got to earn back somewhere so they offer small advances to people like us. They do now acknowledge that it was silly money, don't they? There will be a handful that will undoubtedly have earned out and earned out handsomely. I know Peter Kay's first biography paid for the entire bonuses of the publishing house that year and I have a girlfriend who works at Transworld who thinks Dan Brown is a god because that's who pays her salary. But if you are a publisher with*

£1 million worth of unearned advance (which there will be with those figures), authors further down the line will have advances that get chopped and chopped.

MS – There is a popular belief among authors that if you get a large advance, the publishing house put more effort into publicity because they've got to make sales to try and justify that advance. But publicity isn't everything; it doesn't guarantee astronomical sales. Looking at it for the long term, it's better to have a slow build over time and several books, rather than go up like a rocket and fall like a stick.

Annie Ashworth and Meg Sanders, authors who write as Annie Sanders
www.anniesanders.co.uk

Consumer (or trade) publishing

Consumer or trade books are aimed at the general reader. The hope is to publish books that will appeal to the widest number of people. You get the bestsellers in trade publishing but there are also books that the publishers had high hopes for but that didn't sell well. Trade publishers often have to respond quickly to trends, such as the popularity of a genre, personality or a topical issue (for example, biographies of Michael Jackson after his death).

Children's publishing

Fiction and non-fiction books aimed at the very young to young adult.

Academic, textbook and educational publishing

Educational publishing is less risky than trade because you tend to know your market size. If you have an author who writes a book on 'Introduction to Calculus' or 'Modern British History' there are students in the States who are taking those courses and are told to buy those specific books.

Todd Armstrong, Senior Acquisitions Editor,
Communications and Media Studies, SAGE Publications
www.sagepub.com

These publishing houses tend to specialize in academic and textbooks for schools, colleges, universities and libraries. The lead times on academic and textbook publishing can, on average, be longer than trade books.

Textbooks are commissioned, designed and priced to meet teaching and learning needs. There are differences between the UK and the US when it comes to publishing educational books. US textbook publishers look closely at the curriculum needs because US professors will adopt a particular book for a course from which they will teach. In the UK, there has been a slightly different approach; professors have been less likely to adopt one particular book for their course and would, instead, produce a suggested reading list.

STM (scientific, technical, medical)
Professional books are usually aimed at helping professionals in their work: for example, managers, lawyers, financiers, healthcare workers, etc.

BOOK PACKAGERS

A book packager will deliver a complete book, written, edited, designed and illustrated and, sometimes, printed, to their customer, a publishing house. The promotion and selling of the book is then down to the publisher, not the book packager.

Book packagers work in many different genres, predominantly children's and young adult and especially in illustrated non-fiction; Working Partners is one such packager in the UK. They are popular with books that are considered labour-intensive, such as books with lots of illustrations and diagrams, a high proportion of photographs or numerous authors, or novelty books.

A book packager will commission an author to write the text for them. They are generally paid a fixed fee rather than an advance and royalties; although terms differ from packager to packager (there is more information on book packaging in Chapter 4, pp. 109–13).

In the case of Working Partners, they will invite several authors to write sample chapters to a specific brief. One is chosen and the book is submitted to English language publishers in the UK and the US. For more information, go to their website: www.workingpartnersltd.co.uk

AGENTS

Obviously you hope that the book you are taking on is going to have a long shelf life. You don't want it to die a quick death, particularly if it is a work of fiction. That is what you are striving for as an agent; you are looking at the longer, bigger picture. When you take someone on you're trying to build them as a writer.

Camilla Goslett, literary agent, Curtis Brown
www.curtisbrown.co.uk

In *Get Started in Creative Writing*, Stephen May said having a good agent was like having a native guide through hostile territory. They know the editors in the various publishing houses; they know what they are looking for, where the gaps in the lists are and whether they are looking to expand their list, develop into new genres and so on.

Agents will send manuscripts to selected editors, either one at a time or, if they wish to conduct an auction because they feel the book will sell really well, simultaneously to several editors at once. Equally, editors will get in touch with agents if they have an idea or project that they need an author for.

Many agents are members of either the Association of Authors' Agents (AAA) in the UK or the Association of Authors' Representatives (AAR) in the US. Members adhere to a code of practice. You can identify those who are members by the asterisk against their name in the yearbook; guides in the US also identify members of the AAR.

Do not be put off if an agent is not a member. It may be that they have just set up their agency and have therefore not been practising for the three years that the AAA requires of its members (two years for the AAR) or its revenue may be under £25,000.

What an agent does

You have to remember that dealing with queries is only a small part of what agents actually do. I think a lot of aspiring writers feel that we just sit there reading submissions all day and that is not the case. My first duty is to my existing clients. I send their manuscripts out and work on getting them a deal. A writer may think one contract is amazing but, as an agent, I see my job much more as trying to assist them to have a long-term writing career, which can be a challenge. So there's the challenge of the first contract and then the challenge of staying under contract and I work hard to make sure they are kept under contract with a publisher. Someone who has written a great first story doesn't always follow it up with an equally commercial concept second time around, so there can be a lot of advising and revising on new work.

So, I'm doing a lot on behalf of my existing clients, including liaising with my sister company which sells foreign rights, dealing with all things financial or answering myriad questions from authors, publishers and colleagues. I also do a lot of preparation and travel for conferences (critiques and speeches), website maintenance, and interviews.

Submissions have to be fitted around all these other responsibilities – in the evenings, at weekends, on the train, in coffee shops. But also in specially set-aside slabs of time when I try to ignore the phone and constant demands of email. Submissions have to be treated very seriously and looked at with real focus – a potential gem may be among them.

Sarah Davies, literary agent, The Greenhouse Literary Agency
www.greenhouseliterary.com

A literary agent:

- ▶ *assesses the quality and marketability of a writer's work*
- ▶ *gives editorial guidance to their writers*

- *gives advice about trends, market conditions, practices and contracts*
- *markets an author's work*
- *devises strategies for getting an author's work accepted by a publisher*
- *negotiates deals to get the best terms for their authors*
- *reviews licensing agreements*
- *checks advance payments and royalties*
- *reviews royalty statements, chasing money and keeping the author informed about financial matters.*

Literary or authors' agents earn money only when their clients do; in other words, when they sell a book or rights to a publishing house. That means that they will take on only those authors who they feel have something marketable. Agents put in a lot of unpaid time and effort on behalf of their clients – they need to feel confident that all that work is worthwhile.

Literary agents will negotiate terms with publishers on behalf of their clients. They know the market, both at home and abroad, and will therefore ensure they get the best terms possible for an author's work. More to the point, they understand publishing contracts, which is an art in itself.

Agents sell and license the rights to various media (book publishers, TV, film, etc.) at home and abroad on behalf of their authors. They negotiate what rights a publisher can have and what rights they retain on behalf of their author. For example, they might withhold foreign language translation or merchandizing rights. They can sell to US publishers, film and TV companies, European or other overseas agents. Equally, a UK agent may represent an American author on behalf of their American agents while still in the UK.

Agents receive a commission, on average 15 per cent of the author's earnings from sales of their books at home; this can rise to around 20 per cent for overseas sales. Commissions for TV or film are around 15–20 per cent. So, if an agent secures an advance of £3,000 and charges 15 per cent commission, their share will be £450.

Publishers do not have time to read through the 'slush pile' – unsolicited submissions sent in by aspiring authors – because it does not make them money. Agents *will* tackle the slush pile; it may be a fairly junior person going through it or it will be an in-house reader whose job it is to look at unsolicited work, but they will get looked at.

Learn about the market

> *Most publishers would be honest enough to not take on a book they didn't really like or enjoy just because they thought it was commercial. And many publishers turn down books that subsequently go on to be bestsellers. It doesn't mean they are bad books, it means that they just weren't right for them. Or it wasn't right for the publishing house. If you've got an incredibly good sex and shopping type of commercial women's fiction, don't try and send it to Faber. And the same would go for agents. Be sensible; look at agents' and publishers' websites to see the sorts of authors they are interested in. Do your homework.*
>
> Kate Parkin, publisher, John Murray Publishers
www.johnmurray.co.uk

Learn about the publishing world, so you know what is selling, where to send your work and, perhaps more importantly, where *not* to send it. Agents and editors continually complain about getting inappropriate submissions; with the reference material and information that is available to authors, there should be no excuse for this.

There are some extremely useful publications and websites that list all the agents, publishing houses and general resources for writers. They contain information on:

- ▶ *literary agents – both home and abroad; what genres they work in; list of clients; commission charged*

- *publishing houses – both at home and abroad; what genres they publish books in*
- *book packagers – what genres they work in; what services they offer*
- *societies, organizations and clubs*
- *art agents – what they specialize in; commission charged*
- *picture agencies and libraries*
- *prizes and awards*
- *literature festivals*
- *libraries*
- *creative writing courses*
- *trade journals.*

Look at the *Writers' & Artists' Yearbook*, *The Writer's Handbook* and, in the US, *Writer's Market* to find out who does what. Useful references include:

Writers' & Artists' Yearbook (UK)
The Writers' Handbook (UK)
Writer's Market (US)
Literary Market Place (US)
Publishers' Marketplace (US)
Media Bistro (US)
Writer's Digest (US)
The Writer (US)

Magazines (some are subscription only):

The Author (www.societyofauthors.org)
Flair News (www.flair4words.co.uk)
The New Writer (www.thenewwriter.com) (UK)
Poets & Writers magazine (www.pw.org/magazine) (US)
Writers' Forum (www.writers-forum.com) (UK)
Writers' Journal (www.writersjournal.com) (US)
The Writer magazine (www.writermag.com) (US)
Writers' News (www.writersnews.co.uk)
The Bookseller (www.thebookseller.com) (weekly trade publication in the UK that has listings of books to be published over the next

six months. You can also see who is moving to which company and who has left to set up their own agency/press.)
Publishing News (www.publishingnews.co.uk) (UK)
Publishers Weekly (www.publishersweekly.com)
  (publishes news, gossip and statistics in US, similar to The Bookseller)
Bookbrunch (www.bookbrunch.co.uk).

> **Insight**
> Make sure you use an up-to-date version of the yearbook (published annually). Addresses and details change as do the requirements for submissions.

BOOK FAIRS

Beijing	www.bibf.net
Bologna	www.bookfair.bolognafiere.it/en (children's book fair)
Frankfurt	www.frankfurt-book-fair.com
London	www.londonbookfair.co.uk
US	www.bookexpoamerica.com

Literary festivals are about books and writing. Book fairs are about the business of books. If you want to learn about the industry, it is worth attending the London, Frankfurt (or Bologna – if you are interested in children's fiction) book fairs or BookExpo America, for example. There is a range of free seminars on a variety of useful topics; you can see what ideas, subjects and genres are popular and topical; you will get to meet useful companies (especially if you are considering self-publishing) such as printers, wholesalers and packagers.

> **Did you know?**
> Frankfurt Book Fair is the largest international book fair, with nearly 7,500 exhibitors and over 400,000 titles.

Don't expect to land a book deal by turning up at a book fair and cornering an agent or editor. These are industry get-togethers; ideal places for agents and publishing houses to do deals. The last thing they want is to be buttonholed by an author.

Book fairs can be useful to authors. You can:

- *draw up a shortlist of publishing houses that publish your kind of work and visit their stand to see what they have to offer; are they interested in taking on a new book in that genre?*
- *find out what is popular and selling right now*
- *get the contact details of the right people to approach*
- *get ideas.*

You should:

- *go on a Sunday which is the best day for the public*
- *dress smartly; you want to look like a publisher, not like an author*
- *avoid putting 'author' on your name badge; use a company name – otherwise industry professionals will try to avoid you*
- *take business cards (or some other kind of promotional literature – like a bookmark) to leave with people.*

Insight
Avoid sending in submissions before and after Christmas and before and after book fairs. The slush pile has the lowest priority then.

THE MARKETPLACE

Sometimes, a genre catches light so brilliantly that there are a lot more possibilities within it. So when that happens, as an agent, you will want to see other things in that genre. On the other hand, just going back to an agent who represents someone who is writing in a very similar fashion to you is not necessarily the best thing to do – the agent may feel your work is a little too close in theme to the novel of someone they already represent.

Sarah Davies, literary agent, The Greenhouse Literary Agency

www.greenhouseliterary.com

Fiction categories

commercial/mass-market
literary
action/adventure
children's and young adult
sci-fi, fantasy, horror
crime, thriller, mystery
romance
erotica/adult
historical
war
western
variations on the above, such as 'historical crime'

Non-fiction categories

art/photography/fashion
autobiographies/biographies/memoirs
business/economics
computer/internet
cookery/food/drink
education/academic
gardening
health/beauty/fitness
history/politics/current affairs
home front
humour/gift books
language & literature
mind, body & spirit (MBS)
natural history/pets
personal development/self-help

> popular science
> psychology/sociology
> reference
> sport
> television/film/TV tie-ins
> travel

We will assume that you know what genre you are writing in. If you don't and it is too muddled, it will be hard to market and if your book is hard to market, agents/publishers are not likely to want to take it on.

The best way to categorize what you are writing is to think where it would be put if it were being sold in a bookshop. If you struggle to find the right shelf, imagine how difficult it would be for an agent/publisher to sell it.

A good writer is a good reader. Read widely so you know your market. Look at different categories, series, genres and publishers' imprints (to help you find a suitable publisher). Look at recent titles published; ask for a catalogue from the marketing department of a publishing house or imprint. The trade press, such as *The Bookseller*, is a good source of information on what new books are coming out and when.

New genres are being invented and cross-fertilized all the time. Part of your job as a writer is to keep up with the trends in the industry. That means reading publications that deal with books, publishing and writing; go into bookshops and see what is selling; attend literary festivals.

Insight
Publishing is not a race. Get your work into as good a shape as possible before you try to get published.

Large versus small

Someone said that the worst place to be is a medium-sized publisher because the big houses have got bigger and are snapping up more and more imprints. They are the only ones who can ride through economic slowdowns; they compete against each other to get the next big bestseller, like Dan Brown; they operate at the super-league level. In the middle are medium-sized publishers; they have overheads like everybody but they find it very tough because they have to compete against the big boys. At the other end, you've got the independent publishers who can take decisions quickly, who will chase an author they really want, who can slip under the wire, if you like. It's economies of scale, they want one or two good authors with bankable books; that means that the author is a big fish in a small pond which is nice for the author because they feel wanted and looked after. The rise of the independent is on the up, I think.

If I was starting to do this now, I would consider an independent publisher. They will say 'No' just as easily as one of the bigger publishing houses but I think that their antennae are much more finely tuned; they are more receptive, welcoming, and they are on the look-out for new authors because they have to survive.

Robert Forsyth, publisher, Chevron Publishing
www.chevronpublishing.co.uk

Big is not better than small and vice versa. There are pros and cons to working with a large or small publisher and/or a large or small agency. It will depend on what is important to you and what you want from the relationship with your agent/editor.

The large agencies have a range of agents, each of whom will have a particular area of expertise and interest. They will usually have a separate rights department whose sole aim is negotiating rights around the world. The large agencies, such as Curtis Brown, will have offices in the UK and the US as well as contacts in Hollywood.

Large publishing houses enjoy economies of scale. It means that they can sometimes get press coverage more readily than smaller firms. They may also have close links with large bookshops around the country and a large sales force to service those retailers. Large houses can offer more resources in designing and editing the book and in selling and promoting it. They have bigger budgets and often offer larger advances.

But they are huge corporations, with the focus more on the bottom line; they are increasingly phasing out the niche titles that do not sell as many copies. It can take a long time to get a decision because several people will have to be consulted. You may get asked for your opinion but, with a large publisher, what they say ultimately goes. You will have a relationship with an agent or editor, not with the company itself.

> *People like to go with the big agencies because they come with a lot of extras. For instance, the different departments we have at Curtis Brown [theatre, film, television, actors, presenters] can be very helpful to certain writers. Having all that in-house means there's a lot of creative cross-over within the departments. But then some authors don't need that. A boutique, small agency, where they are one of a small number of authors, is also very nice. I think it's horses for courses and what suits you as an individual.*
>
> Camilla Goslett, literary agent, Curtis Brown
> www.curtisbrown.co.uk

With a smaller publishing house or agency, you will often deal directly with the person who can make a decision. As an author, you are a much bigger fish in a smaller pond. You will potentially have more input into areas such as design and price. You will have a relationship with the people who actually run the company. The budgets will not be as large.

Smaller publishing houses and agencies are able to move quickly to seize opportunities and operate efficiently in difficult market conditions. They are often more willing to publish books that will instantly go to the backlist, rather than target frontlist books.

A smaller house may be more suitable for a particular genre or non-fiction writer because some publishers tend to specialize; a couple of examples of such publishing houses are Mills & Boon in romantic fiction in the UK and Prufrock Press in the US, which publishes titles for parents of children with special needs.

> *Make a short list – a mix of large and small agencies – and don't just necessarily base it on the big names. Younger agencies are often incredibly driven and hard working, and that can be to your advantage. Plus a newer agent may just be starting to build their list, so is more open to submissions and the possibility of taking on new clients.*
>
> Sarah Davies, literary agent, The Greenhouse Literary Agency
> www.greenhouseliterary.com

Timing

The trouble with publishing is that, from time to time, a book will come out that is tremendously successful. It strikes a chord with the buying public and agents/editors will look to jump on that successful bandwagon. But it's a law of diminishing returns: only the first few will be successful. Then you will be told that there is no market for your book because the subject has been over-published. Take heart – the market will always come back. It may not return in the next few months, but if writing in that style or genre is something that is important to you, stick to that rather than try to second guess what you think will sell. Having a passion for your work is a more reliable way of getting published than trying to anticipate what the market wants.

The time it takes to get a book to publication can vary; it usually depends on the genre – a few months from commission for a non-fiction book to 18 months to two years for a novel. Doug Young, Publishing Director, Sport & Entertainment at Transworld, rarely has projects that last longer than a year. As he points out, the more commercial you get, the more time-specific you have to be, particularly if the book is tied in to a television series or something similar.

What is predictable is the *annual* timetable for books and publishers are very aware of timing certain books to meet these dates. There may be a particular sporting event or anniversary (the Olympics or the World Cup, for example) that they would want to tie books into. Seasons come round, obviously, once a year. Almost three quarters of books sold are bought in the run-up to Christmas. Christmas is good for cookery books and presents; the New Year for dieting, self-improvement and gardening publications; Mother's Day, Valentine's Day and Father's Day are also all useful dates where particular books will do well; travel books are popular in early summer; hardbacks get good media coverage in the autumn (during the run-up to Christmas) and spring (there are a lot of literary festivals at that time).

Case study

Maria McCarthy, author, *The Girls' Guide To Losing Your L-Plates: How To Pass Your Driving Test* and *The Girls' Car Handbook* (Simon and Schuster) www.mariamccarthy.co.uk

As I was working on a non-fiction book, I just did a synopsis and three chapters. It's easier to sell non-fiction on a partial; I think it's virtually impossible these days to get fiction sold just on three chapters. Novels can so easily start well and then sink in the middle like a Victoria sponge. But if a non-fiction author can produce some good initial chapters it's far more likely they'll be able to keep it going.

It felt quite weird because, as a journalist, I'm used to getting commissions from newspapers and magazines up front, so I know in advance that I'm going to get paid for everything I write. Writing three full chapters not knowing if it was ever going to sell
(Contd)

*felt rather unnerving but I felt so committed to writing a book about learning to drive (*The Girls' Guide to Losing Your L-Plates*) that I just went ahead anyway.*

I looked in the Writers' & Artists' Yearbook *and I searched for agents who seemed to handle the popular non-fiction, as opposed to something like learned biographies or children's fiction. I narrowed it down to a number of agencies. They say time spent in reconnaissance is never wasted. I had also read in* The Bookseller *that Luigi Bonomi, formerly of the respected agency Sheil Lands, had left together with a colleague to set up a new agency (LBA). That happens with reasonable frequency and it's a good 'window of opportunity' to approach them, as they're more likely to be looking for new clients at that point.*

So I put my first three chapters and synopsis in the post to them. In my covering letter, I think I came across as practical and down-to-earth. I mentioned where I'd been published before and said why I thought the book would work. I also did a selling outline; this was a number of pages: what the market was, why I was entirely the right person to write the book and an analysis of what the competing books in the field were and why mine would be better!

I approached LBA and got an email the very next day saying they were interested. Naturally, I was over the moon! Then I went up to London for an initial chat. At a first meeting with an agency, they just want to meet you and make sure that you are not the sort of person who is going to throw temper tantrums if things don't go your way. They obviously look at your writing to see if that works but they need to see what kind of person you are; your personality does matter. That doesn't mean you have to waft in and be terribly glamorous or assertive; I think just coming across as pleasant and down-to-earth will do.

Publishing can be a rocky road and there are times when things go well and times when they don't. You need to be able to get on with people, to negotiate and keep talking to each other, even if things are going badly.

I think they also need to see you to work out how you will fit in with the potential marketing and publicity of the book. If you turned up and you were ravishingly beautiful and had a celebrity footballer boyfriend waiting outside in his Aston Martin, that would obviously gain you some extra points but don't feel you have to have that in order to be taken on.

It is worth taking a bit of trouble with your appearance. As a working writer, I tend to sit around most days wearing trackie bottoms and no make-up. When I meet my agent or publisher, I like to look a bit more groomed; I think it's more professional.

I wanted an agent who was businesslike and capable and I very much got those vibes at that first meeting with LBA and was delighted when they offered to represent me. After our meeting my agent drew up a contract and popped it in the post and I signed a few days later.

I worked with my agent to tidy up the manuscript a bit and by that point it was late November so rather than send it out in the frantic run-up to Christmas it was decided to wait until January.

My agent told me that we would get some acceptances and some rejections. Did I, she asked, want to be told about them as they came in or leave it to the end? I asked to be told at the end. I sort of guessed that there would be rejections and I thought it would be too depressing to hear about them one by one.

Then came the news that Simon & Schuster were interested. The editor who accepted it had failed her own driving test eight times and that is often how it works in publishing. I think sometimes the difference between a 'yes' and a 'no' can be as ephemeral as that – whether or not the editor feels a personal connection.

(Contd)

I was invited in for a meeting with Simon & Schuster, along with my agent. We just had a general chat. I was told beforehand not to mention money or expect any decision there and then. They just wanted to look me over and see what sort of person I was. So I went in and was very friendly, pleasant and low key. I spoke when I was spoken to, told a few stories about learning to drive and then I shut up. I was lively but not pushy. Then I went off shopping in London while the decision was made. I actually got the call from my agent that they'd offered me a contract while I was washing my hands in the ladies' loo in Selfridges. Afterwards, I turned to the other women and said, 'I've just got a book deal.' I hope they believed me and didn't think I was just some deranged person who loitered in toilets claiming to have book deals.

My agent emailed the contract over and then talked me through it on the phone so I knew what I was signing up to. I was given a deadline for delivery of manuscript by the end of May; the contract was signed in January. With my journalism work, I was having to juggle the book to fit it in. It was hard, hard work with a lot of hours and a lot of research. My editor, Edwina, was brilliant; she held my hand all the way through. I would send in a chapter at a time to her and get feedback. It felt really good; it didn't feel like I was on my own. The agent had, in a sense, done her bit and from now on it was down to my editor and myself.

We had a fantastic relationship. She really got the book and she understood me. She would tell me when I'd repeated myself, would say if my jokes weren't funny but also not destroy me in the process. She was very good at pointing me in the right direction. Not all editorial relationships are necessarily going to be like that; I was very lucky that mine was.

Although I had submitted the book chapter by chapter there was still lots of work to do when I sent the last one in. The editor read it through to check for repetitions and so forth and then there was more work to be done on it. The final checking of proofs didn't end till July.

The book came out in January 2007. The timing was good because it tied in with all that New Year's resolution mindset. The publicity went very well and I did a lot of radio interviews. I had the advantage of a time-specific link to the book; it is potentially quite a funny topic and I had lots of amusing stories about driving test disasters. For publicizing non-fiction work, it does help if you can pull out lots of little anecdotes, either funny stories or things that other people would find interesting or entertaining.

Publicists are quite overstretched so the more you can do yourself, the better. I think it's quite a good idea to ask to see your press release in advance and have a chat with your publicist about what you feel you can do. You could offer to write press releases and distribute them locally to newspapers, magazines and so on; you could approach local radio. I also approached various literature festivals and offered myself as a speaker at those. That's something I've continued – so far I've appeared at Bath, Birmingham, Ilkley, Daphne du Maurier and Warwick Words Literature Festivals – it's a great way to get to see the country!

Publishers quite like you to do your subsequent books in the same field because they can build you as a brand. So, it felt quite natural for me to go on and do another car book (The Girls' Car Handbook).

The path to publication can have its ups and downs. Your editor may move to another job in the middle of your edits, you might not like your book jacket, you may have writer's block. It's important to realize that a completely smooth ride is the exception rather than the norm and to work with your agent and publishers to tackle any problems in a level-headed manner. Save your angst for your nearest and dearest!

10 THINGS TO REMEMBER

1 *Publishing houses are made up of different imprints; imprints are the trade names under which books are published.*

2 *Sometimes, imprints belonging to the same large group will compete directly with each other.*

3 *The frontlist is made up of a publishing house's newly published books.*

4 *The backlist contains the long-lasting titles which keep selling.*

5 *Very few publishing houses will now look at unsolicited submissions, especially for writers of fiction.*

6 *A book is championed by a commissioning editor in a publishing house; it is their job to convince their colleagues (in sales, marketing, rights, etc.) to take the book on.*

7 *Taking on a book is a mix of business (will the book sell?) and personal preference.*

8 *Book fairs are a good place to learn about the business of books; don't put author on your badge, though, because agents and publishers will avoid you.*

9 *There are useful annual yearbooks that contain contact details for publishers, agents, packagers, newspapers, magazines, etc. that should be on every writer's bookshelf.*

10 *Timing is important in publishing; there are certain times of the year when different books will do well.*

2
What are they looking for?

In this chapter you will learn:
- *who to approach*
- *what to send*
- *what not to send.*

> *All good writing is swimming under water and holding your breath*
>
> F. Scott Fitzgerald, author

Having a talent for writing and being able to master the techniques of the craft are important skills for an author. This book, however, is not about teaching you how to write. There are other books in the *Teach Yourself* series that will help you with that (*Write a Novel And Get it Published*, *Write a Blockbuster And Get it Published*, *Write a Children's Book And Get it Published*, *Get Your Articles Published*, *Get Your Travel Writing Published*, *Get Started in Creative Writing* and *Write Poetry And Get it Published*). This is about getting your book into print. And for that, you need to be determined, hard-working and thick-skinned.

First of all, stop thinking that agents and publishers need you. Of course, agents have to have authors with work to sell on to the publishing houses who need to acquire books – otherwise they wouldn't make any money. But publishing *is* a business. Remember too that agents and publishing houses have existing authors whom they already know and represent. They will not just drop an existing author in order to take on somebody new. A new author is a high risk for a publisher.

What makes a publisher publish a book?

> *With fiction in particular, we take the attitude that we're taking on an author rather than a book. The idea being that we will continue to publish them and help develop their career. There are always exceptions but in general, we take someone on with a view to publishing their next book and beyond. Sometimes it turns out that they only write one book! Sometimes, their second book is rejected and they move to another publisher. And sometimes they recognize that their second book should be put in the bottom drawer and they come back with one we do want to publish.*
>
> Carole Welch, Publishing Director, Sceptre
www.hodder.co.uk

A publisher will weigh up the following factors:

- *Does the book fit the company's list?*
- *The author – can they write? Are they reliable? Are they promotable? What is their motivation for writing?*
- *USP (unique selling point) – what makes this book different from any other? Is it the author, the subject matter, the way it's produced? Is there a link to an event, a television series, the author's status (i.e. are they a celebrity?). Is it experimental?*
- *The marketplace – who will buy the book?*
- *The competition – what are the competing books like?*
- *Price/appearance – length of book, size, binding, production, how much it will cost?*
- *Frontlist or backlist – how long is its shelf life?*
- *Investment – how much money will be required? Advance, marketing, promotion against projected sales. Has it got earning power?*

What the publisher wants, the literary agent wants as well. They can sell an author and a manuscript only if they look like being a marketable commodity. With debut authors, agents and publishers are looking for something new and fresh so make sure that you get that new, fresh feeling into your synopsis and sample chapters.

> **Insight**
> Once you have written, rewritten and polished your work until you feel you can do no more to it, put it in an envelope and start thinking about it as a product, not a work of art.

If you are writing fiction, don't send in anything until your book is finished and you have a completed manuscript. An editor or agent may suggest revisions at a later stage but don't submit a 'work in progress'. Literary agents have sold partial manuscripts in the past but they have been *exceptionally* good. A completed manuscript is preferred.

You may have to send only the first three or four chapters to an agent or editor but if you've got a complete manuscript, it has proved you can finish a project. It makes you more marketable because if you have already got one manuscript under your belt, you are able to start on a second.

If you are writing non-fiction, it is much easier to sell the *idea* of the book before you have written it. For non-fiction, you can approach a commissioning editor directly with your idea, rather than go via an agent. Whether you are approaching an agent or an editor, though, your submission must look professional.

Who to approach

> *However cynical you are and however long you've been in the publishing business, you really do not know what is going to come in and it can be tremendously exciting. That is what keeps you engaged.*
>
> Kate Parkin, publisher, John Murray Publishers
> www.johnmurray.co.uk

Research the agencies and publishing houses to find one that feels like a good match for you and your work. Look at the writers you like or aspire to be like and see who represents them.

Check websites of the agencies and publishing houses; they will tell you what they expect to see (for example, Sarah Davies at The Greenhouse Literary Agency only accepts electronic submissions; while Laura Longrigg, director at the MBA literary agency, wants a letter, synopsis and three sample chapters sent by post – *not* by email. Follow the submission guidelines *to the letter*.

Then find the right person in the organization to send your submission to. If necessary, make a phone call to the company and ask who that person is. Never send a submission to 'Dear Sir/Madam', 'The Managing Director' or 'The Editor'; address your submission to a named person.

This is not difficult. Again, the yearbooks and the websites are your best resource. There is no point sending your romantic novel to an agency/publishing house that specializes in children's fiction. Equally, it is no good sending your submission to the right agency but the wrong person. Within agencies, people have their own areas of speciality. For example, at the Caroline Sheldon literary agency, Caroline Sheldon is mainly interested in 'women's fiction, children's books and compelling non-fiction stories', while her colleague, Penny Holroyde, shares that interest in children's books but also wants to see memoirs and historical settings.

It seems such an obvious piece of advice to send your work to agents and publishers who deal in your kind of fiction or genre but practically every agent interviewed for this book made the same point which means that would-be authors are still sending out their work to the wrong people.

> *I always tell people to start with the Writers' & Artists' Yearbook, the latest edition. You would not believe the number of people who are using out-of-date editions! It's a very easy book to use, it's not expensive and it's a real Bible that has a lot of names in it that aren't usually on websites. So if you want to be systematic about it, go through the yearbook, pick out a shortlist and then work through the individual agency websites for further, up-to-date information. What*

*people tend to do nowadays is to go straight to the website
and I wouldn't say that is the most sensible way of getting
the best overall picture.*

Heather Holden Brown, literary agent, hhb Agency Ltd
www.hhbagency.com

What to send

Before you do send anything out, make sure you have got it
absolutely to the best standard you can.

Agents will find it easier to say 'no' to your manuscript if you
haven't sent what they asked for. A new author requires a huge
amount of time and effort from both an agent and a publisher;
that means adding to their already considerable workload so it is
understandable why saying 'no' is so tempting.

*As a prospective author, following a publisher's guidelines
gets you thinking about your project and helps you
understand what a publisher is looking for. You have to make
a persuasive argument for your work. Why should a company
gamble all their money on it? You need to show them.*

Todd Armstrong, Senior Acquisitions Editor, Communications and Media Studies,
SAGE Publications www.sagepub.com

It is highly unlikely that you will be asked to send in a complete
manuscript – so don't. Agencies and publishing houses do not have
room for them and they do not have time to read through every
full manuscript. You will be asked to send either some sample
chapters or a set number of pages. You should, however, mention
whether you have completed your manuscript or not.

The majority of literary agencies will *not* charge a reading fee for
looking at unsolicited manuscripts; the Association of Authors'
Representatives, for example, prohibits its members from charging
a fee. Agencies should state this on their website.

SUBMISSIONS

I have a book on my list that I am really pleased with and that has had some wonderful reviews. But it was submitted to me by an agent with an almost unreadable first chapter. If I hadn't been ill at home, rather than busy in the office, I don't think I would have persisted. But there must have been something about it because I picked it up again half an hour after I had given up on it and I kept going. Then I realized 'Oh my goodness, this is brilliant!' So really think about the opening. What is going to attract someone's attention? It's all about making someone want to turn the page. And that pertains to literary fiction, just as much as it does to commercial fiction. You've got to give the reader a reason to turn the page.

Kate Parkin, publisher, John Murray Publishers
www.johnmurray.co.uk

Agencies and those publishing houses that accept them can receive around 30–50 unsolicited submissions in the post or by email each day; that's anything from 150–200 a week and some agencies receive a lot more. Imagine all those submissions landing on desks and into inboxes, all of them believing they are worthy of being published. If there is anything about a submission that makes it hard to read, it will swiftly go to the rejection pile.

A submission represents you. It needs to be well set out, clean, clear with accurate spelling, grammar and punctuation. If you can show that you care about what you are doing and that you are approaching the job in a professional way, you encourage the agent/editor to have confidence in its contents, even before they start reading. You are, after all, putting yourself forward as a professional writer so make sure your submission is professional.

Submissions will vary slightly from company to company. Literary agents Lutyens & Rubenstein ask for two sample chapters, a covering letter and/or a short synopsis; Curtis Brown want three sample chapters, a covering letter and a synopsis (by post); Blake Friedmann also want three chapters and a covering letter but state that the synopsis should be no longer than three pages. The agencies give *very* clear guidelines. In general, they will consist of the following:

- *a covering letter*
- *the first few chapters (1, 2, 3; not random chapters); if the number of chapters is not specified, send the first three*
- *a synopsis.*

Add to that:

- *a stamped addressed envelope if the agent/editor asks that you do; why should you expect them to pay for the postage? Use a new envelope; not a used one. However, if an SAE is not specified, don't send one. Firstly, it's too much of a temptation to an agent/editor and, secondly, you should not be reusing these submissions so is a large SAE really necessary?*
- *a stamped postcard that the agency/publisher can put in the post to acknowledge receipt; as well as your address, add the title of your book (just in case it gets separated from your submission).*

Agents and editors want to see well-presented submissions (no stains, paw prints, or even smelling of cigarette smoke). If it is presented perfectly, it will get noticed for all the right reasons. You should use a computer; do not handwrite your submission. Make sure that your printer produces clear, sharp and easy-to-read text.

In this day and age, it really should be a computer rather than a typewriter. Apart from the fact that it is so much easier to edit your work, agents and publishers communicate by email; information can be found on the internet and often it is a requirement of the contract that your manuscript be submitted on a PC-compatible disk.

Use a good-quality A4 paper. It doesn't have to be the most expensive paper but it needs to be robust enough to be handled by (potentially) several people and survive being sent in the post.

It must be true to say that the amount of submissions has increased since creative writing courses in universities really took hold. When I started as an agent in 2005, I remember looking through creative writing courses on the computer: when I got to 35 I'd had enough and closed the screen.

Heather Holden Brown, literary agent, hhb Agency Ltd
www.hhbagency.com

Multiple submissions or one at a time?
Ask most industry professionals and they will tell you that agents and publishers prefer to be approached one at a time. Ask an author the same question and the response is very different. An author can spend a very long time waiting for a response. If you sent your submission to 20 agents, one at a time, and waited, on average, eight weeks for a decision from each of them, you could spend over three years before you heard from the twentieth.

So, for authors, multiple submissions make sense. Opinion is divided on whether you own up to this or not. Some (mainly writers) feel that you do not have to let the agent/editor know that you are submitting to others; however, if you get a response and are asked whether anyone else is looking at your submission, you should be honest. If they are asking you that question, it shows that they have an interest in your work. Others (industry professionals) feel that it is only common courtesy to let the agent/editor know that you are approaching others.

Did you know?
In the US, submitting your work is also known as 'getting over the transom'. In the old days, publishers had windows above their front doors, called a transom, which was often tilted open at night to let the air circulate. Hopeful authors would throw their manuscript over the transom at night in the hope that it would get read and picked up by the publisher.

If I want to see more of a particular submission, I usually ask a writer to send me a complete manuscript as a Word document. So, while I am getting stacks of new submissions

*in as emails, I also have a shortlist of ten or so full
manuscripts that I am trying to read. Of course, while you're
reading the full manuscripts, another 50 or so submissions
will come in. It's a tough business that operates completely
differently from most 'conventional' types of work. The fact
is, it would be quite possible to work like crazy for a year
and not sell anything. Using your time in the optimum way,
focusing on absolutely the right projects, is one of the biggest
challenges we face as agents.*

Sarah Davies, literary agent, The Greenhouse Literary Agency
www.greenhouseliterary.com

Keeping track of submissions

While one hopes that the number of submissions you make don't run
into the hundreds, it makes sense to keep a record of where you sent
your work, on what date you sent it out, whether you received your
acknowledgment of receipt from the agent/publisher, whether it was
rejected and, if so, what kind of rejection it was (a straightforward
'no thanks' letter or one with a bit of helpful advice).

*Inevitably, a lot of common sense comes into this.
Do your research. Make sure you know the individual
that you are going to contact; 'know' in the sense that
you've looked up what they've already published in the
past, what their taste is and where they fit into the whole
system. That's the absolute minimum that you should know.
Just spraying around ideas (and proposals) willy nilly is a
waste of time. You should have your script well mapped out
in your mind before you approach anyone. People want to
know in a nutshell what your proposal is about. It's just like
the old Hollywood 25-word pitch. Anyone who has to pitch
a proposal should watch the opening scene of Altman's film,
'The Player'. It's very funny but about right.*

*I think the pitch is also a measure of the mindset of the
individual who is pitching to me. Obviously, it's important
that they can write and that they have a good idea. But is
it something I can pitch well in turn – in my acquisition*

meeting? You pitch to me, if I 'get it', I can make sure everyone else around me gets it and they can sell it effectively to the retailers and, one hopes, the retailers can then sell it on to the consumer. The more crafted the package the more easily it can be passed on from one to the other and the more likely it is that you will get a publishing deal.

Trevor Dolby, publisher, Preface Publishing, an imprint of Random House

www.prefacepublishing.co.uk

Introductory or query letter

Everybody will read your query or covering letter. If you are lucky, they will go on to read your synopsis and maybe even the sample chapters but they will *all* look at the letter. This is effectively page one of your submission.

Your covering letter needs to give a sense of who you are, your ambitions, what genre you are pitching at and a brief pitch of the book you are trying to submit. Nowadays, the writer is very much part of the package of a published book so you do need to give a sense of yourself in the letter. You should be pleasant, direct, simple and straightforward.

The letter is also a business proposal. You are hoping to sell a product to an agent/editor. You should show that you have knowledge of the company that you are writing to; do not send out a generic covering letter.

Writing a query letter is an art form in itself. You have to get quite a lot of information onto, ideally, *one page*. That can be quite a daunting thought but if you can manage to compress the following information into an interesting and enticing format, you stand a greater chance of grabbing the attention of an agent or editor.

Insight

Think of the query letter as a shortened version of the conversation you would like to be having face to face with the agent in terms of the information you want to get across. Be business-like and to the point.

Your letter should include the following:

- *the title and subject of your book and the angle you will take*
- *roughly how many words it contains (see Word count, Chapter 4, p. 108)*
- *why people will want to read the book*
- *why you are the right person to write this book: do you have a suitable background, relevant qualifications (especially needed if you are writing non-fiction), media experience? What is interesting about you? Do you have any publishing history?*
- *if your book is the first in a series or if you have other ideas to follow up on this one*
- *whether the subject matter is topical*
- *benchmark against bestselling authors.*

The aim is to give the key idea of your book. To do this, think of the 30-second rule. Sales reps have, at most, 30 seconds to sell a book into the shops. Anything that takes longer than that...they will have moved on to the next book.

Having a constraint in your writing can force your creativity. Try and encapsulate your book into one or two sentences. Think Twitter if you like. There is a (probably apocryphal) story that the film *Alien* was sold to Hollywood as '*Jaws* in space'. It's pithy and to the point and you get an immediate sense of what the film is about.

> *It's always good to have some kind of pitch (such as 'It's a cross between Dan Brown and Jilly Cooper' or whatever) and an uncomplicated synopsis. You can then gauge immediately what you're reading – which is a good thing when we have around 50 unsolicited manuscripts coming in each week. When a writer is submitting, they should always look at it as if the agent was wandering round a bookshop and reading the blurb on the back of a book; that's what you're really aiming for. That immediate hook so that you know what you're in for and want to start the book.*
>
> Camilla Goslett, literary agent, Curtis Brown
> www.curtisbrown.co.uk

THE TITLE
An eye-catching title is a major part of a book's success. People spend around eight seconds looking at the cover of a book before they make a decision whether to buy it or not. If you are lucky, they spend 12 seconds reading through the blurb and the opening page. You will need to put careful thought into your title.

Shorter titles tend to do better; yes, there are exceptions to the rule (*Salmon Fishing in the Yemen*, *A Short History of Tractors in Ukrainian*, etc.) but shorter titles are more memorable.

If you are writing non-fiction, you should consider having a clear and explanatory title; many people look for books on the internet and a title that clearly states what the book is all about (*Speak Spanish with Confidence*, for example) is more likely to get picked up.

Also for non-fiction, a strapline or sub-title spelling out the benefits of reading your book is also helpful. Lynne Truss's book *Eats, Shoots & Leaves* had the strapline 'The Zero Tolerance Approach to Punctuation'. Good straplines will appear on Amazon and Google.

If you are still not convinced that you have the right one, put [working title] after the main title.

BIOGRAPHY
The agent/editor needs to know a little bit about you. You need to include whether you have had anything published before (this shows you have a track record at writing) and anything else that may be of interest and that can make you a saleable author. Put in any writing or public speaking experience that is relevant to the book. If you have a website or blog, put that down; that shows you are able to self-promote and potentially already have a following.

This has to be condensed into one paragraph of your covering letter. If you feel that there are other elements in your CV that are worth mentioning or expanding upon, have a separate sheet of paper.

Why are you the best author to write this book?
This is useful for the publishers to know from a publicity point of view. Do you have any endorsements? If you know a published fiction writer who has looked at your work and is prepared to say something positive about it, then use that. You only have a short time to sell yourself so you need all the help you can get. That is not to say that you *must* have an endorsement: positive comments from your mother, best friend or neighbour will not count.

Do not:

- *grovel, demand or gush; it's a business letter*
- *use capitals; it's the written equivalent of shouting*
- *tell the recipient that they are going to love your book/you are the best thing since Rowling/Nabokov/Cussler – you are just setting the reader up to be disappointed*
- *ask for feedback*
- *tell them what you want the cover of the book to look like*
- *say that your work is copyrighted or include a copyright symbol on your manuscript*
- *do not crack jokes; humour is subjective*
- *send in a photograph of yourself.*

Do:

- *write a coherent, enticing, professional, friendly letter*
- *make use of paragraphs (and bullet points if you feel they help get the information over clearly and quickly)*
- *explain why you sent your submission to that particular agent (you liked their authors, their website, etc.); it shows that you are interested and have done your homework on the company*
- *say you will wait to hear back from them before sending it elsewhere or explain that you have sent it to x other agents but will keep them informed of any developments*
- *get someone to read it through for you; another pair of eyes is always useful.*

> **Did you know?**
> In 2008 Orion, one of the UK's leading trade publishers, received over 1,000 manuscripts from agents proposing new authors. They bought seven.

Synopsis

First-time novelists need more than one book inside them because one thing the industry knows is that regular repeating authors do best. There are an awful lot of authors who have been in the bestseller lists for years and years (John Grisham, Maeve Binchy, James Patterson, Jeffrey Archer and so on). What I am looking for when I take on a new author, is someone who is in it for a career; I think that's terribly important.

I would be very unlikely to take on a novelist for just one book. It's such a lot of work to develop a relationship with a new writer, to get their books to sell... you don't want to invest all that effort for just one book. When I was at Random House, we published the crime writer, Karin Slaughter. When her first novel turned up, it was accompanied by four or five brilliantly worked out plots for the next books in her proposed series. And she said she had more. It was clear that this was a completely professional and dedicated writer; she had entered her world so completely. We offered her a multi-book contract, which is extremely unusual for a first-time writer.

It is all about confidence, about the sense that an author has stories in them, who wants to write and who has other ideas that interest them. That suggests a fertile imagination, an engagement in the craft and a willingness to commit themselves to a future as a writer.

Kate Parkin, publisher, John Murray Publishers
www.johnmurray.co.uk

A synopsis is not a blow-by-blow account of what happens in each chapter. A synopsis means 'a brief description of the contents of something'. It has to be detailed enough to grab the reader's attention but short enough to make them want to read more.

This is also an opportunity to show that you know your work really well; that you are in control of it, that you know how to plot its structure and that you are a good enough writer to break it down to its component parts.

A synopsis is like the extended blurb at the back of a book but with the ending included (if it is a work of fiction). This is not the place to be coy about the twist in the tail; the agent/editor needs to be able to judge the book as a whole, so tell them how it ends. Equally, you do not have to list every twist and turn of the narrative. The main aim is to intrigue them, grab their interest and make them want to read the book.

Writing a synopsis is a skill but it is one that can be learned. If you are writing fiction, have a look at the *Oxford Companion to Literature*. There you will find a large number of brief summaries of well-known works. Also look at film reviews, which are good examples of how to summarize a creative idea.

> **Insight**
> Make writing a synopsis a positive experience. Show that you really know your work. Use it as an opportunity to go back, study what you have written and improve it if necessary.

It can sometimes be discouraging to see submissions that are poorly written with grammatical errors and typos. The initial presentation is so important, and so we always prefer to review material that is in the best shape it can be. It can also be frustrating to review manuscripts from folks who believe that writing a children's book is easy. Writing is a craft and skill that authors can spend their lifetimes honing, no matter who the audience is intended to be. We also expect the author to have a handle on who their audience is, and where their project will fit – is it middle-grade or teen, for example.

Children's Editorial Group, HarperCollins US
www.harpercollins.com

Always submit what the agency or publishing house is asking for. If they want a one-page synopsis, give them one page; if they want three, do three and so on. If you give them what they want, you reduce the annoyance factor and the chance that your submission gets put to one side before they have read it through completely.

If there is no specific guideline as to length of synopsis, then it is up to you. It depends very much on the type of book you are writing. A book on how to learn Spanish may well take only one page to cover all the relevant points while a literary novel may take a few pages and an academic book even longer. You are aiming to get all the important points of the book down in a clear, logical style.

This may, of course, mean that you have to produce several versions of your synopsis, some slightly longer than others. This should not be a problem, though; you are a writer after all.

For fiction:

- the synopsis needs to be double-spaced and printed on one side of A4
- introduce the main characters and any other characters pivotal to the plot (but not all)
- introduce the main plot
- highlight the high points
- where is it set? When is it set?
- how does it end?
- you don't need to do a chapter-by-chapter breakdown
- write it in the present tense, even if the book is set in the past tense
- have you a particular format in mind? Are there illustrations?
- what is your target market? Give facts and figures
- are there any ties with anniversaries/special events?

For non-fiction:

- *the synopsis needs to be double-spaced and printed on one side of A4*
- *give an overview of the central argument or theme (i.e. the subject and how you will develop it)*
- *list a table of contents*
- *outline: a chapter-by-chapter breakdown covering the main points of each chapter (no more than a paragraph per chapter usually); this shows you can plot the book and that you have enough material to produce a decent book on the subject*
- *competition: comparison with other similar books on the market*
- *have you a particular format in mind? Are there illustrations?*
- *what is your target market? Give facts and figures*
- *are there any ties with anniversaries/special events?*

If you are writing non-fiction, agents and editors aren't necessarily going to know much about your subject. So what you need to do is give them an overview of it and convince them that there is room for another book on whatever your particular subject is. If you wanted to write a book about asthma, for example, you could give an idea of how many people there are in the country who suffer from asthma. By doing that you are instantly giving the agent or publisher an idea of the potential purchasers of the book.

Maria McCarthy, author
www.mariamccarthy.co.uk

MARKET POTENTIAL AND READERSHIP

It is not enough to hope that your manuscript will speak for itself – it won't. You need to present a good argument that your book will sell. Give agents and, therefore, editors, all the information they need to make a positive decision. Who is going to buy this book and why? You will have mentioned this briefly in your covering letter; now you need to expand on this.

No one will take on a book, however well written, unless they know it is going to sell in requisite quantities. You will be describing the primary market for your book; in other words, where it is going to sell the greatest numbers. Do not rely on 'the general reader' as the person who will buy your book. The publishers need to know that there is a specific audience who are the potential buyers. There is no need to try to match your book to lots of different markets; for example, if the book is about learning ballroom dancing, the main audience would be people who want to learn to dance. You don't have to throw in young adults, people who want to lose weight, the newly retired...and any other group you think might be remotely interested in dance.

If you believe that the book will have a substantial secondary market (an academic course or a professional organization, for example), then give the details as well. If you feel that your book will have an international audience, then say so.

THE COMPETITION
List similar titles in the marketplace. The fact that there are other books on the same subject as yours is not a problem. Competition is a good thing. Agents and editors are often wary of books that have no competition at all; it is much more comforting to know that it fits into a recognizable genre or deals with subject matter that has already proved successful with the buying public. What you must do is explain why your book will be different and will improve on these other competing titles.

Insight
If the choice is between two similar books, the agent/editor will go with the writer that has a ready-made potential readership. If you can provide information on who may buy your book, your submission will look more attractive.

ANNIVERSARIES/TIE-INS
This will not apply to every book but, if you can link your book to an anniversary or event, then you are already providing a useful hook that could generate media interest.

Sample chapters/opening pages

I receive more and more proposals via email, but hard copies are acceptable as well. A big turn-off is a proposal that is sloppy, incomplete, poorly assembled, and hasn't been proofread/copyedited; if I see tons of spelling mistakes or it's poorly written, it's an immediate rejection.

Amy Vinchesi, editor, Watson-Guptill, an imprint of Random House

www.randomhouse.com

The first chapter is always important in a book. But so are the first paragraph and the first sentence. The first page of a novel should be brilliant if it is to jump off the slush pile.

The reader, in this instance the agent or the publisher, will want the interest that they felt on reading your covering letter and synopsis to be underlined. These chapters will show the quality of your writing.

You need to grab the attention and interest of your reader from the start. It's no good if the story really gets going by Chapter 5 – if that's the case, maybe you should consider getting rid of Chapters 1 to 4.

Tips on presentation

- *Chapters should start on a new page. Justify left-hand side only. **Don't use a blank line between paragraphs**; indent first line of new paragraph. Blank lines should be used for change of subject, or time, or scene, or viewpoint. Consistent use of spellings, capitalization, sub-headings, etc. **Decide whether you're using 'ise' or 'ize'.***
- *Organize pages (publishers call them folios) – number straight through from beginning to end; don't start each chapter with p. 1.*
- *Put your name and the title of your book on each page; use the 'header' or 'footer' option, small print.*
- *Poetry – type it exactly the way the poem would appear in the printed version.*

(Contd)

> *Illustrations/diagrams – if your work requires illustrations, maps, and/or diagrams, and you expect to provide them yourself, include a selection with your sample chapters. You could send a rough copy/example with your submission, rather than spend time and money on high-quality originals (which run the risk of getting lost while out with an agent/editor). Unless your book is about photography, you would want to give an **idea** of the quality; copies will be fine for that.*

I think an important tip for anyone who wants to get published is always go to the agency website. All too often writers submit work that is outside our interests and specialisms – for example, age groups or genres we just don't represent. This is something that drives all agents mad. Aspiring writers need to take time and trouble to target their work correctly. And it makes me tear my hair out because it means that around 15 per cent of material that comes in is simply not relevant to me and that is such a huge time waster.

When I receive material that just isn't for Greenhouse I often write back to the sender to enquire where they read about us, with the aim of getting that listing removed or corrected. Usually the answer is: 'Oops, sorry, my fault. I misread the information.'

So one thing I would say to aspiring writers is do your homework, go straight to the website for up-to-the-minute instructions because agencies' submission guidelines are subject to change and you want to make sure you don't waste either your time or theirs.

Sarah Davies, literary agent, The Greenhouse Literary Agency
www.greenhouseliterary.com

Don't:

- *send a synopsis without sample chapters, and vice versa*
- *try to stand out by using coloured paper or coloured text*
- *use italics or comedy fonts*

- *use fancy folders, ring binders or plastic folders (too slippery)*
- *try to be gimmicky; you are aiming for 'professional', not wacky*
- *cram in your text with small point sizes and margins*
- *staple your work together (it's difficult to read stapled pages); don't use paperclips (too easy to pick up extra pages that don't belong to the manuscript when it's been lying on a desk); don't use pins (they can draw blood)*
- *try to catch out agents/editors by putting in a trap to check that they have actually read through the submission*
- *be tempted to stray too far from these guidelines; they are used because they work; they are easy to read; they work for agents and publishers*
- *suggest your own illustrator; agents/editors like to choose their own so this could put them off*
- *produce a mock-up of the book.*

Do:

- *print on one side of the paper*
- *leave a decent margin (at least 4 cm (1½") all around the text): editors need the space to make corrections, amendments and instructions to the printer*
- *use 12-point type and a font that's easy to read (e.g. Arial, Times); use black ink*
- *indent the first line of each paragraph*
- *make sure the pages have printed straight*
- *have a title page with your contact details, i.e. the title, your name (or pen name) and address in the bottom right-hand corner*
- *use a couple of rubber bands to bind your papers together*
- *put the pages into a wallet-type folder (more than one if necessary)*
- *put the title of the book and your name and address on the outside of the folder.*

A proposal should be no more than 20 pages long, i.e. short enough to speed-read but long enough to get an idea of the writer's style and the book's potential.

When you have finished your letter and got your chapters and synopsis ready, print them all off and then read them through again before sending them out. Proofreading a printed page is very different from reading on screen.

> **Insight**
> When proofreading, read from the bottom of the page up, a line at a time. Cover up the lines that you have checked as you work up the page. This helps you to pick out any typos or spelling errors that you might miss if you read the text conventionally.

Checklist

Before you send anything out, make sure:

- *people's names are spelt correctly. Check everything is spelt correctly. If you don't get it right, it doesn't give the reader a feeling of trust and confidence in the writer*
- *grammar, punctuation, syntax are all correct*
- *your covering letter is businesslike and gets to the point*
- *you have included a stamped addressed envelope/postcard with the correct postage*
- *the presentation is clean and professional*
- *you keep a copy of your submission letter, your sample chapters, your synopsis – don't send your only copy.*

The closer you get to sending your proposal out, the harder it is to let it go. But it has to go out at some point. Get it to the best standard you can and then send it on its way.

As an agent, you have to be very straight with people and I think writers appreciate that. If you do believe something is terrible you've just got to say that you don't think it's working and give your reasons why. It's up to the writer to take that away and either agree with you and see that you've got a point or fight for what they believe in. I think anyone appreciates honesty. Ultimately, you have to get on with each other; you have to like your authors or admire them in some way. This has to work as a relationship because, hopefully, it's one that's going to last for quite a long time; if all goes well it can last decades.

Camilla Goslett, literary agent, Curtis Brown
www.curtisbrown.co.uk

Case study

Isabel Losada, author, *New Habits* (Hodder), *The Battersea Park Road to Enlightenment* (Bloomsbury), *For Tibet With Love: A Beginner's Guide to Changing the World* (Bloomsbury), *100 Reasons To Be Glad* (Summersdale), *Men! Where the **** are they?* (Virgin – Random House), *The Battersea Park Road to Paradise* (Watkins Publishing) www.isabellosada.com

I'd once edited a book but now I had one that I was writing myself. The compulsory first three chapters were finished and I started to write to agents with what has since been called 'misguided eternal optimism.' You can imagine my excitement when I was taken on by an enthusiastic agent at one of the three top London literary agencies. She was fantastically positive about the book I was writing (The Battersea Park Road to Enlightenment), *experienced in the business, and was interested not only in selling the book but also in helping me make it as good as possible. I very quickly came to adore her.*

I had just submitted chapter 6, the Tantric Sex chapter, when she called me in for a meeting. She closed the door and told me she had been fired by the agency because she hadn't been turning over

(Contd)

profit quickly enough. I was stunned; halfway through the book and I didn't have an agent any more. I approached practically every other agent in London, none of whom were interested. So I went back to the umbrella company of the first agency and said, 'It's not my fault you fired this agent. Don't you have an obligation to represent me?'

They agreed and one of the other agents took me on. She was very old school in that she submitted to one publishing house at a time and told me, 'Under no circumstances do I ever follow up the submission in any way, I wait for them to get back to me.' This method is very respectful of the publishing houses but makes the poor author contemplate their old age pension.

I think she submitted my book in various forms to practically every single publishing house in London. But because she wouldn't let me speak to any of them, I had no idea why it was being rejected. 'They said it wasn't for them', she'd say if I enquired.

After 18 months of this and with about 18 rejections from publishing houses, she told me to give up, 'Put it down to experience; put the book aside and good luck with life.' She showed me the door. I still had a book that, bizarrely perhaps, I was convinced that everybody would want to read but I seemed to be alone in this view since I now had no publisher, no agent and enough rejection letters to form a collection. However I found there were advantages to NOT having an agent, too. Freed from the shackles of representation, I was able to phone all the editors that had rejected the book and find out why they had turned it down.

I discovered that, first of all, they remembered the title, then they remembered the content, they were very complimentary about my writing and usually the book had got as far as the editorial meeting. I had known nothing of this when I was with an agent as I had been forbidden to speak to any of the editors.

I managed to get all the various rejection letters sent through to me and what I noticed was that they all contradicted each other. For example:

- *Rejection A: 'We absolutely loved this book but we felt that the author should have inserted more information about the various subjects that she explored.'*
- *Rejection B: 'We absolutely loved this book but we felt that the author had included too much information and not enough personal narrative.'*
- *Rejection C: 'We found that there was too much personal narrative in this book and that she really needed to concentrate on varying the ending of her book.'*
- *Rejection D: 'We felt that, although she was a wonderful authorial voice, this would be more suitable as a series of magazine articles.'*

All completely contradictory and left me feeling completely bewildered. I thought, 'Right, I need to get myself another agent.' But obviously that was difficult because I'd already had rejections from every publishing house in London and no agent will take on a book that everybody's already turned down.

So I took myself off to the London Book Fair whereby, if you are blessed with the gift of the gab, you can manage to get yourself into areas where authors are not supposed to be...which I did. I met two fabulous agents, both of whom invited me to send them my writing, both of whom read the manuscript, asked me who had rejected it and showed me the door again when I was honest about where it had been submitted. Agents obviously don't like something that's already been touted round.

I set about going back to the 18 publishing houses that had turned it down, resubmitting it myself. If it had been submitted as one chapter, I submitted the whole book; if it had been submitted as a whole book, I submitted one chapter. Basically, I did the opposite

(Contd)

of what had been done previously. Eventually some unknown reader at Bloomsbury read it and got excited. She split up the chapters and passed it around and then everyone got excited, they interviewed me and eventually sent a large bunch of flowers and an offer. They were one of the publishers that had originally rejected the book. But I didn't remind them. I went back to one of the agents, told them I'd got the deal and, unsurprisingly as I had an offer in my hand, they were then willing to take me on.

It was about two years from the time that I had finished writing the book until I eventually had a publishing deal and an agent but it had been a long hard slog and the really hard work starts at that point.

One of the problems with my book is that the category was something like 'narrative non-fiction – semi-autobiographical humour MBS [mind, body, spirit] and travel.' This doesn't help. If I'd give one tip now it would be that before you even start writing your book you should go into the bookshop and work out where it's going to be found. If it's not fiction, you may have a problem. And if you've written something really original, then you've definitely got a problem. Books have got to go on a shelf somewhere but if you've written something that is difficult to put in a category then it's also difficult to market.

Much as I would love a shelf, in a bookshop, which specifically says 'Bestselling works by Isabel Losada', I have to rely on my books being put in amongst other subjects. My books have appeared in 'Religion', 'Travel', 'Popular Psychology', 'Mind, Body, Spirit' and 'Biography'; they've also appeared (misplaced) in 'Fiction'. They've literally appeared all over the shop and that has been a huge problem. In fact, one of my titles was so lost in one of the sections, it was retitled; it then appeared in 'Philosophy' where it disappeared altogether. So my first advice to prospective authors is to write fiction. If you're not a fiction writer, make sure you know which part of a shop your books are going to go into. My second piece of advice is persistence – joy, persistence – joy, persistence – joy, persistence – joy...

If you are SURE your book is going to sell (because you know who to and why) then you can persevere. One of my inspirations was that I'd read that Jonathan Livingston Seagull *had been turned down 98 times; so at 18 rejections I felt I was just starting. In the end, my book that no one wanted did fantastically well. It earned out the advance before publication and went on to sell 100,000 copies and be published in 16 languages.*

Selling subsequent books has not been easier... but that's another story.

10 THINGS TO REMEMBER

1 *Explain why you have targeted a particular agency or publishing house; it shows that you have done your homework and have an interest in what they do.*

2 *Networking is important and useful – try to get someone influential (another writer; an expert) to endorse your work.*

3 *Literary agents will only take on a manuscript that they feel passionate about. If they don't have strong feelings for it, it makes it very difficult for them to go on and sell it.*

4 *The first instinct of an agent or publisher will be to reject your work so you need to stand out and show them that they can make money from you.*

5 *The covering letter has to convince an agent/editor that this is a person they want to work with.*

6 *Try reading the letter back to yourself, pretending that you don't know this person. Do you like what you see? Are you intrigued?*

7 *Practise writing a synopsis by summarizing a famous book or one that you know well.*

8 *A good proposal should leave no question unanswered.*

9 *Editors and agents remember the bits that don't work (for example, spelling errors; incorrect address; too many chapters or too few), so don't give them the opportunity.*

10 *Finalize off screen. Words do really look very different on a printed page. When you read on screen, you read what you think you wrote, not what is necessarily there.*

3

Persistence

In this chapter you will learn:
- *how to deal with rejection*
- *why submissions are rejected*
- *how to learn from rejection.*

It is impossible to discourage the real writers – they don't give a damn what you say, they're going to write.

Sinclair Lewis, author

Joanna Trollope once said it had taken her 20 years to become an overnight success. She stuck at her writing and refused to give up. Successfully published authors are resilient and tenacious. Many writers have had a great book but it was the wrong time for it; others have had bad books but the timing was just right. Things can go wrong for a variety of reasons but these writers just kept plugging away. You need to have these qualities to survive as an author.

So, you sent in your submission two months ago and you have not heard a thing. What should you do?

This will not be a fast process. It takes time. Even when you get taken on by an agent and editor, the wheels of the publishing industry grind rather slowly. It *is* frustrating but be prepared to wait for a decision.

Instead, while you are waiting for people to get back to you, start working on your next project. It could be an article for the local magazine or newspaper; it might be the outline for your next book. Whatever it is, don't waste time and energy worrying about what is happening to your submission; channel it into something positive.

Don't bombard an agent. There's a kind of etiquette here; you send your very best work and if you are rejected you don't immediately go back with another one. If you are rejected, you might ask, 'In the future, would you be interested in reading something else?' You certainly shouldn't swamp agents with multiple submissions.

Never write back to an agent on rejection and say, 'That's your loss!', as I have had some people do.

Do not write to an agent, telling them you are brilliant or how exactly like Tolkien or Philip Pullman you are, because you are setting yourself up to disappoint.

Just set out your stall clearly and simply and let your writing do your work for you because it all comes down to the writing in the end.

Sarah Davies, literary agent, The Greenhouse Literary Agency
www.greenhouseliterary.com

> **Insight**
> The larger the agency or publishing house, the more people there are who may have to be convinced to take on you and your book.

On average, the wait for a response is around two to three months; some companies will take longer though. You should be polite and allow the agent/editor enough time to get to your submission and read it through; after all, they have busy jobs, working with their existing authors, and the slush pile can be quite large. Equally, if you have been waiting for a long time, it is perfectly reasonable either to ask for your submission back (if you want it returned) or to explain that you will be approaching other companies from now on (even if you have sent your submission out to more than one company).

Agents and editors do receive a tremendous amount of unsolicited work every week (the Darley Anderson Agency, for example, receives over 1,300 submissions each month). They work hard to keep on top of the slush pile. However, it is important to remember that just reading through unsolicited submissions is not their main job; they have many more pressing concerns, not least the authors they already represent. It is also worth realizing how courteous agents and editors are; they actually bother to write back when it would be much easier to just bin the submissions they don't like without even contacting the people who sent them in.

Be prepared for rejection

Writing comes with a price – rejection. *Every* writer gets rejected at some point – remember that. If you meet an author who claims that they have never had a rejection, they are either the most extraordinary exception to the rule or they are not being entirely truthful with you. You may have read of the (now) famous authors whose work was rejected time and time again, among them Beatrix Potter, George Orwell and Agatha Christie. C.S. Lewis received over 800 rejections before he sold any of his writing; *Zen and the Art of Motorcycle Maintenance* was rejected 121 times; while the *San Francisco Examiner* rejected Rudyard Kipling's submission in 1889, explaining that they were sorry but 'You just do not know how to use the English language.' Rejections are not pleasant but they will not kill you and you can learn from them.

It is not known whether D.H. Lawrence learned anything when Heinemann rejected *Sons and Lovers* in 1912 on the basis that its 'want of reticence makes it unfit...for publication in England'. Lawrence was not happy and wrote back, 'Curse the blasted, jelly-boned swines, the slimy, the belly-wriggling invertebrates... the snivelling, dribbling, dithering, palsied, pulseless lot that make up England today.'

At least Lawrence was given a reason why they turned his manuscript down. Other authors are not as lucky. Don't expect to be given reasons for rejection. If there are any compliments (or criticisms) about your work – take them at face value. Editors and agents tend not to give praise if they don't mean it. If they have taken the time and trouble to give an indication of what they think about your work (even if it is a fairly negative comment) take it as a good sign. It is easier and quicker to send out a standard 'thank you but no thank you' letter; anything else is a positive. If there is advice that comes with rejection, take it and learn from it. Don't send an angry or sarcastic letter/email back. Publishing is a small world and word will get around if you are abusive and unhelpful.

Equally, if you have had a rejected submission:

- *do not keep resubmitting it in its 'improved' version to the same agent/editor – unless specifically asked to do so*
- *don't phone up asking to discuss your book*
- *do not use the phrases from one rejection letter in your approach to another agent/editor (for example, 'my book did not fit the list at Curtis Brown'); phrases such as 'does not fit our list' are quite standard*
- *give yourself a bit of time to feel demoralized, miserable and unwanted and then pull yourself together and do something positive with your book.*

Insight
If you hector, stalk or harass agents and publishers, they will think twice about taking you on as a client.

REASONS FOR REJECTION

I probably get 10–15 unsolicited manuscripts a week that are just addressed to 'Dear Editor'… or not even that sometimes. I just delete them right away. As editors, we're looking for a reason to say 'No' because we've got so much to do. If you address somebody by their name, it shows the editor that at least you've done some sort of research, as opposed to casting a wide net and sending your work to everybody under the sun.

Go to a publisher's website and you will find what other books they publish. If they have one that is in direct competition to yours, they're probably not going to sign another one. However, say you went to SAGE's website, for example, and saw that we didn't have a book in conflict communication. If that was the book you wanted to write, your cover letter would jump out at me. I would be really impressed because it matches the need of the house and the editor; it shows that you've done your homework.

Todd Armstrong, Senior Acquisitions Editor, SAGE Publications
www.sagepub.com

In practical terms, literary agencies and publishing houses have to turn down most of what is sent to them. Partly because they would not be able to take on 50 or 60 new authors each week. And partly because they are trying to peer into the future a year or two ahead and guess what will be selling in the book world then – and they do not always get it right.

Try to remember:

- *a rejection is not personal. It is an **individual** reader's response to what you sent in to them at that time*
- *generally, manuscripts are turned down because they are not what one person is looking for at that particular moment.*

Insight
Give distance to the rejection before you do anything about it. Read your manuscript in a different place from where you wrote it. This gives you some perspective.

If you realize that rejection is part of the job, how you deal with it can become a positive and enriching experience. One writer no longer uses the word 'rejection'; she calls them 'remarketing opportunities'. Try not to dwell on the negativity of the rejection. Treat it as a red alert, warning you that something is not quite right yet.

So try to work out why you didn't succeed. Read between the lines of the rejection; it is not easy if you have had a 'thanks but no thanks' response but ask yourself the following:

- *Was it **really** the best it could be in every way?*
- *Were all the facts (contact details, etc.) correct?*
- *Did you check that the agency/publisher was taking unsolicited submissions?*
- *Was your presentation professional, clean, tidy?*
- *Was your pitch strong enough?*
- *Had you researched the market properly?*
- *Were there any spelling mistakes; was the grammar and punctuation spot on?*

It is important to do your research about the publishing company. If an author comes in and says they don't know anything about Random House, I think that a) their agent hasn't done a very good job of preparing them, and b) I'm not impressed that they have made no effort themselves. It's a bit like a job interview really. If someone goes for an interview and hasn't bothered to do any research about the company, it always strikes me as a bit odd.

Doug Young, Publishing Director, Sport & Entertainment, Transworld
www.transworld-publishers.co.uk

It is not necessarily that your writing is not good enough. It could be that your work was just too similar to that of an author they already have on their books. Why would they want something identical to a book they have just sold? If they tell you that they already have a similar author on their list, you should be greatly encouraged by that. It means that they can see potential in your work.

It may be that your work is not right for the market right now. Publishing houses will not be buying the kinds of book that are currently in the bestseller lists; they will be looking for something different. You have to be original and write from your heart. Agents and editors can tell when you are writing about what you love or feel strongly about.

If they said they enjoyed reading your submission but they just didn't feel strongly about it, again, you should feel encouraged. Maybe your work just didn't 'speak' to that person. There is no point in an agent representing an author whose books they do not like. They need to feel passionate about a book in order to sell it. It is very much about individual tastes and preferences. If one person didn't like it, another may love it.

If they said that the plot didn't engage them or that they found it hard going, or slow, or any similar comment, then you need to do a rewrite.

Insight
If you do not have an email address, get one. Most communication is done by email nowadays. If you don't appear to have an email address, it may put an agent/editor off.

It may be that you have written something good but that it is not the right book to launch your career as a published author. Helen Corner (Cornerstones Literary Consultancy) refers to this in greater detail on p. 74. It is very easy to think of your current work as the best thing you have ever done but it may be the book that helps you develop as a writer – in which case, it was not a waste of time. You may need to consider putting it to one side and begin to work up your next project.

So, take a long hard look at what you sent out, be prepared to rework it and send it out again or put it aside and start anew. Agents and editors tend not to want to work with writers who may have a book in them but it is just not there yet. They want as near to the finished article as possible. Michael Ridpath wrote and rewrote his first thriller, *Free To Trade*, three times before he sent out a synopsis to agents. It was picked up by literary agent Carole Blake, who got five publishing houses bidding for it in an auction (won by Heinemann for a six-figure deal) and sold the rights to 35 territories.

> **Insight**
> Good writers of great books get rejected – many times. Even when they are published, they will get their fair share of bad reviews. Rejection goes hand in hand with success.

Know your craft

> *Writing is terribly hard and lonely and authors have to be highly disciplined. They have to write regularly, and, in order to get it 'to market' (whether that means to literary agents or publishing houses), writers have to totally absorb themselves in their work. The authors that are getting work accepted by publishers are sometimes doing six, seven, even eight drafts of their book to get it to a high enough standard.*
>
> Heather Holden Brown, literary agent, hhb Agency Ltd
> www.hhbagency.com

Writing is a craft and something that you can learn about and improve on all the time. Reading, whether books that are similar to yours or not, also helps to format the shape of your work in your head. What worked for you? What didn't work? Learn what makes them successful – or not.

The other books in the *Teach Yourself* series are full of advice on technique and crafting your work. Understand that one of the joys of being a writer is that you cannot write the perfect book so you are always learning. And if you are learning, you are improving. Never be complacent about your work and never stop learning.

Being your own editor

> *For first-time writers in particular, self-editing is an imperative part of writing a book that is often overlooked when they first start out. It can be a labour-intensive and lengthy process but as long as the author feels like they're improving and we see that they're improving, then it's a worthwhile and rewarding thing to do.*
>
> Helen Corner, Cornerstones Literary Consultancy
> www.cornerstones.co.uk

Whether you are still working on getting your book accepted by an agent or editor, or you have been picked up by someone, you need to develop your skills as your own editor. Of course you will get help when your book is picked up by an agent/editor. Many literary agents will work with their authors to shape their work, especially to help them turn a good idea into a great commercial idea. Equally, editors will work with writers to edit their work. But you need to get your work in the best shape it can be, whether you are putting it in front of agents/editors for consideration or you have been asked to rework something.

There is no such thing as a bad first draft – it is a *first* draft. The good thing is that you've actually put your words down in some shape and form. Now you can begin to work on it to improve it. Writing and editing are two very different skills and are best kept separate; don't try to edit while you write your first draft and vice versa.

Insight
When you are editing your work, pretend it is someone else's. Break your editing into 20- to 30-minute sessions.

Networking

> *Where editors do commonly offer guidance or advice pre-submission is at writers' conferences, where editors often give keynote speeches, offer workshops, or conduct one-on-one consultations for writers at all levels, from those just getting started to established writers looking to further hone their craft. We do expect authors to revise their own manuscript on their own and get it into the best shape they possibly can before seeking publication – writing and critique groups can be an invaluable resource for that type of revision.*
>
> Children's Editorial Group, HarperCollins US
> www.harpercollins.com

Writing is very solitary but you need people to become a better writer. Listen to and observe others, look at things from different angles, be aware of other beliefs and soak up ideas. Don't spend all your time sitting in front of your computer or scribbling in your notebooks.

One way to get out and meet people is to attend literary festivals and writers' groups. Not only do you learn about the craft of writing but you can meet agents and editors, learn about the publishing industry and exchange news, information and advice with like-minded people. Your name starts to become known to people, both within the industry and with the reading public. It is much easier and more effective to start a query letter with 'We met at the such and such festival/fair...'

Tips on networking
- *Attend writers' groups/workshops – you will meet like-minded people who understand what you are about.*
- *Join associations and societies, e.g. the Romantic Novelists' Association, the Society of Authors, the Authors' Guild. Katie Fforde, for example, found her agent while she was on the New Writers' Scheme of the Romantic Novelists' Association.*

- Enrol on *creative writing courses*. Ian McEwan was one of the first writers on the University of East Anglia's MA course on creative writing, run by Malcolm Bradbury and Angus Wilson. Marina Lewycka's first novel, A Short History of Tractors in Ukrainian, was picked by a literary agent when she did a course at Sheffield Hallam University. Going on a writing course is not necessarily a short cut to getting published, but you will meet like-minded people and being in a creative atmosphere is extremely stimulating.
- *Do plenty of writing in any format* (blog, local paper, articles) – it puts your name in front of people.
- *Offer to give talks or interviews on local radio or television programmes;* again, your name is becoming known as a writer to a wider circle.

Feedback

> *Consider waiting to give your manuscript to a friend whilst you yourself can still see mistakes in it. You don't want to run out of their goodwill, and you need someone to read it to find the mistakes that you – as the author – find it hard to see. Be very clear about what you are asking of a friend when they read your manuscript. Proofreading is work – you are asking them to draw back from the content to look for typos and grammatical errors, etc. It is a much lesser task to say: 'Here's the introduction, can you give me a first impression? Do you think it makes an impact? Does it represent my work in the right way?' You'll have friends who have different levels of interest in the content of your book, and different strengths when it comes to appraising your work, so use them accordingly.*
>
> Katherine T Owen, self-published author, It's OK to Believe

Most authors lead a rather solitary existence when they are writing so it can be helpful to look outside your study, shed or garret and get the opinions of others. Ideally, get someone whose judgement you trust and who is interested in and appreciates writing. You could ask another writer; it can help if their work is different from yours, rather than being in direct competition. Be specific about what you want from this person. Ask them:

- *where do you think it is good?*
- *where do you think it is bad?*
- *where do you think it is slow?*

If you have asked someone for feedback, make sure they actually do get back to you with their comments within a reasonable period of time. It may help to put it on a slightly more businesslike footing. Rather than asking them to comment on your work as a favour, offer them a bottle of wine or a meal. Make it a business transaction.

If writing for children, offer to give a reading at a school or library. Ask yourself afterwards:

- *Did I hold the children's attention?*
- *Did they understand the language?*
- *Have I pitched it at the right age group?*

As with any feedback, what you choose to do with it is up to you. You can ignore it, disagree with it or take it on board and review your work. Just don't get so much feedback that you begin to drown in it!

> *The usefulness of writer's groups? It depends. If you just want to write as a hobby, then writers' groups can be great. I think it's very important to be clear in your mind whether you are doing it as a hobby or you want publication. If it's the latter, writers' groups can sometimes throw you off course; I've heard of people writing far too much to please their group rather than being true to themselves and keeping commercial focus.*
>
> Maria McCarthy, author
> www.mariamccarthy.co.uk

> **Insight**
> When rewriting, read your work aloud. Rewrite if you find it difficult to read or stumble over words; it will be just as difficult for a reader.

Literary consultants

I think nowadays the literary consultancy is another useful step, a way of winnowing the wheat from the chaff for the agents. There are so many manuscripts around that a third step is needed and the literary consultancy helps you get your work right before you send it to the agent. I think it is money well spent. If you're really confident in your book, then yes, you could send it out straight to agents and publishers because you never know – it might just fall on the right desk at the right time and get bought without you having to spend the money. But after that first round of almost inevitable rejection, it is worth sending it to a consultancy and spending a bit of money. If you're serious about it. Anyway, the learning process is half the fun of it, isn't it?

Bryony Pearce, author
www.bryonypearce.co.uk

A literary consultant will assess and give feedback on a writer's manuscript for a fee. There is a range of literary consultancies in the UK. Choose them carefully. It would be very easy to take a writer's money even though their work really has no hope of ever getting published. Literary consultancies should, like an agent, be there to help you make money (i.e. sell your work) rather than just take your money. Writers' forums, word of mouth and agent referrals are a good way of finding a good literary agency.

The following have all been rated by agents and editors as offering reputable service:

Cornerstones (www.cornerstones.co.uk)
Hilary Johnson (www.hilaryjohnson.demon.co.uk)

The Literary Consultancy (*www.literaryconsultancy.co.uk*)
The Writer's Journey (*www.juliamccutchen.com*)

> *We only take on writers we feel we can work with. I can't imagine doing it any other way. Two reasons: one, writers are often at the creative writing stage, even if they are talented, and to receive feedback too early can be damaging. So we like to work with writers who are at self-edit stage. The second reason is that there are raw manuscripts out there. If we took on everything, we wouldn't keep our readers and it would end up being vanity editing. We have quite a strong policy about that.*
>
> *First port of call is for an author to contact us. We look at their first chapter and synopsis, and see what stage they're at. We then either take them on or suggest an alternative route, perhaps a creative writing course or something like that.*
>
> *If, having looked at their material, we do want to take them on we then figure out the best service which might be a report, workshop or brainstorming session. For instance, we may recommend a general report if they're pretty much at a high standard already. Or if we think they need more, we'll put their work through a more detailed editorial process.*
>
> *We are always hungry to see new talent and we ask our readers to flag up manuscripts with real potential. We have an internal grading system and if one of our editors gives a manuscript the thumbs up, we will let the author know that, following revision, we would like to consider submitting it to agents. Then my colleague, Kathryn Robinson, and I will look at the first 50 pages and if we like what we see call in the whole MS [manuscript]. If we love it, we'll then work with the author at no charge for however long it takes – assuming the author can follow our editorial direction (and the best writers take it one step beyond).*
>
> *If the MS is at a high standard already we can move quickly. One of our authors, Ava McCarthy,* The Insider,

we placed with an agent within a week, and the agent got a sizeable publishing deal two weeks later. Another author, Sarwat Chadda, The Devil's Kiss, we worked with for a year or so before we got him an agent and who then got a transatlantic publishing deal. When we work with authors with a view to passing them through to agents we don't charge them for our time or contacts but we do receive a one-off 10% fee on the initial worldwide advance (so no ongoing royalties or subsidiary rights).

Because we don't charge agents to take on our authors, they are generally open to looking at our authors' work, they give us a quick turnaround, and we often get more feedback than an author would if they submitted their own work. We sometimes end up working together – author, agent and us – which is an enjoyable process.

I suppose you could call us an agent's agent, in terms of filtering and passing new talent to them that's already been shaped to a high standard. However, an important part of our job is to manage an author's expectations and they're primarily coming to us to learn how to shape and self-edit their MS – a vital writing skill that can be taught. But no one should come to us expecting to pay for a fast route to getting published.

When I first set up, there was one other literary consultancy. Then, more started springing up: freelance consultants with a small number of readers, and some companies like ours, so yes, it is becoming a firmer, more established rung in the publishing industry. As far as I know we're the only consultancy to have a filter system but where we still provide feedback on the opening pages even if we don't take on an author. We're all about teaching authors the skills to edit their own work and have spent years dissecting the components of great writing; we run specialist workshops on how to self-edit and submit and our book, Write a Blockbuster And Get it Published *(Hodder), is based on these.*

Authors should be wary of any company that seems like it's not a personalized service, or where pound signs speak louder than anything else, usually in the £1000s. That's why word-of-mouth recommendation – via an agent, publisher, writers' forum or community, or writing magazines – is a good indication of a reliable company; if in any doubt, contact the Society of Authors.

A good literary consultancy is all about finding the right route for an author. It depends what stage they are at with their writing; whether it is even the right book to launch them. It can be hard to say to an author that the book they've been working on for years doesn't seem to be improving and the best solution is to put it to one side and start a new one. It's important to work out which book should launch an author especially with the unforgiving EPOS (electronic point of sale) system. If a first book doesn't sell that well it can damage an author's career before it's even begun. No book is ever a waste of time, though, and every draft should take an author's writing to the next stage. It's a bitter-sweet moment when an author no longer needs us, but ultimately we're all striving for the same thing, which is publication and ongoing success.

Helen Corner, Cornerstones Literary Consultancy
www.cornerstones.co.uk

The first meeting with the agent

Quite often, there is one agent who will just stand out for you because they want you from the start – it's like a match made in heaven. I would say it has to be someone you feel comfortable with. You need someone for whom you have a respect, a mutual respect, and a liking; where you know from their reputation that they do good deals and that they work hard for their authors; that they're energetic and that they have the kind of profile that you feel comfortable with.

> *It's got to be somebody you like – a kind of chemistry – so that you will enjoy working with this individual for a long period of time; I think that's very important.*
>
> Sarah Davies, literary agent, The Greenhouse Literary Agency
> www.greenhouseliterary.com

Let us assume that you have reached the stage where all your hard work has paid off and an agent that you have approached contacts you and asks for a meeting.

WHAT QUESTIONS SHOULD YOU ASK AN AGENT?

If an agent shows interest in representing you and wants to meet, don't get so excited or grateful that you forget to ask the agent some questions of your own. They will not be offended; again, it shows that you have thought things through and done your homework. This is a business relationship primarily and you want to make sure that the person handling the business of getting you into print knows what they are doing and offers the kind of service you expect.

- ▶ How long has the agent been in business?
- ▶ Is the agent a member of the Association of Authors' Agents (UK)/Association of Authors' Representatives (US)?
- ▶ Do they have specialists in foreign rights?
- ▶ Do they have specialists in movie and television rights?
- ▶ Will the agent handle your work personally?
- ▶ Do they do editorial work or are they specialists in contracts and negotiation? Or do they do both?
- ▶ How closely will the agent keep in touch with the author regarding work being done on their behalf?
- ▶ Is there a standard agent–author agreement?
- ▶ Will the agent consult you about any and all offers? If you should part company, what is the policy for handling any unsold subsidiary rights?

The agent will be looking at you as a person. Agents and editors are no different from the rest of us; they want to work with people who are going to be nice to deal with. Is this author going to be able to cope when they receive setbacks? How are they going to act when they become successful?

Some agents will encourage an author to meet another agent because they feel it is important that the author has chosen them because they feel they can work together. Some authors choose their agents because they feel a bit scared of them; believing that if they are tough with them, they will be tough with publishers. Others have been known to pick their agent because they wanted to be able to have regular face-to-face meetings so they went with agents that were based near where they lived.

Remember that the agent ultimately works *for* you; they act on your behalf. They are experts who know the business, have contacts with editors and publishing houses and can work with you on your book to turn it into something special. But they can also be guided by you. This first meeting is your opportunity to ask questions, find out what they can do for you, who their contacts are (they should have a strong list of editorial contacts) and what strategy they propose for your work. If you feel that the agent shares your vision of your work, that they will champion your book for you, that is a good sign.

> *If you get an offer and you've met the agent and you've got on with them, why not go with them? You don't know if your manuscript is still sitting on the other slush piles. You've got to go with a gut feeling but if you've got someone who is willing to work with you, has got the contacts and knows how to represent their authors, what are you waiting for? It's the authors who realize that they are very hot property with several agents keen to represent them who can sit back and wait.*
>
> Camilla Goslett, literary agent, Curtis Brown
> www.curtisbrown.co.uk

When you do find an agent, you will sign an author–agent agreement. This will set out:

- *what commission the agent will charge for the different sales of rights*
- *what rights the agent will handle*
- *what money will be charged (be wary of agents who charge for editorial services)*
- *how the agreement can be ended (there is usually a set period of notice).*

Some agents will offer editorial feedback. Work with them. An agent, particularly for a first book, is an author's creative ally. If you get editorial feedback from your agent, do not dismiss it out of hand. You have the right, as the author, to reject any editorial suggestions or revisions but remember that the agent knows the marketplace. They have taken you on because they feel your work will sell, but that does not mean that your work is currently perfectly formed and ready to go. Many agents are former editors and understand what makes a book work; they can take something that has promise and help you turn it into something quite special.

The first contact with the editor

> *A lot of agent/editor relationships have built over long periods of time; you find particular editors and agents who share each other's tastes. Many of my bestselling authors have come via an agent called Darley Anderson. So I will automatically take seriously anything Darley sends me because his track record of knowing what I like and what I publish well has been amazing over a 25-year period.*
>
> Sue Fletcher, publisher, Hodder & Stoughton
> www.hodder.co.uk

When your agent is happy with the manuscript, they will submit your work to a commissioning editor at a publishing house. Some editors have the seniority and expertise to be able to get the whole publishing house team on their side and take on a book pretty much on their say so; while other more junior editors, with slightly less experience, may have to solicit support from their colleagues (in sales, marketing & publicity and so on) before going into the acquisition meeting (editorial committee, publishing meeting – the name is slightly different depending on the publishing house). You can have as many as eight different readers at a publishing house considering a proposal.

> *I wouldn't submit to publishers and editors that I'm not happy for the author to end up with. What you're talking about is the potential relationship the publishing house has with the author, the culture of the company, how they handle their backlist and the strength of their sales and marketing. It's a gut feeling, too. I always like to take an author for a meeting in the offices of an editor/publisher because it's like going to someone's house. You get a nice feeling (or not) about them. It's the same; it's instinctive.*
>
> Heather Holden Brown, literary agent, hhb Agency Ltd
> www.hhbagency.com

It is at this point that the publishing house will look at the book's format, the market for the book, what the competition is and when the book could be published. There may be a reader's report to consider. Financial considerations will be looked at: expected sales revenue, how much it will be to cost the book, what the hoped-for profit margin will be if the book sells out.

There is a lot to be thought about. This is why it is important that you consider your book from a business point of view – that's what the publishing house will be doing when they are deciding whether to take you on or not. Your book may get rejected at this point – either an outright rejection or the editor may suggest changes before it is resubmitted.

Accepting a publishing house

> *When authors come in, I want them to be knowledgeable and ebullient; know how they want to present themselves;*

what it is that they've got to offer. Are they articulate? Do they fit the image that the book wants to portray (if it's a book about grooming, for example, you don't want them looking like a badly tied parcel)? We took on a travel writer who knows more about the history of travel writing over the last 50 years than anyone I've ever met; he's read everything; he's got first editions of everything so he's steeped in that subject. And because he's so knowledgeable, there's probably another book in him. He talked articulately about where he felt his book fitted into that particular genre. So for the editor, there's a confidence that you've got a real author.

We're not looking for books, by and large, we want authors. I'm looking for people I want to be working with in 10 years' time. I'm not suggesting that authors come to the meeting armed with another five ideas. What they need to do is convince me that they're serious about this business; that this is not just one good idea that they've stumbled in on. I still may commission one good idea, of course, but it's not guaranteed.

Trevor Dolby, publisher, Preface Publishing, an imprint of Random House
www.prefacepublishing.co.uk

If the book is accepted, the publisher will make an offer to the author and/or the agent if the author has one. While any author will no doubt be thrilled to be taken on by a publisher, it is important that they are happy with what the publisher is proposing.

The aim is for both parties to get a good deal. If you have an agent, they will do the negotiation for you. If you are dealing with the publisher directly, you should expect to discuss:

- *the amount of the advance*
- *when it is paid*
- *timescale for delivery of the manuscript*
- *what rights the publisher wants to retain*
- *whether the subsidiary rights are set against the advance.*

Advance – the larger the advance, the longer it takes to start earning royalties but that may not necessarily be important to you. If you do not feel that the advance is reasonable, you can always ask if it can be increased.

Payment – the advance will be paid in stages (signature of contract, delivery of manuscript, on publication). Some publishers prefer to divide the payments into quarters, with the final payment on publication of the paperback version. You can ask that payments are made up to publication, rather than afterwards.

Timescale – you know your schedule and what is realistic. Publishers always want the manuscript as soon as possible; authors always want more time than they get. If you believe that the deadline is too tight, say so. It is better that you are honest rather than say 'yes' to an unrealistic timescale and risk missing the deadline which could, in a worst-case scenario, negate the contract altogether.

Rights – authors' agents try to hold on to as many rights as possible. The more the author holds, the more there is to sell elsewhere. Bear in mind that this is difficult to do on your own if you have no experience of selling rights; there are agents (listed in the yearbook and handbook) who specialize in this.

As well as being happy with what you are being offered in terms of money and timescales, you should also consider whether the publishing house is right for you. The editor will explain to the author what the publishing house proposes to do with the book (further editorial work, publicity, publication date and so on). As Heather Holden Brown points out, it has to *feel* right. Do you feel you could work with these people? Do you share the same expectations for the book?

When both parties are happy, the publisher issues the contract (see Chapter 4). On signature of the contract, the first part of the advance is paid. At this stage, the agent steps back and allows the author and editor to begin working together.

Publishers, like authors, want to work with people they like and who are easy to work with. If your first book was a success and you were a pleasure to work with and your second proposal is a good one, you'll get another deal. That doesn't mean that everybody is fawning over each other all the time; it means that you are straightforward, practical and communicative; you have good ideas and you do things when you say you'll do them. And it works the other way too. If your editor was a pain in the a**e and now, only when the book is successful, are they all over you, you can make the decision not to work with them next time as well.

Trevor Dolby, publisher, Preface Publishing, an imprint of Random House
www.prefacepublishing.co.uk

Case study

Bryony Pearce, author, *Angel's Fury* (Egmont)
www.bryonypearce.co.uk

At university, I did English Literature but I think analysing so many amazing authors just killed my ability to write for myself. After I'd been working for a while in London, I was desperate to start writing but couldn't put pen to paper. So I did a short story writing course with the National School of Journalism, feeling that I would have to write something then. I didn't do it with a view to getting my work published; I did the course because I so desperately wanted to do something that I loved again and that would make me happy.

I decided to expand one of the stories I wrote on the course into a novel (Windrunner's Daughter). I certainly didn't have a particular audience or market in mind. It was more a case of I wrote the book, then looked at it and realized it would appeal to teenagers.

I didn't use any friends or family to read what I'd written – that would be far too embarrassing! What I did do though is talk to

(Contd)

another children's writer who lives near me called Nik Perring who wrote I met a Roman last night, what did you do? *He read the first two pages and he gave me some advice on writing a synopsis and covering letter.*

Windrunner's Daughter *was written over a few years; the main part of it while I was pregnant with my daughter, Maisie. I sent it off to publishers and literary agents and got rejected...a lot. I even had rejections from people who clearly hadn't read my work. They would reply referring to my 'stories', 'We don't want to take on your stories.' It's a novel, it's not a collection of short stories. It was a bit demoralizing.*

Although I didn't set out to see my book in print, once I'd made my mind up that I wanted to be published I was determined to do it. Every time I got a rejection, I allowed myself a day to feel really, really despondent. Then I picked myself up and said, 'Right, you've got to do a rewrite.' And that's basically what I did. Gave myself a day, then looked at it, tried to see what was wrong with it and fixed it. I think you have to be so stubborn, so thick-skinned and persistent and willing to rewrite. The feedback I was getting was that the second half wasn't working so I realized I had to delete it and write it again. The number of times I sat down at my computer and deleted chapter after chapter of Windrunner's Daughter; *I literally just deleted the whole half of the book a couple of times and rewrote it. Not just tweaks, a massive rewrite.*

The rejection I got from the literary agent, Caroline Sheldon, wasn't the standard 'We hate your story; go away' letter. It said, 'Sorry we are rejecting you but have you considered going to the literary consultancy, Cornerstones, to get a report?' which I did. Cornerstones said the book had a lot of potential but it needed rewriting. So I rewrote and rewrote and rewrote.

Helen Corner, at Cornerstones, then suggested that I enter the 'Undiscovered Voices' competition which is run by the Society of Children's Book Writers & Illustrators (SCBWI British Isles) to highlight debut fiction writers. So I did and I was one of the

12 winners. After winning, I received two offers from agents in quick succession and I chose to go with Sam Copeland now at Rogers Coleridge & White. Having been in the position of getting rejection after rejection, to suddenly having two offers, I was completely over the moon. And then I thought 'Oh no, now I've got to choose between these two amazing agents. And upset somebody. And I've got to make a rejection now!'

Windrunner's Daughter *got rewritten so many times but it kept getting rejected; although Sam called them 'fantastic rejections'! Eventually, while it was out with a set of publishers, I decided to write another book,* Angel's Fury, *which I did in about seven months while I was pregnant with Riley.*

I got rejections for this as well but then two publishing houses said they were interested so I went down to London to meet them. I was eight months pregnant, on crutches and it was my birthday. The first meeting went well and I came out thinking that if I didn't get an offer from them, I wouldn't understand why. At the second meeting later that afternoon, I was flagging and could barely keep my eyes open. Coming out from that meeting, I thought if they didn't make me an offer I would know exactly why!

In the end, I didn't exactly get an offer from either publisher. The first meeting had been with the publishers, Egmont, who said that there were lots of changes they wanted made. But, as I was eight months pregnant they didn't want to give me a contract and push me to deadlines that I wouldn't make. I said, 'Tell me what are the changes that you want and if I do them would you be willing to look at the book again?' They said 'Yes, absolutely,' obviously expecting me to get back to them in three years' time. I actually had the telephone conversation with the editor about the rewrites while I was in labour. Then, I rewrote the book and got it back to them before Riley was three months old.

Fantastically Egmont then took me on. They sent me a lovely email with their offer, saying how pleased they were with the book. One
(Contd)

of their comments was that I'd 'handled the rewrites like an utter professional'. I think that was one of the things that swung it in my favour. The fact that the editor now knows that I may have a brand new baby and be on crutches but I'm still going to turn round a book rewrite for her; she can rely on me to do it so I think that helped.

It's been wonderful working with Egmont. Philippa Donovan, my editor, is lovely. We are very much on the same wavelength and the changes that she has asked me to make have improved the book dramatically. So it's been a fantastic experience; partly because I'm learning a lot and partly because it's improving the book. Every time I make changes it is getting better so it's turning into something I can really be proud of. And Philippa is lovely. She's on the phone when I need her; she's there to talk me through the changes if I want that; she's completely happy to do that.

It feels like a partnership between the two of us. I've provided the rough script and she's used the benefit of her expertise to show me how I can make it the best it can be. I'm using the benefit of my talent, I suppose, to provide something for her that I hope is going to sell well – and make her publishing house some money and therefore help her out. We're helping each other out really.

The original offer from Egmont is for a one-book deal but the publishers have said that they want first look at anything else I write. I am in the process of writing the next book and have shown the synopsis to Philippa. She likes it and I'm hoping that when she sees the rest of the book she'll like that too.

I will go back to Windrunner's Daughter. I still think there's something there because so many publishers asked to see it based on the first three chapters. Having had my second novel picked up and had the editorial comments come back on that book, I now know what's wrong with Windrunner's Daughter and I should be able to rewrite it properly.

I have been learning a craft. I feel very strongly that this is important. Belief in yourself is, obviously, crucial but being willing to learn from the people in the industry is hugely important. You hear stories of authors who are so entrenched in their work that they refuse point blank to listen to anyone else; they won't make changes, they won't learn. That's so arrogant. Who has nothing to learn?

What did I really want from this? It was a fulfilment of a lifetime dream; I'd always wanted to write. It has gone at my own pace and I've sold my book. You can't really ask more than that, can you? If I can get a photograph of someone in the street reading my book or me standing next to a display of my books in Waterstone's, then that's all I really want from it. The money is a very welcome bonus but what I'd really rather have is a fan letter saying how much they liked my book.

10 THINGS TO REMEMBER

1. *Don't jump on the bandwagon and try to write something you think will sell. Write what you feel strongly about.*

2. *Expect rejection; every writer gets rejected – many times. The most successful writers get the most rejections because they are the most persistent.*

3. *If you get a rejection, don't believe it. It is one person's opinion on that day. Use rejection to help you improve your manuscript.*

4. *They may say that other agents might be interested in your work. It's not a brush-off; this is a subjective business and it may just not appeal to that particular individual.*

5. *Be prepared to edit your work – which can often mean cutting out some of your favourite bits. Make every word count.*

6. *The larger the agency or publishing house, the more people there are who may have to be convinced to take on you and your book*

7. *Literary consultants will assess and give feedback on a manuscript for a fee.*

8. *When editing, read your words aloud. If you stumble over words, they will be as difficult to read as they are to speak, so consider rewriting.*

9. *The author/agent relationship is a mix of business and mutual respect and liking. You need to trust and get on with your agent.*

10. *Before you sign on with a publishing house, make sure they understand you and your work. It's not just about the size of the advance.*

4

Legalities and practicalities

In this chapter you will learn:
- *what rights affect writers*
- *what a basic publishing contract contains*
- *about ISBN, PLR and other publishing acronyms.*

No man but a blockhead ever wrote except for money.

Samuel Johnson, author

In this chapter, we will look at the basic legal elements that are part of publishing a book. Publishing and bookselling are no different from any other business and are affected by general legislation as well as regulations concerning consumer protection, trading standards, price fixing, copyright, obscenity and libel.

Negotiation, and negotiating the contract in particular, is a huge part of what we do for an author. There really is no way an author on their own is going to be able to negotiate an optimum contract for themselves with a corporate publisher. Finance, and being able to advise on tax, move money in a timely way to where it should be, advise people on tax forms (if you're a Brit and paid by an American house or vice versa) – these are all part of an agent's job too. I'm very fortunate to have a strong back-office team to work with me on all these issues.

Sarah Davies, literary agent, The Greenhouse Literary Agency

www.greenhouseliterary.com

Rights

As the author, you hold the rights to your work. When you agree to have your book published, you give a publishing house the exclusive licence or 'right' to make use of your work. Signing over all your rights to the publishers is unusual; it tends to happen with book packaging, when an author is commissioned to write for a flat fee. If the idea was not yours (it was the publisher/packager's) and you are happy with it, then that is absolutely fine.

You can also give copyright to the publisher while the contract is in place; this is called copyright assignment (see below).

The primary right is to publish the book itself; all other rights are secondary (or subsidiary) to the right to print. Agents generally want to hold on to as many of these secondary rights as possible, while the publisher wants to gain control of as many of these rights as they can. The contract (and the negotiation that leads up to the final contract) lays out who has what rights.

The secondary rights are attractive (and lucrative) to agents and publishers because nothing has to be physically produced when they are sold.

COPYRIGHT

Copyright exists as soon as you or anyone else records anything original to you on paper, film or disk; therefore you don't have to actually physically register copyright. Nor do you have to put the copyright symbol on your manuscript (or sample chapters) when you submit to agents or publishers; you are automatically covered by the law.

Copyright protects authors, giving them legal ownership of their work. It establishes that an author's work is their own personal property. Because they own it, the author has the right to sell or license it to others.

Insight
Be aware that some competitions state in their rules that entrants give up their copyright or moral rights.

If the copyright was assigned to the publisher, the author's name is next to the © on the title verso page; under an exclusive licence it is the publisher's name here. Assigned copyright will revert to the author when the contract is terminated; the reasons for termination will be laid out in the contract (such as the book going out of print, which is what you would hope to have in a contract).

In the UK, Europe and the US, copyright is protected during your lifetime and for 70 years after your death. So you could quote Queen Victoria and Benjamin Franklin without permission, but not Winston Churchill or J.D. Salinger (agencies not only represent living authors but the estates of dead ones, too).

Did you know?
The Association of American Publishers reported that US publishers lost around $600m in 2008 from copyright piracy.

Copyright is your intellectual property, which means you can sell it outright, but that means you then have no further claim on that work and, therefore, cannot make any money from it.

If you sell on your copyright, your work no longer belongs to you. You cannot even rewrite it because that would count as adaptation. You may not be allowed to reuse characters from the original work. Even if you do give up the copyright, you are still entitled to attribution as the author of that work.

- ▶ *There is no copyright in ideas or in the title of a work (but obviously avoid calling your work something like* Harry Potter *or* The Da Vinci Code*).*
- ▶ *Copyright exists in the expression of ideas (i.e. when they are written down).*
- ▶ *Copyright can be held jointly.*

(Contd)

> ▶ *A work must be original in order to be covered by copyright.*
> ▶ *If you have created your work during working hours, as part of your terms and conditions as an employee, the copyright will belong to the employer.*
> ▶ *Copyright in translation belongs to the translator.*
> ▶ *Breach of copyright is still illegal even if no financial gain has taken place.*

Insight

If you are putting your work online, it is worth putting a copyright notice on it. While laws vary from country to country, the copyright mark shows that you are claiming the rights to your work and that it is not available for everyone to use.

Under the Universal Copyright convention (1952) all books should carry a copyright notice. You can find the information and logo on the title verso page. A new edition of a book has a new date in the copyright line. If you are self-publishing:

▶ *make sure that the copyright symbol © is on the correct page*
▶ *put the year the book was first published*
▶ *put the name of the copyright holder.*

Look at the wording of the copyright statement in printed books and ensure you include it in your book if you are self-publishing (see Chapter 6, p. 151).

If you and a co-author are self-publishing a book, write and sign an agreement on how you both want the copyright to be shared. It is usually a 50/50 split but, if one of you has put in less or more than the other, you may wish the split to reflect the work. Settle the issue now, rather than when the book is published.

In the US, authors have to register their work as proof of ownership. The US Copyright Office is the authoritative source for information, procedures and searches, including texts of relevant laws (www.copyright.gov).

> **Insight**
>
> If you are worried someone might steal your idea, send a copy of your manuscript to yourself via registered mail, making sure that the package is clearly date stamped. Leave it sealed and you can then use it in a court of law if necessary.

The Authors' Licensing and Collecting Society (ALCS) in the UK and the Authors Registry in the US manage the collective rights for writers. They make sure that writers are compensated when their work is copied (e.g. photocopied). For more information on registering with these agencies, see Chapter 10, p. 256.

MORAL RIGHTS

Moral rights are covered in the UK by the 1988 Copyright, Designs and Patent Act. They include:

- *paternity – the author's right to be clearly identified as the person who created the work; same duration as copyright*
- *integrity – the right for the author to prevent any distortion or mutilation of their work that could damage their reputation; same duration as copyright*
- *false attribution – prevents the author from being credited with something they didn't write; lasts for life + 20 years.*

The right of integrity is automatically granted but you have to assert your right of paternity in writing. You can assert your right of paternity by putting 'The moral right of the author has been asserted' on the inside cover page (title verso page) which contains the ISBN number, copyright information, year of publication, etc. Look at printed books to see examples of this.

Moral rights are separate from copyright. You can waive your moral rights but if you do, you give up the right to have that work attributed to you. Your work can then be changed in any way; your permission does not have to be sought.

Contracts

Contracts will vary slightly from one publishing house to another but all should contain:

- *date of agreement*
- *names and addresses of publisher and author*
- *title (or working title) of the book*
- *author's obligations*
- *publisher's obligations*
- *detailed specification of rights assigned*
- *provision for revised editions*
- *specification of royalty*
- *specification of accounting periods*
- *warranties and indemnities*
- *termination and reversion of rights*
- *miscellaneous sub-clauses pertinent to particular agreements.*

The contract will be between the licensor (the author who owns the rights) and the licensee (the publisher).

If you do not have an agent, you really should consider becoming a member of the Society of Authors (or the Authors Guild in the US) who will check through the contract free of charge before you sign it. They also give advice on negotiating items that an author may want changing. See Chapter 10 for more information on the Society and the Guild. If you are a member of the Society (or the Authors Guild), let your publisher know before they draw up the contract.

The Society and the Writers' Guild of Great Britain have drawn up a Minimum Terms Agreement (MTA) which gives a basic code of conduct for publishers to adhere to when drawing up a contract. Not all publishers have signed up to it but many of the larger houses have.

Equally, the offer of a publishing contract makes you a much more attractive prospect for a literary agent so you could try approaching one who could negotiate better terms for you as Isabel Losada did.

> **Insight**
> *All* contracts are negotiable, no matter what the publisher tells you.

Let's look at some of the elements of a publishing contract in more detail:

Format
This states whether it is hardback or paperback, the approximate UK retail price and an estimated first print run.

Rights granted
This clause will show whether the contract assigns rights to the publisher or licenses them to publish an author's work, i.e. whether the author retains full copyright and the publisher buys the licence to publish the book. It will explain what rights are assigned to the publisher and which to the author/agent. *Copyright & moral rights –* see pp. 88–91. The clause states that the author owns the copyright.

Typescript and delivery of the work
Details of the work, which include title and length. States the agreed delivery date for the manuscript. It also states what the author has to provide in the nature of original artwork, photographs, illustrations, maps, etc. (not relevant for all titles). If the contract states that the book is a 60,000-word historical crime title, that is what you must deliver.

Proofs
This clause deals with correction of proofs. As the licensor (the author of the work), you are entitled to see the proofs.

Printing and publication
The publisher agrees to print and publish the book. It may include an agreement that the author be consulted over cover design, illustrations, etc. There should also be a commitment to publish

the work in a set period of time (12 months, for example); the commitment to publish should not be subject to approval or acceptance of the manuscript.

Quotations and illustrations from other sources
See 'Permissions' on p. 100. It is usually the responsibility of the author to get and (if necessary) pay for the permissions. If a publisher has to do the research themselves, they may set the cost of the permissions against the author's royalty.

Warranty and indemnification
Publishing houses ask authors to indemnify themselves against the risk of libel, invasion of privacy and infringement of copyright. Publishers often insist on altering the text to remove anything they think might be actionable; if you think that may be the case, you could add the proviso that you get final approval on the text. Some authors take out professional indemnity insurance to cover the risk.

> *When I was going down for my meetings with Egmont, my agent said if they made an offer, I would get an advance. So I asked how much? 'It will be small,' he said. My friend, Sarwat Chadda, got a six-figure book deal for his first book. My agent paled. That's when he realized what my yardstick was, so he had to beat my expectations down to the point that I would have been grateful for two chocolate bars and a hundred quid. So when I did get a bit more than that I was grateful!*
>
> Bryony Pearce, author
> www.bryonypearce.co.uk

Advance
One tends to read in the newspapers about eye-popping advances. They are the exception rather than the rule. They can be as little as £500 or go as high as six figures plus. If your first book is a success, the advance may be larger for the second book.

The advance is divided up and the author receives each instalment at a specific point in the delivery of the book: the first instalment on signature of contract; the second on delivery of manuscript; the third on publication (there might be a fourth if the book was originally a hardback and is subsequently published as a paperback). Advances are usually non-returnable unless you fail to deliver the manuscript.

If you have an agent, the advance is paid to them; they will take off their fee (usually 15 per cent) and then the rest if passed on to you. The agent will usually pay the amount owing to income tax as well.

Royalties
Authors usually receive a percentage of sales of their book after the advance has been covered. Royalties can be based on:

- *the cover price of a book, or*
- *the net sales revenue (i.e. the amount of money the publisher gets after trade discounts have been applied to the cost of the book).*

For example, if the recommended retail price is £20 and the average trade discount is 50 per cent, the net sales revenue will be £10. So:

- *if the royalty is 10 per cent of the cover price, the author would receive 10 per cent of £20 = £2 per copy sold*
- *if the royalty is 10 per cent of the net sales revenue, the author would receive 10% of £10 = £1 per copy sold.*

First-time authors often get quite a low royalty rate. Royalties paid to an author can increase with book sales. The publisher aims to cover their costs with the first print run; as sales continue to rise, the book is reprinted and the costs (and the losses) to the publisher go down. For example, a hardback royalty of 10 per cent on the first 2,500 copies may rise to 12.5 per cent on the next 2,500, then 15 per cent as sales increase. Home, mass-market paperback sales have a royalty of 7.5 per cent; after 30,000 copies have been sold that rises to 10 per cent (although fewer publishers are distinguishing between hard and paperback nowadays). Export sales usually attract a lower royalty rate than home sales (publishers have often given a higher discount to the export market). There will also be a royalty paid on highly discounted books (such as those sold in supermarkets, large bookstore chains, wholesalers) which is generally a lot lower than other royalty rates.

> **Insight**
> Make sure that you are offered a rising scale of royalty rate; if it is not in the contract, ask for it to be included. The publisher will have an idea of the break-even point (i.e. the point at which they stop making a loss and start to make a profit). That is where your royalty rate should increase.

Agency
If you are represented by an agent, this clause authorizes the publisher to pay any money to the agent on the author's behalf.

Cheap editions and remainders
This section will set out the minimum time the book has to be available for sale before being remaindered. It states that the author will be told when books are to be remaindered and allowed to be bought at the cheaper rate.

Reversion of rights
This clause outlines what will happen if a publisher no longer actively exploits the rights to a book. Rights do not always automatically revert to the author. There should be a clause that terminates the contract if the book goes out of print or drops below an agreed level of sales.

Subsidiary rights
This is an agreement which allows a third party to produce your book in a different format: for example, translation rights, foreign English-language markets, large print, film rights, electronic rights (see Chapter 7 for more on this), anthology rights, audio books, periodical rights (first serial – extracts printed in magazines/newspapers before publication; second serial – extracts printed after publication).

Territorial rights
A book printed and published in one country can be sold to any number of other publishers in other countries:

- ▶ *English-speaking rights give licence to publish an English edition of the book in a different English-speaking country.*
- ▶ *World rights means a publisher can distribute, or license the distribution, in any country in the world.*

Reserved rights
If any rights are not specifically granted to the publishing house in the contract, they are owned by the author.

Competing works
This prevents the author from writing a similar (and therefore competing) work for another publisher. Make sure that the definition of 'competing work' is very clear.

Accounts
If the author finds an error on the royalty statement, they have the right to ask an independent auditor to look at the publishing company's accounts. In reality, this rarely happens; paying an accountant to pore over the accounts of a publishing house costs a lot of money. If there is an error in the statement, contact the royalty department and ask if it can be sorted out. Mistakes can happen so don't be confrontational.

Author's copies
Sometimes referred to as presentation copies. This tells you how many free copies you can expect to receive. It is not usually a huge amount (possibly 10 copies); US publishers tend to be more generous than their UK counterparts.

Option on next work
This means that the author has to show the publisher part or all of their next work; it is more common with fiction. It does not mean that the publisher is obliged to take that next work. It is easy to be flattered by this but do not get tied in to having to show *all* your future titles to this one publisher. If the clause is in, ask that

it be restricted to one book, on terms that are mutually agreed (not on 'the same terms' as the current title) and have a time limit on enforcing this.

Avoid having a phrase that says you have to offer the publisher a whole manuscript; that means you have to write the whole book before you can show it to them and get a decision on whether they want to go ahead or not. Suggest an outline and sample chapter as a better option for you.

NEGOTIATION

Discussions over advances and rights often begin before the contract is issued. If you do not have an agent, should you drive a hard bargain with the publisher? Or do you feel that you should just accept whatever they offer?

As Sarah Davies says at the beginning of this chapter, negotiating an optimum contract with a commercial publishing house is something agents do every day. Authors generally do not. However, if you do not have an agent and there are parts of the agreement that you feel strongly about (you would like a slightly larger advance or a lower quantity threshold where the royalty increases), you can but ask. If a publisher wants you badly enough, they will probably be happy to agree to some terms but not all; perhaps they will agree to meet halfway?

If there is something you do not understand, just ask. The intention is not to confuse you or hide things but a contract is a legal document and the language is not always the easiest to understand. A good editor will explain the details.

> *The recession undoubtedly caused advances to come down, though exceptions remain – especially for debut authors who have a fresh slate and for authors whose books seem to be sure-fire winners. This isn't necessarily a bad thing for authors – instead of a book selling well but the publishers still perceiving it as a disappointment because it didn't earn its advance, if a book earns out a lower advance everyone*

should be happy – the author will earn royalties, the agent will earn commission on those royalties, and the publisher will have recouped their investment and feel confident about publishing the author's next book.

Carole Welch, Publishing Director, Sceptre
www.hodder.co.uk

If you would like a more detailed breakdown of what publishing contracts contain, read *Understanding Publishers' Contracts* by Michael Legat (Robert Hale) and *From Pitch to Publication* by Carole Blake (Macmillan). The books cover the meaning of each clause, hardbacks, paperbacks and American agreements.

[I had been offered] a contract with a major publisher. There would be a marketing and publicity campaign with a nationwide tour and an initial print run of 12,000 copies. However, a few days after that meeting, another major publishing house got in touch and said they would like to meet me. I was keen to follow this up and delayed the signing of the contract on offer. We had a good meeting, they appeared enthusiastic but eventually turned it down. In the meantime, the first editor suddenly left her job. The unsigned contract went on hold until a new editor was in place who then decided not to pursue it. I blame myself for not signing it at the time. It was a salutary lesson...a bird in the hand and all that!

Mo Smith, author, *The Purple Spoon* (self-published) and *The Lazy Cook's*
Family Favourites (Allison & Busby)
www.lazycookmosmith.co.uk

If you are self-publishing and choose to use experts, such as a designer or printer, use a basic contract to cover your agreement. It could just be a one-page written confirmation of what has been agreed between the two parties. This would cover:

- ▶ *when the work should be finished/delivered*
- ▶ *payment*
- ▶ *who has copyright*
- ▶ *what work is required.*

BOILERPLATE AGREEMENTS

A boilerplate agreement is a standard contract drawn up by a publishing house and a literary agency who have dealt with each other on a regular basis. It avoids having to go down the route of quibbling over standard clauses.

Other legalities

Libel
A statement made in writing or in print which defames the character of an identifiable living person by holding them up to ridicule or contempt. Be careful with the names of characters and company names. Try to check that you haven't accidentally named a real-life person or business. If you think you may be writing something that could be libellous, get professional legal advice.

The Society of Authors has a guide to libel which is worth reading and they can advise on insurers who offer libel insurance. The Society also has a professional indemnity insurance scheme for writers.

Permissions
If you wish to quote from another writer's work or use an illustration of some sort, you should get permission from the publisher of that work. There is often a cost involved.

You do not need to get permission if the quotation is considered 'fair dealing' – where you can legitimately use published material 'for the purposes of criticism or review'. That means you can use a line or two to help you make a point but you must acknowledge the source of the quotation.

The Society of Authors considers as fair dealing:

- ▶ *use of a single extract of up to 400 words, or*
- ▶ *use of a series of extracts (of which none exceeds 300 words) to a total of 800 words from a prose work, or*

- *use of extracts to a total of 40 lines from a poem, provided that this does not exceed a quarter of the poem,*

and also provided that:

- *the words are quoted in the context of 'criticism or review' of the work quoted*
- *the work (except photos) is used for the purposes of reporting current events.*

To seek permission for use of an extract from someone's work, you need to:

- *contact the publishers of the first edition of the work (write to the permissions department at the publishing house), or*
- *if you need to track down the rights holders, approach the Association of Authors' Agents or the Authors' Licensing and Collecting Society (ALCS) (contact details are in the Appendix).*

Plagiarism
This is using work covered by copyright that is held by someone else, not getting permission for that use and passing it off as your own without crediting the original author.

- *Plagiarism covers ideas as well as finished work.*
- *If you steal someone's work, you can be prosecuted for copyright infringement or sued in court for loss of earnings and reputation.*

Proving that your work has been plagiarized can be difficult, unless large chunks of your work are reproduced. There are also cases when some authors have plagiarized works without knowing it.

Tips on avoiding plagiarism
- *If you use other people's work(s) in your book, get permission and/or keep a list of all the sources you use so that you credit them clearly.*
- *Use work that is out of copyright (but you must still credit the writer).*

(Contd)

- *Be careful who you share your ideas and work with.*
- *Open forums and blogs are easily accessible so be careful what you write on them if you wish to use them in your work.*
- *If you think you might have unwittingly written something that sounds familiar, type it into a search engine and see if it throws anything up.*

Industry classifications

Books are classified with standard subject headings. Go to the Book Industry Communications (BIC) website (www.bic.org.uk) which runs the classification scheme for the UK book trade and other English-language markets to find out what your book should be listed under. You will need this information if you are planning to publicize your book and send the information out to retailers and wholesalers.

Children's books have a whole separate marketing category (also found on the BIC website). You have to choose just one value from each of the five sections listed that cover different aspects of the book. The five sections cover:

- *interest level (indicating the age range for which the book is intended)*
- *broad subject (for example, poetry and song, early learning, fiction)*
- *type/format (for example, activity book, printed book, annual, electronic)*
- *character (whether the book has an established children's character or not)*
- *tie-in (tied in to a film or television programme or not).*

For example, a book labelled C1M79 is an ordinary printed poetry book for seven- to nine-year-olds, that has no established character and is not a tie-in book.

ISBN (International Standard Book Number)

The ISBN is a 13-digit product identification number found on the back of most books; it is required for booksellers and libraries. Books may have similar titles, but each ISBN will be different.

There is no legal requirement to have an ISBN but if you are self-publishing and want to sell your book on Amazon or via a bookshop, you need to obtain one. ISBNs cannot be bought singly. You have to buy them in batches; the minimum number is 10. They are available from:

- *www.isbn.nielsenbookdata.co.uk (UK)*
- *www.isbn.org (US)*
- *www.bowker.com (US).*

They cost around £112/$240 for ten ISBNs and take about ten days to be processed. You will receive an information pack when you order your ISBNs – this will outline your responsibilities as a publisher and the rules that pertain to the ISBN.

APPLYING FOR AN ISBN

- *You need to get an ISBN number before you print your book.*
- *When filling out information for an ISBN, you will have to put down the book's title, format and length.*
- *You will also need to put down the publisher's name (either your name or the name you give your publishing company).*

Insight

Your contact details will be needed when you register for an ISBN. These will be used by wholesalers and bookshops to order books. If you are self-publishing, make sure your contact details are kept updated.

All communications regarding the book will go to whoever registers the ISBN. So if you use a self-publishing company and they supply one of their ISBNs, the book trade will contact them and not you. This is absolutely fine if you do not want to handle sales and distribution yourself. If you have a publisher, you will receive an ISBN with your book. Each book is allocated one ISBN; each version of a book (hardback, paperback, ebook, etc.) requires a separate ISBN.

Nielsen BookData (Bowker in the US) supplies the ISBNs and will retain the information. The book trade uses this information so make sure it is kept up to date.

Barcodes
The barcode incorporates the ISBN. The Bookland EAN is the most widely used barcode in the publishing industry because it can be used worldwide. When you register for an ISBN, you can get information on EAN barcodes. You can get your barcode from the ISBN agency (for a bit more money) or you can go to a third-party provider who will create a barcode for you.

GS1 UK is a not-for-profit organization that offers a free service to convert an ISBN into a barcode. For more information, go to www.gs1uk.org.

The big book retailers and wholesalers will require books to have an EAN barcode. The standard position for the barcode is the bottom right-hand corner of the back of a book. You will receive your barcode in the form of a high-resolution graphic file.

Nielsen BookData (UK)
Nielsen BookData is the provider of book information to the book industry in the UK. Some bookshop chains, like Waterstone's, will take information only from them. It is the responsibility of the publisher to make sure that Nielsen BookData has an accurate record of their titles and to provide updates when anything changes.

Nielsen BookData does not charge for a basic record (which includes a jacket image) but you can opt for a subscription-based enhanced service. The basic full record includes:

- *ISBN*
- *author*
- *title*

- *subject classification (+ BIC code – see p. 102)*
- *imprint and publisher*
- *UK availability (whether it is in print or not yet published)*
- *format (paperback/hardback)*
- *territorial rights statement (which must say that the book is for sale in the UK)*
- *UK publication date.*

It takes about six weeks for new submissions to be put into the BookData system. If you want further information or to check whether your details are in the system, you can call the BookData Publisher helpdesk (tel: 0845 450 0016) or email: pubhelp.book@nielsen.com.

Nielsen BookData has an online editing service, called Pubweb, which you can access via the website (www.nielsenbookdata.co.uk).

Books In Print (US)
In the US, when a book has an ISBN, it can be registered on Books In Print (at www.bowkerlink.com). Books In Print, like BookData, is the main directory that bookstores, online retailers and libraries use when looking for books for their customers. It is published in October each year.

Cataloguing in Publication
Cataloguing in Publication (CIP) is basic cataloguing data prepared before publication by the national library of the country where the book is being published: for example, the British Library or Library of Congress. It is usually found near the bottom of the book's copyright page.

A publisher has to send information on a book at least four months in advance of publication, including the book's ISBN. It is a way of letting libraries know about new books. The CIP programme is free of charge to participating publishers.

Library book deposits
By law, all publishers (including self-publishers) must send one copy of every book they publish in the UK to the Legal Deposit

Office at the British Library within one month of publication. In the US, you will have to send a copy to the Library of Congress (ebooks that have no printed edition do not have to be sent).

Publications are recorded in an online catalogue and are available to all users. Within the terms of the Legal Deposit Libraries Act 2003, 'publisher' is to be understood as anyone who issues or distributes publications to the public. Items published in the UK and in Ireland are liable for deposit, as are items originally published elsewhere but distributed in the UK and in Ireland.

In addition, the following five libraries should also receive a copy:

The Bodleian Library, Oxford
University Library, Cambridge
National Library of Scotland, Edinburgh
National Library of Wales
The Library of Trinity College, Dublin

You don't have to send five separate copies to five separate addresses. Send the five copies in one parcel to the libraries' agent, the Agent for Copyright Libraries (see Appendix for contact details). Remember that you have to give away these six books when you are calculating how many books to print off.

Public Lending Right (UK)
Public libraries are an important market to publishing houses, especially in fiction. They are also important to writers because it is possible to earn some money from the Public Lending Right (PLR).

The PLR is a publicly funded payment made to authors whose books are lent by public libraries. Each loan generates a tiny payment but they add up to a considerable overall sum (£7 million was paid to 24,000 authors in 2006–2007).

Payment is made once a year and is proportionate to the number of times a book is borrowed. It is recognized in 28 countries; the United States is not currently among them.

The PLR is something published authors are rarely told about, certainly not by their publishers. There is nothing sinister in that; it is just an oversight. As the author, it is your responsibility to register your published book yourself with the PLR office. You can either download a form from their website (www.plr.uk.com) or send for a registration form. PLR currently covers only books, not audio or ebooks.

Pseudonyms

Otherwise known as a 'pen name', a psuedonym hides the real name of the author. It can be useful if you write in more than one genre and want to be distinguished between each one. Catherine Jones is a writer of romantic fiction; she also writes under the pseudonym of Annie Jones when collaborating with another author and as Kate Lace for Little Black Dress when writing funny, contemporary stories. Rosemary Laurey writes romantic fiction but she has two alter egos: Madeleine Oh for her erotic novels and Georgia Evans for her fantasy books. It can be a useful tool to keep your various writing personas in place.

A pseudonym also comes in handy if, when you start writing, you find that there is another author with a name that is the same as or similar to yours.

If you are considering a pseudonym:

- *check if anyone else has 'your' name*
- *make sure your name reflects your readership (a young name for a youthful audience, for example)*
- *pick a name that will be placed near that of a bestselling author in bookshops and libraries.*

Michael Ridpath had been a successful writer of financial thrillers. When he decided to change genre, he asked his agent to send his submission out under a pseudonym because he wanted people to focus on the book rather than his (known) name.

> **Insight**
> Consider where your book will be placed. If you choose a name that starts with a letter at the beginning or end of the alphabet, your books will appear at one end or the other of bookshelves. If you choose a name beginning with a letter from the middle of the alphabet, you will be placed on the middle shelves.

Other practicalities

Word count

You will need to know how many words there are in your manuscript. Computers will give you a figure and your editor will do a count after the text has been edited.

However, computers do not give the figures that the production department is interested in. A computer's word count includes headlines and sub-headings. When it comes to typesetting, these headings are in a different size from the main body text so will be counted separately to make sure they have enough space.

One quick way of estimating your word count is to count each word on a sample page and multiply that number by the number of pages in your manuscript. As a rough guide, 250 is the average number of words on a double-spaced A4 page.

If your book is illustrated, count the number of pages of illustrations (an approximate number is fine) and subtract that from the total number of pages. Find the average number of words on one of the remaining pages and multiply as above.

> **Insight**
> Look at other books in your genre. Your manuscript should be around the same length, give or take ten per cent.

Case study

Robert Forsyth, publisher, Chevron Publishing
www.chevronpublishing.co.uk

I wrote my first book, which was about a German fighter squadron in the Second World War. I've always been interested in military history and I enjoyed writing it. However, I hadn't really thought about publishing it at all. I was having a drink with a friend who asked me what I was going to do with it. He suggested we publish it. And that's how we started the company.

So far, we've done over 150 titles. I've gone from writing a book, to writing books for other publishers, to publishing under my own imprint and now I'm involved in book packaging. Virtually all of what I do now is specialist, boys' toys kind of stuff: aircraft, weaponry, military and so on. We commission, edit, design and we do the repro. We tend not to get involved in print unless I'm doing a book myself; we generally leave that to our publishing client.

Although we do specialize in a particular subject, what I'm describing applies to the packaging industry as a whole. Book packagers work for a range of publishing clients who come in all sorts of shapes and sizes; they can be general mainstream and they can be very specialist. The publishers need to sustain their book publishing lists and book packagers are an extra pair of eyes and ears in the market.

For example, if a publisher becomes aware that the 70th anniversary of the first flight of the Spitfire is coming up, they will get in touch with someone like me. We ask them about the kind of format they're looking at (hardback, softback, x number of pages, x number of illustrations; is there a budget for graphics, colour, maps…?). Then the haggling starts, which is when the publisher tells you how much they want to spend and we tell them what we can do for that budget.

(Contd)

Book packaging and specialist publishing are subject-driven, not author-driven. There are, of course, in our specialist world, authors who are very highly regarded and people will buy their books. Generally, however, I as the reader have an interest in the Spitfire, for example, and that interest is going to fuel my purchasing decision, not who wrote it.

We will know a small number of authors and experts whose name will be credible enough to appear on a book, who we can approach and ask if they would be interested in the project. We'll tell the author how much we have got to pay them and how long they have got to write the book. Generally speaking, the writing period can be anything from six months to a year. At that point, if the author says 'Yes', contracts are issued.

So the author becomes one element of the production process. However, that author may not have any photographs to go with the text. It is also unlikely that the author will know how to commission colour graphics, colour artwork and so on. The role of the packager (and the value of the packager to the publisher) is that we will go off and do that for them. So, the author, the photographs, the illustrations, the editing process and then the design are all components of the ultimate product which we then put together.

In this particular case, we would normally contract an author direct; in other words, it's a fixed fee with the author and it normally constitutes an advance on signing of contract; then, a second-stage payment on delivery of all materials to us (when we make sure that the author has actually done the book that we were expecting). We then deliver it to the publisher and the balance of the fee is paid on publication; so it's a three-stage payment to the author. However, authors are all different. Some people work on the basis that they want as much money as they can get up front; others will say that they don't want any advance because if they get the money first, they won't have an incentive to finish the book. They want to get paid when they deliver. As the commissioning editor with the packager, I have to work with each author separately.

While the author is producing the copy, we will have sourced photographs, scanned them in and made sure they look good. In our particular line of work, our market demands quality so we place a massive emphasis on it. So we work very closely with the author to maximize reproduction values; we commission any artwork that is going in the book.

We then edit the book. I tell a lot of our authors that they just have to think of me as the person who has either bought the book online or wandered into a bookshop and I've taken their book home and I'm reading it. If I don't understand something, the reader isn't going to understand something. So if I query something in the text, don't take offence. A lot of authors bristle when an editor does this; they think editors have one mission in life and that is to surgically slash apart their manuscript. That is not an editor's role. Editors are there to fine tune and make a work acceptable for what could be a global readership.

Then we proofread. While that is being done, we start the design process. We issue a set of proofs to the author to make sure we've done a good job and he's happy with the book and we then send a set of proofs to the publisher to make sure they are happy. We then submit the book as a DVD or CD and deliver that to the publisher with our bill, they pay and the book is published.

Sometimes, the publisher wants us to deliver a printed book, on a pallet. So we then get involved in print, which usually means sourcing it from countries such as China, the Far East, or Poland. Normally, though, the publisher arranges their own printing. Very rarely do we get involved in sales or marketing of the book; that's down to the publisher. We are a production company.

In the scenario I've just described, the publisher buys the rights entirely. It is accepted publishing practice, if you like, that when a publisher says they've got an idea and commission someone to go away and produce that book, it 'belongs' to them. To put it crudely they are actually making you guns for hire; you go off and get your
(Contd)

posse which includes your author, your designer, your illustrator and so on. You are working for a client. Some publishers are more generous than others; if they get massive interest from the States they might give you a percentage of earnings of foreign rights. Unfortunately, that happens less and less now.

The other path you can go down is that the fundamental process is exactly the same but it works the other way: the author comes to us. I then wear a different hat and look at the idea as an editor in a publishing house would.

So, for example, an author I've never heard of comes to us and says he's got an idea for a book about subject X. I say that it sounds interesting and ask for an outline synopsis, idea of title and, very important for us, what the word count is, at least the word count of the narrative text; because we have to get an idea very quickly on the kind of size of book we will be working with: will it be a huge book or will it be a slim volume? Does it have photographs? Is it going to be illustrated? The first thing I try to do is get inside the author's head and work out what he wants us to produce. I then ask, why should I want to buy this book? Some authors get a bit shirty about that. You really want to know what their motivation is for writing the book; what do they think the USP is.

If I like it, I would then have further dialogue with the author, fine tune a few points, maybe raise a couple of issues with him. For instance, I was talking to a military history author who wanted to do a book on one month in the Second World War. It was a pivotal month, there was a lot happening during that time and he wanted to cover events in Europe, the Eastern Front, Western Front, the home front and the Pacific. I felt he didn't need the Pacific in the book; I'd need the book in a year and that would have involved a huge amount of work on his behalf. We discussed it and, in the end, we decided that the book would be interesting and work just as well without that element in it. So there's this dialogue with the author and the more you can get what you think is a good idea, the more likely you are to be able to sell it to a publisher.

I then have to map out a book proposal, based on my conversation with the author, and I take it to a publisher. All publishers are different: some will come straight back and say that yes, they like it; others will have various meetings (board meetings, appraisal meetings, sales & marketing meetings) before deciding whether to take the book or not. Sometimes, it can take a year to get a book commissioned. They sound out their US distributors, their European sales force; they are very prudent and check ideas out. Then they come back and either say no they don't want to do it – in which case you have to find another publisher or you give up the project – or they say yes and the book is commissioned and whole process that I described above kicks in.

In this particular instance, the author gets a royalty because it's the author's idea. Again, we don't stray into the arena of sales and marketing; once the book is commissioned our job is very much that of a production house. The publisher would sort out any author signings, talks, advertising, etc. Our job is done when we deliver the book as a DVD to the publisher.

There is also a third strand to book packaging, when we generate ideas ourselves. For example, we did a series on vintage motor sport and the history of British racing green and Italian red and so on. We got it commissioned by a publisher, we went off and found the authors, the photographs and so on. That really is the whole packaging process and what I've outlined is the same whether it's a book about airplanes, horses or whatever.

10 THINGS TO REMEMBER

1 *Copyright is protected during your lifetime and for 70 years after your death.*

2 *Copyright exists as soon as you or anyone else records anything original to you on paper, film or disk; therefore you don't have to physically register copyright.*

3 *Assigned copyright reverts to the author when the contract is terminated.*

4 *All books should carry a copyright notice.*

5 *In moral rights, the right of integrity is automatically granted but you have to assert your right of paternity in writing.*

6 *If you do not have an agent, you should consider becoming a member of the Society of Authors (or the Authors Guild in the US) who will check through the contract for free before you sign it.*

7 *If you wish to quote from another writer's work or use an illustration of some sort, you should get permission from the publisher of that work.*

8 *Books are classified with standard subject headings. Go to the Book Industry Communications website (www.bic.org.uk) to find out how to classify your work.*

9 *There is no legal requirement to have an ISBN but if you want to sell your book on Amazon or via a bookshop you will need one.*

10 *By law, all publishers must send one copy of every book they publish in the UK to the Legal Deposit Office at the British Library within one month of publication.*

5

In production

In this chapter you will learn:
- *how to prepare your manuscript for your editor*
- *how to deal with feedback*
- *how to work as a writer.*

An editor should tell the author his writing is better than it is. Not a lot better, a little better.

T.S. Eliot, poet

You need to understand your editor, what they are doing, what they need to do and the processes in their lives. Any aspiring writer should read Scott Berg's biography of Max Perkins. He was one of the great editors of the twentieth century who discovered and published many great authors, from Hemingway to Scott Fitzgerald. He changed the editor's role from the Edwardian era when manuscripts were pretty much delivered and published to the modern role of an editor, which is much more of a working partnership between author and editor. For sheer enjoyment, aspiring authors should also read, amongst much else, Diana Athill's Stet.

Trevor Dolby, publisher, Preface Publishing, an imprint of Random House
www.prefacepublishing.co.uk

This chapter looks at production: both the production of your manuscript – how to prepare it for submission – and how a publishing house turns that manuscript into a published book.

The author is very important because getting a book published is a long and quite intimate process. As an editor, you have to feel that you can work with an author; that they are going to be reasonable, helpful and supportive because there will be a lot of things they will be asked to do to support publication of their book. I think you also have to feel that the author has a very clear vision of what they're writing and for whom. It's an intensely collaborative process. It is all about trying to do the best, most positive job possible.

The writer has to understand that the editor only has the book's best interests at heart, that they are helping to make it as good as it can possibly be, while the editor has to remember that it is the author's book and not theirs. What a good editor does is offer a very experienced reader's eye. It's a tremendously sensitive time for an author when an editor first comes up with notes and an opinion. The author has been locked away writing their book and suddenly their creation is being minutely examined. I am always very conscious of how hard that must be and how sensitive they must feel.

At its best, editing is a wonderful, exciting, collaborative process. The author starts with the book on their own, then it's the author and the agent, then it's the author, the agent and the editor. And from that point it just blossoms out until the whole entire publishing house is engaged in that particular piece of creative work. Thereafter, it develops a life of its own.

Kate Parkin, publisher, John Murray Publishers
www.johnmurray.co.uk

Once a contract is signed with a publishing house, the editor will be working backwards from a proposed publishing date. They need to make sure that the author delivers the manuscript on time, that copy editors, illustrators, designers, typesetters and printers are all ready for their input at a set time in order to meet that publishing date.

Time is money, both for you as the writer and for your editor, representing the publishing house.

> *If I commissioned a book as a packager and an author let me down, I would think very hard about using them again. It's the worst thing you can do to be late. If you cause pain, you won't be used again.*
>
> Robert Forsyth, publisher, Chevron Publishing
> www.chevronpublishing.co.uk

Preparing your manuscript

> *I look out for my authors; I cherish the relationship with them. As an editor, you are interacting with people who have very interesting ideas and are interested in communicating those ideas or stories to others. It's a very collaborative process and that's what I love about the job.*
>
> Todd Armstrong, Senior Acquisitions Editor, Communications and Media Studies, SAGE Publications
> www.sagepub.com

If your manuscript looks professional, you will appear professional. Anything that makes life easier for editors, typesetters, etc. will be appreciated.

Tips on presentation
- ▶ Don't send your only copy.
- ▶ It's usual to send an electronic copy these days. However, if hard copy is needed, guidelines follow the same advice given in Chapter 2 on submissions.
- ▶ If it is in hard copy, editors want to see well-presented manuscripts – definitely not handwritten.
- ▶ Number pages straight through from beginning to end; don't start each chapter with page 1. Imagine what would happen if someone were to drop the lot on the floor; the reader wants

(Contd)

> - *to reassemble them as quickly as possible, not try to guess in which part of the manuscript the various page 1s belong.*
> - *If you want acknowledgements, a list of contents, a dedication, a list of other books you have published, either leave these pages unnumbered or use small roman figures (i, ii, iii, etc.).*
> - *You need at least a 4 cm (1½") margin on the left-hand side where editorial comments and typesetting instructions can be written.*
> - *Create a title/cover page, showing the title, your name (or pen name). Add your name/address in the bottom right-hand corner and put it on the first and last pages of the manuscript.*
> - *If the instructions are clear, there are fewer misunderstandings and mistakes; that means the work can be processed quickly and accurately. This keeps costs down and maintains quality.*
> - *If you have photographs or illustrations, put an identifying mark on the back of each illustration and a corresponding one where it is meant to be in the manuscript. Put the list of illustrations, with captions, on a separate piece of paper.*

Meeting deadlines

A date for delivery of the manuscript will have been agreed on signature of contract. When you negotiate this date, always give yourself at least three weeks longer than you think you will need – just in case.

Keep your editor informed of how you are progressing. If you look like you will be late, let your editor know *as soon as possible*. Everything has been geared up to a particular publication date and missing that can have serious repercussions for both the author and the publishing house. If they know there is going to be a delay, they *may* be able to delay the publication date. At the very least, the production team, printer and sales force will need to reschedule.

When the commissioning editor, copy editor and author are happy with the marked-up typescript, it is sent to the production department for design and typesetting. Junior editors will work with the production department to make sure that the book is progressing as planned.

What happens when the manuscript arrives at the publishing house?

The editor has a very important role – as an advocate for the author within the publishing house. Maybe that's something that has changed over the years. People's image of an editor, going back to Maxwell Perkins and Scott Fitzgerald, is of a rather erudite person with fantastically good grammar and a comprehensive general knowledge, who is going to hone your prose into a thing of beauty. That is still part of it nowadays. But on the commercial fiction side, which is where my expertise lies, while that is important it's not actually the main part of the job. In some cases, we use freelance editors to tidy up the manuscript rather than somebody like me doing it. My job is to be an advocate for the book within the company. So that everyone in the company takes it seriously, understands its potential and understands what we expect of it. I'm a sort of cheerleader for my authors and for their books as well as the person who says, 'I think this character is really awful and the book will be better without her.'

Sue Fletcher, publisher, Hodder & Stoughton
www.hodder.co.uk

Your manuscript receives a *structural edit*; in other words, the book is looked at as a whole (narrative pacing, characterization, general style; for non-fiction, illustrations, appendices, bibliography, notes, index). It will be checked for length and quality. If the publisher has a particular house style that they like to see in their books, the changes will be made here.

As editors, part of our job is to help an author make a good book great, from tackling the broad strokes of the story to

> the line-by-line detail. What writers should keep in mind is that they and their editor are working as a team, with the common goal of publishing the best book possible. So when a lengthy editorial letter lands on their desk or in their e-mail, our hope is that the author will understand that our feedback represents not only a fresh perspective and fresh eyes, but also knowledge of the market, an understanding of trends, and years of experience helping writers tap into their best work. It's not our expectation that an author will make every change we suggest, and we know that it's not always easy to answer the big questions set forth, but we do expect an open mind and an open dialogue and an understanding that no manuscript is perfect right off the bat.
>
> Children's Editorial Group, HarperCollins US
www.harpercollinschildrens.com

The copy editor (desk editor) is often a freelance editor employed by the publishing house. The copy editor may also be responsible for the structural edit. For the copy edit, they check the manuscript line by line, word by word. The process is designed to catch all errors and inconsistencies in the text: facts, spelling, punctuation and sense. They will also be looking for any comments that could potentially be libellous. Some do it on screen, others on typescript. Any queries are put onto a marked-up manuscript, which is sent to the author to be checked. The author is then asked to answer any queries that may have arisen.

Some of the points will be out-and-out errors; others will be suggestions from the copy editor. Apart from the obvious mistakes (someone has green eyes in Chapter 3 and hazel in Chapter 5), you do not have to agree to all the suggested changes. You will have to go through the marked-up manuscript, make any changes (or not, if you don't agree with them) and send the manuscript back to the editor.

> *Be open to the idea that the publisher might want that book to be arranged or targeted in a slightly different way. The focus that you have as a writer, the kind of thing that's*

driving you passionately, may be key as far as you're concerned. But from a commercial point of view, a publisher might suggest you take an entirely different route but to the same end. Now you may choose not to believe them or take their advice but it's just as well to be aware that some people might see your subject differently.

Doug Young, Publishing Director, Sport & Entertainment, Transworld
www.transworld-publishers.co.uk

As an author, you may need encouragement, praise or a whip cracked. It will depend on your temperament and the relationship you have with your editor. Most editors are very good at reading what kind of people their authors are and dealing with them accordingly. Remember, though, that your editor is not working exclusively with you; they will have other authors that demand their attention.

FEEDBACK

How should authors handle sticky moments during the editorial process? I think it depends on your general demeanour. How do you deal with disputes in your everyday life? It's going to be similar to how you handle disagreements in the editorial process.

Maria McCarthy, author
www.mariamccarthy.co.uk

Insight

As far as some authors are concerned 'feedback = criticism'. Don't be too oversensitive or stubborn about criticism. If you are flexible and accommodating, the editor will want to work with you again and it can be a pleasant experience for both of you.

Give your editor the courtesy of listening to their professional editorial feedback. You don't *have* to make the changes if you don't want to. Editors will often dovetail their comments with feedback from the copy editors so that the author gets only one set of comments. It is in the interests of the publishing house that the author is happy with what gets sent off for typesetting.

> *Working with your editor is all about straightforward collaboration. Making sure you have a dialogue with them. It's asking the right questions and remaining in contact with each other; for example, phoning up your editor and telling them when you've got a really thorny problem that you're not sure how to get out of, can they help? It's that sort of thing, involving your editor and making sure that they feel they can involve you. All authors work differently but I don't think writers should just deliver their manuscript on time with a nice email, Word file attached, saying 'I hope you like it; give me a ring when you've read it.' Simply don't do that – collaborate with your editor.*
>
> *Any editor worth their salt will want to work with an author, particularly a first-time author. The more you collaborate as the book is produced, the better it will be. I'm not suggesting sending one page in at a time. I'm suggesting that you send in, very early on, a couple of chapters and get a critique from your editor because they don't want to get to the end of the book and find they've got something they're not expecting. An editor will be really grateful for that because it makes their life easier, it gives them the necessary knowledge they need and makes them feel secure.*
>
> Trevor Dolby, publisher, Preface Publishing, an imprint of Random House
> www.prefacepublishing.co.uk

Insight

Iris Murdoch refused to be edited. That is not to be recommended for most authors. The editor is, at this point, thinking primarily of the reader, rather than the writer. If they are suggesting making changes, it is because they think it will improve the reading experience for the person who buys the book.

It is *extremely* rare that the manuscript will get rejected in its entirety. If this happens, it is important to establish exactly why it has not made the grade. Get the comments in writing, and then find out what the editor would like you to do; ideally, you want the opportunity to rewrite it.

If they do not want a rewrite, you can either try to insist that it gets published or (if the idea was yours in the first place) take it away and get it published (or self-published) elsewhere.

Hopefully, you can avoid anything like this taking place by, as Trevor Dolby suggests, collaborating with your editor.

> *It's true that editors have to balance looking after an author and representing their publishing house but it doesn't often feel as though there's a conflict between the two because we're all after the same end, which is to publish their book as successfully as possible. Of course, sometimes an author might feel their book is not, for example, getting as much of a marketing push as another and that's something the editor has to explain. Sometimes time is a factor: for example, an author might want their book cover to be changed or a quote added, but to do so would delay the book's production. This is where agents can be very useful arbiters, explaining to the author the mechanics of the business and reassuring them that their publisher isn't just trying to be awkward.*
>
> *Prima donnas aren't fun to work with. I consider myself fortunate because I don't have any authors like that. I have to say that, on the whole, I get the impression that there are more prima donnas in commercial genres, perhaps because they are often more financially successful than literary novelists so feel more able to call the shots. But then there are plenty of extremely successful commercial writers who are not like that at all – and some extremely successful literary novelists too.*
>
> *Obviously, it's like any normal relationship; you don't want someone to be a complete pest but, on the other hand,*

authors are going to be interested and want to know what's going on...and they should know what's going on. It's up to the editor to keep them informed.

Carole Welch, Publishing Director, Sceptre
www.hodder.co.uk

The *front matter* (or prelims) and *end matter* of a book – the first few and last few pages of the book – will usually be done by the publishers. These are the pages that give:

- *the book title and author*
- *the name of the publishing house*
- *the copyright notice*
- *the ISBN*
- *Cataloguing in Publication (CIP) data.*

Other pages may be:

- *contents*
- *acknowledgements*
- *list of illustrations.*

PROOFS

The author returns the amended marked-up manuscript; it is often sent back again for a final check in its revised form before going to the proof stage. The first proof is seen by the author and a proofreader (often another freelancer). At this stage, it is important to check for any typographical errors that may have crept in during the typesetting process. Editorial changes should have been done during the manuscript stage. Anything that the author wants to revise that is in excess of 10–15 per cent of the typesetting cost, they will be expected to pay.

When the proofs come back, a junior editor will collate them and mark them, using standard symbols, on a master copy. As an author, you will not see this master copy or need to understand the special symbols.

This second proof is then checked against the first proof to make sure that all the amendments have been made. The index, if there is one, is usually compiled at this stage. This set of proofs is returned to the production department to be turned into final proofs. Everything is checked and made ready to print.

> *I think it's really important that once you've done a deal as an agent you step back slightly; in other words, you shouldn't interfere too much with the editor and the writer and their relationship. Yet you always need to be there for your author. The editor will phone and update you and tell you what's going on. You'll always be a part of it, at some stages more than others. The editor is the person who has bought the book and they did so because they are enthusiastic about it.*
>
> Camilla Goslett, literary agent, Curtis Brown
www.curtisbrown.co.uk

DESIGN

Think about what makes you pick up a book when you are in a library or bookstore – very often it is purely because you like the look of the cover design. Work on the cover design begins months in advance of the publishing date. Hardback jackets and paperback covers are used as the main selling tool. Most buying decisions are made by trade buyers before a book is printed – and often all they have is the cover to go on.

If you are with a publishing house, you can make comments or suggestions on the book cover (as early on in the process as possible) but the final decision will lie with the publisher. They know what works in the market so it is not helpful to insist that they use a picture that your five-year-old son painted. We will look at designing your own self-published book in Chapter 6.

> *I always want to see the first draft within 18 months of signing the contract because we can realistically work back from that. In educational publishing, books usually have*

15 chapters because there are 15 weeks in a semester; as a student you will do one chapter a week on your course. This gives my author a chapter a month to write. A chapter will be 30 manuscript pages and that's a manuscript page a day. As I tell my authors, if they break things down to smaller parts it becomes more manageable.

When I was the history editor at Simon & Schuster, I found some authors would start revising their textbooks and then suddenly want to add on a chapter to their Modern American History to reflect recent events. I'd have to point out that despite all those developments, professors would not be given an extra week to teach it.

I really don't want the books to be longer than 256 pages, which will be roughly 100,000 words. This is for a couple of reasons. Unless it's for an introductory course, the tutor will probably use more than one book for the course; so they need to be able to get through all the material in the given time. If my author's book is too long, it just won't be able to fit in to an academic course's timescale. The other thing is the cost factor. Paper is the most expensive component of a book. Remember, the publisher incurs that cost before they sell any copies of the book. And they incur that cost whether that books sells right away or sits in the warehouse for three years. So length of book is very important.

Todd Armstrong, Senior Acquisitions Editor, SAGE Publications

www.sagepub.com

PRODUCTION

The production department handles all aspects of book production including text design. The production processes are:

- ▶ *typesetting*
- ▶ *printing*
- ▶ *binding*
- ▶ *packing and distribution.*

Typesetting

The typescript usually goes to a freelance typesetter to be made into page proofs. They process the text, either by rekeying it or by taking computer disks supplied by the writer, inputting any editorial changes from the marked-up hard copy and then producing the typeset pages. They tend to use applications such as QuarkXPress or Adobe InDesign. Once laid out, they will supply paper proofs or PDF files for checking by the publisher and author.

Printing

Traditionally printing was done as offset lithography; printers use offset metal plates treated so that certain areas attract the ink and repel water; while other areas attract water and repel ink. Litho is still used for large print runs.

Digital printing has become more popular than offset lithography and is used for short runs and print on demand. Wholesalers can now print off books using digital files supplied by a publisher.

The size of the print run is dictated by the market. Retailers are not keen to subscribe to a book by an unknown author up front; they want to see how it performs before they put in a huge order. So, they will order a few copies (if you are lucky) and then wait to see what happens. This affects publishers (and self-publishers) who will print fewer copies on the first print run; they do not want to be left with a huge number of unsold books.

Binding

Binding can be:

- ▶ *perfect binding*
- ▶ *slotted/burst binding*
- ▶ *wire stitching*
- ▶ *sewn limp.*

(See Chapter 6, p. 154 for more detail.)

Packing and distribution

The books are packed in quantity by the printer, shrink-wrapped and parcelled up either in boxes or on pallets. They are then either sent to a specified warehouse belonging to the publisher, from where they are sent on to the main retailers and wholesalers, or sent directly to the customers (retailers/wholesalers).

> *Publishing is a very collaborative process. It's not just me reading and enjoying a book. It's me enjoying a book and being evangelical about feeling it could be shared profitably with a very wide audience. After all, you can define 'publishing' as bringing something to public attention.*
>
> Sue Fletcher, publisher, Hodder & Stoughton
> www.hodder.co.uk

SALES

We will look at the process of selling books in Chapter 9 but it is worth mentioning the sales process at this stage. The sales department is an integral part of the publishing team. They are responsible for getting books into bookshops so that people can buy them, which in turn earns you money. Sales representatives ('reps') go to bookshops selling the up-and-coming titles; they operate several months in advance of publication.

There are also freelance sales reps who will take a percentage of the orders they take plus any reorders from the same shop. They will not always take on one book from a self-publisher but if you contact them and convince them that your book is saleable, you may persuade them to take you on. With these pre-orders, the publishing house has an idea of how big the first print run should be.

Insight

It is unlikely that you will get to meet members of the sales team unless you are one of the publisher's major authors; then you may get to go to the annual sales conference. Whether you meet them or not, remember that they have a huge role in helping to make your book a success. You can help them by delivering a good book and doing as much as you can to promote yourself and your book.

Selling rights
Part of the selling process also comes from the rights departments, which sell the publishing rights to other publishers (i.e. in other countries) and/or serializations in newspapers and magazines.

What happens if your editor moves on

It is not uncommon for editors to move to different publishing houses. It can be upsetting for an author if their editor leaves in the middle of a project. However, the contract is with the publishing house, not with the editor. You will have to finish your current book with that house. When you have finished (and if your contract allows it), you can always take your next proposal to that editor (if you enjoyed working with them).

If it happens to you, remember that the publishing house has committed itself to publishing your book so it is in their interest to make sure it reaches publication. If you are concerned that you might find yourself in this situation, you could always ask who would take over in such a scenario at your first meeting with the editor – and then ask to meet them.

Case study

Annie Ashworth and Meg Sanders, authors who write as Annie Sanders

Fiction: *Goodbye Jimmy Choo*, *Warnings of Gales*, *The Xmas Factor*, *Busy Woman Seeks Wife*, *Gap Year for Grown Ups*, *Getting Mad Getting Even* (all Orion)

(Contd)

Non-fiction: *Trade Secrets, Trade Secrets Christmas, Trade Secrets Parenting* (Orion), *How To Beat The System* (Orion), *Fat Club* (Granada Media), *The Chain, The Madness of Modern Families* (Hodder & Stoughton) www.anniesanders.co.uk

MS – We only got an agent when we started writing novels. Prior to that we were writing non-fiction and we managed pretty well without an agent, I think; although looking back, there were probably things that would have gone better if we had had an agent.

AA – I agree; we were so naive. We were just glad to get the work. When it came to finding an agent, we spoke to people in publishing, asking if they recommended anyone because the most important thing is to get an agent who specializes in your genre.

MS – If you don't have contacts in publishing, find a writer whose work you admire, look in their acknowledgements and see who their agent is. And, of course, the Writer's Handbook *is invaluable.*

AA – We targeted three or four agents. We had a very positive response from one but the agent we have now stepped in within 24 hours of receiving our manuscript. It takes a very brave author to say 'Hang on a minute, I'll wait and see if anyone else comes along!'

MS – Also, she was so decisive about our book, whereas others weren't so sure. They had been suggesting we changed certain things... Stuff that we didn't necessarily feel comfortable with changing. It's good to have an agent that shares your vision; I don't think we'd have done as well with the other one.

AA – So we signed with her. Ironically, just a month before that, she'd had lunch with the editor who eventually published us who said she was looking for a book just like the one we wrote. So it was absolutely 100 per cent the right place and the right time. We were really lucky in that respect.

We sent in three chapters and a synopsis to the agent and we then had to write the whole of the book before she'd submit it. So we did that in three weeks.

MS – It was crazy, I remember, we were working until three or four in the morning! The relationship we have with our agent is the one that we want. I think there are different types of agent who give different types of support. Some agents hold your hand, read your manuscripts, suggest ideas for books and are very editorial. Whereas our agent is much more contract orientated; she's a Rottweiler in that respect.

AA – She comes from a rights background, not an editing one, and that could be a consideration for someone looking for an agent. Most authors, I think, submit to their agent first and then the publisher. We submit to the publisher and cc the agent in; her interest and skill lies in the more commercial side of things. A good agent should check that you're going to deliver on time and should be on your side.

MS – We have each other to talk to about the book so we don't need that tremendous editorial support that some people do. They say writing is a very lonely business; well, it's not when you're writing as a pair because we can talk to each other all the time about it. We know that we are just as interested in the book as each other and we understand it in as much detail. So that's one huge advantage of working together and perhaps makes us slightly less in need of moral support.

AA – Yes, I've been to author events where the agent has come with the author and that's something that would never happen with us...because it doesn't need to happen.

MS – I think there are as many different relationships between writers and editors as there are between writers and agents. But some editors are much more hands on than others.

(Contd)

AA – In our case, that 'third eye' of the editor is so useful. Because they know the market, they know you, your strengths and weaknesses. When we submit a manuscript the editor will come back and say, 'It's really strong there but I think you should build it up here...' It's a bit like a teacher, handing back your homework. And they're usually right. But there have been a couple of times when we have disagreed with her suggestions. There was one whole character in a book that we fought to keep and I'm glad we did. I thought she was valuable. And if your editor respects you, she should accept that. It's a bit of give and take.

MS – Almost invariably, when you get big changes suggested, you think, 'No, I can't do that! That can't happen.' But then you just have to back off and let the idea of change percolate through your subconscious – and often the changes make sense. It's just that you have a concept of your story as being all in one and you can't see how to start pulling it apart without it falling to pieces.

AA – Yes, that is the danger. It's like a knitted sweater; if you unravel too much the whole thing falls apart.

MS – I don't know if the editorial hand is heavier nowadays than it used to be. But I know there was a book that was published in the States which did extremely well. I read the first one and loved it. A sequel came out and it was just dire. Apparently, in between times, the author and the agent had fallen out and there's a suspicion that the agent had had a big hand in rewriting the first one.

AA – William Golding's Lord of the Flies *was unpublishable when it first came in and was heavily edited, so writers mustn't think that what they deliver is impossible to salvage...because a good idea is salvageable.*

MS – Do you know what is so great about having an editor? You get very close to your manuscript and it's difficult to step back and see the overall structure. Maybe that's an advantage of submitting a complete manuscript rather than doing it in bits and pieces. The reworking might be more but the editor gets a really fresh look and is able to see that big picture. A good editor will pick out what's working in a manuscript.

AA – An awful lot of authors will submit their first chapter to their editor just to say, 'This is the route I'm taking, this is the tone.' Really well-known authors. We don't do that; we just write the whole thing and send it off and wait for the feedback. Maybe it works for some people to have the reassurance.

MS – I think an awful lot of people don't do what we do. I think we're unusual because there's two of us.

AA – Yes, they do leave us alone!

MS – In fact, when we were signed originally the editor who took us on said she overcame a 25-year prejudice against working with joint authors. And that's why our publishers only wanted to give us one name.

AA – If you haven't got a publisher, you've got all the time in the world with your first novel. But if you're on a two-book contract, like we are, one book a year, there are deadlines to hit.

MS – Everything works back from publication date and it's very mechanistic at that point. Forget art!

AA – You can be terribly self-indulgent when you're writing but you've got to remember that you are writing for someone else to read it. You have to write for the market. Most of us read in bed; don't give me 24 characters whose names begin with 'C' in the first chapter, I can't be bothered. I don't want to read books where I have to work hard.

MS – Reading is also very important for a writer. Although I must say I can't really read while we're writing – at least not anything in our genre. It's like washing a red sock in with your whites; you can't prevent it seeping into your writing and I think that's to be
(Contd)

avoided at all costs. I'll read detective stories or something when we're writing but I can't read another women's commercial fiction book because I'll get it too mixed up with my own ideas.

AA – Unless you are very successful, there's always this sense that you have to be eternally grateful for being published. People tell you all the time how lucky we are and Meg will turn back and say, 'Luck's only part of it actually!' You do have to be able to produce the goods.

Compared to what most people do for a living, you get pretty short shrift if you whinge about it. I'm surrounded by people who think it's a 'la la' waste of time and/or a very easy way to make money. Although if you are making money out of it, it's a very nice way of doing it.

MS – Somebody said they loved writing because they got to meet such interesting people. The people that they had created, in other words. So you can do that as a writer, enter a world that you want to be in, with people you like to spend time with. That's very nice indeed...and you can do it in your pyjamas.

10 THINGS TO REMEMBER

1 *Never send the only copy of your manuscript.*

2 *Presentation of the manuscript is important; pages should be numbered, margins should be at least 4 cm (1½") so notes can be written by the editor; double spacing throughout.*

3 *Photographs or illustrations should have an identifying mark on the back and a note in the manuscript so that the editor/ typesetter knows where they should go. They should not be stuck into the hard copy of the manuscript.*

4 *A manuscript will be looked at for style, pacing, characterization, length. This is the structural editing process.*

5 *A copy editor will check through for inconsistencies and errors.*

6 *Editorial feedback is designed to improve the book; the editor looks at the manuscript with the reader in mind.*

7 *The proof should be checked carefully; mistakes are expensive to rectify once the manuscript goes to the second proof stage.*

8 *Authors can make suggestions on the design of the cover but the final decision will lie with the publisher.*

9 *The size of the print run is dictated by the demands of the market; retailers are not keen to put in a huge order for a first book by an unknown author so the print run will not be huge.*

10 *Authors do not usually get to meet the sales reps, the team responsible for going out and selling the book to the retailers.*

6
Self-publishing

In this chapter you will learn:
- *how to be your own editor*
- *about vanity publishing*
- *about print on demand*
- *where you can get help from professionals*
- *how to set the price of your book.*

> *If you are in difficulties with a book, try the element of surprise, attack it at an hour when it isn't expecting it.*
>
> H.G. Wells, author

In this chapter, we will look at how you can identify your market, prepare your book for publication and the various routes there are to self-publishing.

Self-publishing used to have a poor reputation; it was seen as the last-ditch attempt of authors who could not get published anywhere else. Production values were poor and retailers never used to take self-published books on.

All that has changed and self-publishing has come of age. Publishers and retailers take self-publishing more seriously – as does the book-buying public. If the quality of the book (both in content and production) can rival that of a traditionally published book, the self-publisher can market their title with confidence.

One of the advantages of self-publishing is that you can go at your own speed. Once you have decided you want to get your book published, there is no time spent hawking it round agents or traditional publishing houses, hoping someone will pick it up. You just get on and do it yourself.

Everything changed when my husband suddenly had to have a life-threatening operation and I became his carer. Shortage of time and energy caused me to rethink my style of cooking, producing healthy meals very quickly, and with these newly created recipes I called myself 'The Lazy Cook'. I was wondering how to promote this new range of recipes when a friend said, 'Why don't you publish your own book? If you had 100 printed everyone in the village would buy one – make it your millennium project!'

All I had at that time was a portable typewriter on the kitchen table but I set to and wrote 'Enter the New Millennium with Lazy Cook Mo Smith'. My enthusiasm for this new book was such that I didn't have just 100 copies printed but 1,000! I collected them from my local printer at the beginning of November, leaving me just a few weeks to sell them all, which I did.

Encouraged by the success of my first attempt at self-publishing and still having many recipes to promote, I asked myself 'Why not do another book and aim for sales in major bookshops and supermarkets?' This meant that it would have to be perfect bound, with a barcode and an ISBN. For the title of this second book I chose 'Lazy Cook in the kitchen – mouthwatering recipes for the time-pressured cook'. I opened a Lazy Cook bank account to make it more businesslike and on advice I patented my 'Lazy Cook' title including the hammock logo. A neighbour put me in touch with a designer who suggested a cover. For the barcode I looked in the Yellow Pages and found a company who were helpful and inexpensive. An ISBN was more of a problem, a friend offered to supply one but that meant I would then have to put his name alongside 'Published by'. Proud of my attempts at self-publishing I felt unable to accept his offer. Again I turned to Yellow Pages and looked for a large printing company and asked, 'Can you supply me with an ISBN?' The reply came, 'No, but I know a man who can' – problem solved. Choosing the recipes and planning the layout of the book was interesting, typing the recipes was a long-winded chore and remains so.

Two important decisions remained – the price of the book, I decided on £5.50 per copy with a percentage from each sale to be given to charity, and a first print run of 5,000 copies. My husband pointed out that 5,000 books weighed quite a lot and that we couldn't keep them in the house. I hadn't thought about storage. On my next visit I mentioned this to my printer who replied, 'I'll store them for you'.

Mo Smith, author
www.lazycookmosmith.co.uk

It can be quite daunting. Suddenly, you are no longer a writer but a publisher, editor, agent, sales rep and marketing and publicity specialist all rolled into one. What you do not have is the support and assistance of someone (an editor or agent) who knows the publishing world and can guide you step by step. On the plus side, you are in charge of how your book gets into print; you control the decisions and the timing and you can produce a printed book exactly the way you envisaged it.

You also control and decide what you want to do with your book. It may be that you just want to have a copy of your book on your shelf, maybe you want to give a few copies to friends and family or sell to a niche market, or perhaps you are determined to sell as many copies as you can and make a profit.

If it is the latter two, you need to have a realistic idea of potential sales; plan your distribution and be proactive when it comes to researching your market. You also need to compete with traditionally published books; that means that your production values have to aim to match the technical standards of book production that the publishing houses achieve (error free, well produced, edited). If you don't like the thought of marketing and selling your book, then self-publishing is probably not for you.

> *I think the most important thing for an author is that they have something they want to say, either in fiction or non-fiction. Writing a book represents a colossal effort. Anyone who can sit down and spend that length of time in their own head, feeding on their own resources, is to be admired.*
>
> Kate Parkin, publisher, John Murray Publishers
> www.johnmurray.co.uk

Self-publishing is not a new phenomenon. Bestselling self-published authors include:

Rudyard Kipling
Edgar Allan Poe
Ezra Pound
Upton Sinclair
Walt Whitman
Mark Twain

Insight

Self-publishing can help you to develop your writing. You can get a book out of your system before moving on to your next project.

Being self-published

When considering whether to take on a book, a publisher will ask themselves the following questions. If you are serious about self-publishing, you should do the same.

- *Who are you writing for? What is the target market?*
- *What genre?*

- *Where would you put the book on a bookshelf?*
- *What is special/different/unique about the book?*
- *Why would anyone buy it rather than another title?*
- *How will it be marketed?*

In a self-published book your name must appear as the publisher on the copyright page; this can be your own name or you can give yourself a publishing house name. The book's ISBN must also be registered to you, as the publisher, by the ISBN agency. Copies of the book are then yours to do with as you wish. You must include the standard statement about copyright on the inside page:

All rights reserved. No part of this book can be reproduced, stored in or introduced into a retrieval system, or transmitted, in any form, or by any means (electronic, mechanical, photocopying, recording or otherwise) without the prior written permission of the publisher.

This means that you own the rights (television, film, translation, etc.) and these rights cannot be exploited unless you give permission.

As your own publisher, you need to get the design and presentation of your book right; you need to consider:

- *size*
- *length*
- *format*
- *usability*
- *fitness for purpose*
- *quality*
- *accuracy of content*
- *the look (the design) both internally and externally.*

Did you know?
G.P. Taylor was told that a Christian parable, with black magic set in the eighteenth century, would not be of any interest to publishers. He self-published *Shadowmancer*. It cost him £3,500.

> Recommendations from friends, neighbours and his parishioners meant that the book became popular. So popular that it was bought by Faber and the book spent 15 weeks on the UK bestseller list. The US rights were reputedly sold for over £300,000 to Putnam's.

SET A BUDGET AND A PRICE

How much you spend is entirely up to you but you should put aside a set amount of money before you start. You will not be able to set a budget and price the book in one session. You will have to collate the information and re-adjust figures as you progress until you are happy with the costings. Costs for producing your own book can range from as little as a few pounds to a few thousand.

Pricing the book is related to the cost. While it is worth going round bookshops and looking at online retailers to see what other publishers are charging for their books, remember that as a first-time author you do not have a track record with the buying public. They are not waiting for your book with bated breath. So don't price the book so high that you put them off.

Look at the *type* of book you are intending to produce and see how similar titles are priced and produced. This will give you an idea of what the market expectations are: some books will work if they are cheap and cheerful, while others will be expected to have higher production values and therefore will command a higher price.

You will also have to bear in mind that booksellers demand a discount off the retail price of a book; we look at discounting in more detail in Chapter 9. For now, remember to factor discounts into your costings.

Insight
Pitfalls to look out for are underestimating your costs, overestimating demand and underpricing your product.

The total production cost for your book will be made up of fixed costs and variable costs.

Fixed costs
These will not change no matter how many books you have printed. They may include:

- *payments to freelancers (e.g. illustrator, designer, indexer)*
- *ISBN registration*
- *permission fees (if using other material, e.g. image for book cover)*
- *legal fees (if you have to check through for libel).*

Variable costs
These will depend on how many books you have printed. They can include the cost of:

- *printing*
- *paper*
- *binding*
- *storage*
- *delivery/distribution/postage.*

Other variable costs that don't depend on the print run are:

- *advertising, including flyers, bookmarks*
- *publicity and promotion*
- *website design and maintenance.*

Unit cost
This is the average cost of producing each copy. You calculate this by dividing your total costs (fixed and variable) by how many books you have had printed (or are thinking of getting printed). The more you have printed, the lower the unit cost but the total cost will still increase.

Remember that your potential customer will not be worried about whether you have printed enough books or what your costs were to get the book out. They will consider only whether they are prepared to pay that amount for your book. Trying to keep the variable costs low by opting for cheap paper, for example, could put buyers off.

Net sales revenue
This is the amount of money a publisher (or self-publisher) will receive after the trade discounts have been taken off. For example, if a book has a recommended retail price of £20, it may be sold to a bookseller by the publisher at a 50 per cent discount. In other words, the bookseller pays the publisher £10 for the book. So £10 is the net sales revenue for one copy.

Total revenue
To work out the total revenue of a book, you have to make a sales forecast. This involves setting a price for your book so that it is competitive within the market.

- *If you price a book too highly, you won't sell many copies and your total revenue will be low.*
- *If your book is underpriced, you miss the opportunity to maximize your income for that title.*

If your book doesn't sell well but you priced it high enough, you may still retain some profit. With too low a price and a garage full of books that nobody is buying, you will be out of pocket. The overall cost of your books should be divided by the number you sell, *not* the number you print. Work out the break-even number you need to sell.

Being a publisher

There are various ways to go about it: you can do it all yourself (layout, design) and take it to a local printer; or you can go to a company which will produce and publish your book for you; or you can use a web-based company, which allows you to download software and lay out your book and then, for a price, will produce and print it for you.

USING EXPERTS

Buying in external services is something all publishing houses do. As a self-publisher, you will do the same. Some of the roles you can take on yourself, or you may choose to bring in professionals at each stage. If you decide to use professional services, get as many competitive quotes as you can.

Editors and proofreaders

Using a professional editor or proofreader will bring a fresh set of eyes to your work. Costs will vary but the Society for Editors and Proofreaders lists suggested minimum hourly rates that will give you an idea of what to expect. The National Union of Journalists has a freelance fees guide as well as prices for design, translation and so on.

Many editors and proofreaders will work in particular areas of specialist knowledge, so if your book is aimed at professionals or academics in a certain subject area make sure you get an editor or proofreader who has the same speciality.

What the copy editor and/or proofreader needs to know

- *What will you be sending them?*
- *Will there be illustrations/photos? If so, has permission been sought and agreed?*
- *Is there any outstanding material to come?*
- *What do you want the copy editor to do: the minimum, restructuring and/or rewriting?*
- *What do you want the proofreader to do: read against a copy/previous draft or just read one copy blind?*
- *Who is the target audience?*
- *What is the deadline? When do you want delivery?*
- *What payment/fees are you offering: hourly rate, page rate or lump sum?*

USING FRIENDS

Halfway between using a professional editor/proofreader and doing it yourself is asking a friend to look at your work.

It should be someone you trust and you must be very specific about what you are asking them to do. Ask them:

- *where do they think it is good?*
- *where do they think it is bad?*
- *where do they think it is slow?*

BEING YOUR OWN EDITOR

A self-publisher needs to build in quality control at every step. You will be judged against 'professionally' published books.

> **Insight**
> Most writers believe their work is ready to be sent out when they finish the first draft. It almost never is. Don't send your first draft for feedback or to go to print. Revise it and make it the best you can before you go to print.

Copy editor

A copy editor goes over the text carefully to check for any mistakes or confusions. You need your manuscript to be:

- *consistent – spellings, hyphens, capitalization, quotation marks, speech marks, parenthesis, etc.*
- *clear – have you made any misleading or contradictory statements? Is there repetition?*
- *understood by its readers (i.e. if you are an American writer aiming at a British audience, have you allowed for cultural confusion/differences?)*
- *legal – a copy editor will identify any issues regarding copyright, libel, obscenity, etc.*

For guidance use the *Oxford Style Manual* (or the *Chicago Manual of Style*). They are used by publishing houses and offer guidance on words and how to use them.

Index

Most non-fiction books come with an index. Traditionally, if your book was with a publishing house, it was the responsibility of the author to provide the index; nowadays, it is more commonly outsourced to a professional indexer.

An index has been described as a road map, guiding readers to where they want to go. It is a skilled art. As well as analysing text, indexers need to be able to represent concepts using a few words, create cross-referencing and utilize headings and sub-headings. If you are producing a book that needs an index, do consider using someone who has experience in this.

The Society of Indexers (or the American Society for Indexing – contact details are in the Appendix) will have a list of members as well as a table of recommended fees to give you an idea of costs. There is also advice on the websites on how to commission an index.

Design

The design of a book includes:

- *size*
- *cover design, front and back, including the blurb*
- *layout (inside the book)*
- *font and typeface*
- *illustrations.*

A well-designed book is a pleasure to read; get the look, the design and the feel right and people are more likely to pick up and buy your book.

Look at books to see what you think works and what you like; you should consider the following:

SIZE

Books come in a range of sizes. Standard book formats (the following are approximate measurements):

Paperback/classic	**Demy octavo (C format)**	216 × 138mm
Hardback	**Royal octavo (C format)**	234 × 153mm
Paperback/mass-market	**A format**	178 × 110mm
	B format	198 × 129mm

Look at other books in your genre to see the sorts of shape and size used. Novels are usually in an A or B format paperback. Again, look through a bookshop and see how size gives an indication of the type of paperback it is: literary or mass-market. There is a wider choice in size for non-fiction books.

Tips on book sizes
- *Make sure that your book can be stacked on a shelf comfortably.*
- *Is it easy to hold and read?*
- *If you are planning to post out your book yourself, does it fit comfortably into a standard Jiffy bag or envelope?*

Other book sizes are:

A4	297 × 210mm
Demy quarto	276 × 219mm (often hardback format)
Pinched crown quarto up to	248 × 175mm
A5	210 × 148mm

In the UK, the dimensions are given with the head to tail (top to bottom) measurement first; while in the US and Europe, the width measurement comes first.

COVER DESIGN – FRONT

Authors should always make sure that their book has a spine with writing on it. Obviously when we first have a new title, we have it face up on a table but after a while it's going to end spine-up on a shelf and if you can't see the book it will be lost forever.

Alex Milne-White, Hungerford Bookshop, Independent Bookshop
of the Year 2009 (British Book Industry Awards)
www.hungerfordbooks.co.uk

The cover will need to have some kind of protection. Hardbacks often have dust jackets; paperbacks are usually laminated. If you want your book to be seen on a book shelf (in a shop or a library), as Alex Milne-White suggests, it needs to have 'perfect binding'. This means it will have a spine that shows the title, author and publisher, which helps sales. It is more expensive than other forms of binding but books with perfect binding tend to last longer.

People take about eight seconds when looking at a book to decide whether to buy it or not. A catchy title and a well-designed cover sell the book because they make someone pick it up; once they have it in their hand, they will read the blurb on the back and maybe the first page.

The design department in a publishing house will aim to produce a cover that is striking enough to be picked up by someone browsing as well as clear enough to be reproduced in catalogues and online. If you can, take a leaf out of the publishing houses' book and get your design organized well in advance of publication. Publishers will use the cover design to promote and sell the book.

If you are unsure about your skills as a designer, consider getting help from a design professional.

Tips on cover design

If you are briefing a designer, you should consider the following points.

- *Say what your budget is.*
- *Decide how many colours you want – printers will quote on full colour, three, two or one colour (white does not*

> *count as a colour; therefore, black and white is a one-colour print process; red, black and white would be a two-colour process). Full colour is more expensive to print than using three.*
> - *The design should be aimed at attracting the readership you have identified for your book (should it be contemporary, quirky, traditional?)*
> - *Make sure the title and author's name are clearly marked.*
> - *While you may not have your self-published book in a sales catalogue, you should plan to have a thumbnail image of the cover on your website and on retail sites such as Amazon. Therefore the design needs to work as a small image.*
> - *Try to work out a clear idea of what you want from the design before you brief a designer; if they produce a draft design and you don't like it and want something completely different, it will cost you money every time the designer has to go back to the drawing board.*
> - *Study other books in your genre to get some ideas. Find out what you think is effective and works well and what elements you do not like.*

COVER DESIGN – BACK
The blurb
In the 1990s, Penguin and Orion conducted research into a book's blurb, which revealed that it was a key factor in a person deciding whether to buy a book or not.

In fact, the Book Marketing Society (BMS) now has an award for 'Best Blurb of the Year' to recognize the work of those who write the all-important cover copy. As the BMS says, this is perhaps the most underrated discipline in the publishing industry but one that is so important.

Tips on blurb-writing
> - *People have very little time when reading the blurb, so make it short – no more than 120 words.*
> - *It needs to be relevant, have impact and intrigue the reader.*
>
> *(Contd)*

> - *Sell the atmosphere rather than **tell** the story.*
> - *Consider using a review quote (but don't make them up!).*
> - *Bullet points can help to get across the key benefits of a book, especially a non-fiction book.*
> - *Fiction blurbs can afford to be a bit more emotional.*

In addition to the blurb, you will need to include on the back cover:

- *the ISBN and barcode*
- *the price and publisher information (next to the barcode)*
- *any reviewers' comments*
- *information about you as the author (useful if your book is non-fiction)*
- *a photograph of you, the author, is not necessary but it can help with marketing the book; the photograph needs to be good quality so consider getting one done professionally (you can always use it in your marketing and on your website).*

Insight
Short sentences can be really effective when you are writing your blurb.

LAYOUT

> *When designing the layout of your book, look at the books you've already got. Look at the order of the title page, the copyright page, the preface, the acknowledgements and the contents. Do you want footnotes or endnotes? Do you have an appendix? Make sure you have included everything a professional book would have. Note that the copyright page is usually centred.*
>
> Katherine T. Owen, self-published author, *It's OK to Believe*

A page layout usually consists of two facing pages, based on a grid, within which you place the text and any illustrations.

Tips on layout
- *The structure should be clear and consistent.*
- *Finding your way around the book should be easy and uncomplicated.*

Front matter
These are the first few pages right at the start of a book before the actual text begins. You do not have to have a set number of front matter pages but you must include a right-hand title page and a left-hand copyright page.

Right-hand pages are known as recto. Left-hand pages are known as verso. The title page will be recto (right); it is required and should include:

- *full title*
- *author's name*
- *publisher's imprint (your name or your publishing/imprint name).*

Title verso (left) follows; it, too, is required and should include:

- *copyright information*
- *year of publication*
- *ISBN*
- *assertion of moral rights*
- *if the book is a work of fiction, a disclaimer here saying it is fiction*
- *publisher's address*
- *country of manufacture.*

Other front matter pages are optional and could include:

- *list of contents*
- *acknowledgements (right-hand page)*
- *list of other books by the same author (left-hand page)*
- *dedication (right-hand page)*
- *preface/forward (right-hand page).*

If you want to paginate the preliminary pages, which include title pages, contents, illustrations, acknowledgements, etc, you should use Roman numerals or italics (I, II, III/i, ii, iii, etc.). When you start the book properly and reach the introduction or opening chapter, switch to Arabic numbers (1, 2, 3, etc.).

Back or end matter
The pages at the end of a book can be used for appendices, index, bibliography or notes. You could also use them to advertise your website or other books that you have published. Some self-published authors use the last inside page of the book as an order sheet which can be cut out or photocopied to order more books.

FONTS AND TYPEFACES
The following are some of the most commonly used fonts and all are in 11-point size:

Arial *is a sans serif font.*
Times New Roman *is a serif font.*
Garamond *takes up a bit more room than other fonts.*
Palatino *takes up less space.*

You can experiment with fonts; most computers now have a dazzling array but the aim should be clarity, ease and comfort when reading. Avoid quirky, hard-to-read fonts. Study published books to check the style. Even though you are self-publishing, your book will be judged against the standards of 'professionally' produced books; mimic their style. Pay particular attention to:

- *quotation marks for speech – should be single not double*
- *justified text*
- *indents at the beginning of paragraphs*
- *hyphenation at the end of lines.*

Widows and orphans
- *A widow is the last line of a paragraph at the top of a page.*
- *An orphan is the first line of a paragraph at the bottom of a page.*

Good typesetting will make sure there are no widows or orphans in the text. When you proofread your typeset work, look out for them and amend any you find.

Dropped caps
This allows you to drop the capital letter over a number of lines of text – not a requirement but it can look stylish for some types of book.

For example, if we repeat that last sentence you can see that the 'T' is a dropped cap over two lines of text:

This allows you to drop the capital letter over a number of lines of text – not a requirement but it can look stylish for some types of book.

ILLUSTRATIONS
Obviously, illustrations and photos are not necessary for all genres but they can add value (to a cookery book, for example). There will be a cost to reproduce the photos and illustrations (as there will if you work with an illustrator or a photographer to produce new work for your book) so you need to work out whether that extra cost will contribute to selling more copies.

Tips on illustrations
- *Do the illustrations add value?*
- *Do you need permission to reproduce them? (if so, you may have to pay for that permission)*
- *Can you reproduce them in sufficient quality?*

The cost of getting permissions will depend on what size you plan to use; a quarter-page illustration will be cheaper than a half-page one, and a front cover illustration will cost more than one in the body of the text.

You can source illustrations and photos from the Picture Research Association; they have a list of photo libraries and freelance picture researchers. If you want to use an illustrator, contact the Association of Illustrators for a list of members and to get an idea of costs. One way of avoiding having to get permission would be to take the photographs yourself.

If you are producing the book yourself, you will have to scan the images so that they are in a digital format. The images can then be inserted into the text using typesetting software.

Binding
Hardback and paperback books are bound differently; hardback binding is more expensive.

Types of binding:

- *perfect binding: the spine of the folded section is trimmed off, glue is added and the cover is put on*
- *slotted/burst binding – same as perfect but grooves are cut into the spine*
- *wire stitching – you cannot open the book out flat and there is no spine*
- *sewn limp – expensive but hard wearing; pages are sewn together.*

Did you know?
James Redfield self-published *The Celestine Prophecy* in 1993. He gave away 1,500 copies to bookshops and individuals. Six months later, the book had sold 100,000 copies thanks to word-of-mouth recommendation. Warner Books bought the book which got into the *New York Times* Bestsellers List and stayed there for three years.

Print run
Booksellers want to see how a title performs before they put in a large order. They tend to order a few copies (if you are lucky) and then wait and see how they sell. As a result, publishing houses now print fewer copies on the first print run because they do not want to be left with a huge amount of unsold books.

As a self-publisher, you should think about the numbers you want to print for the first run:

- *Print too few and you could run the risk of losing sales while waiting for reprints if the book proves popular.*

▶ *Print too many and you could have problems and costs regarding storage.*

Remember that you will want to send some books out as review copies (publishing houses send around 30–50 but that would not be practical for a self-publisher) and also keep some for gifts and as a record of your achievement; some might be incorrectly bound and a few might get damaged in transit so you need to build in these books to your overall quantity because they cannot be sold.

Printer
Find a local printer who is used to book production and who is willing to help you through the process; not all printers have the correct machinery or expertise for book printing. Ask to see examples of book production that they have done before. Check whether they will do short print runs or have a minimum print run. You do not have to go with the first printer you contact; they are used to giving quotes for jobs so ask for a few to compare and contrast.

For your meeting with the printer, take along some examples of books that you like and would consider having as your final production copy. The printer will be able to tell you how much each version would cost and what is the best option for you. They will also be able to help you choose the right weight of paper for your book. If they don't do the kind of binding you want or only do very large print runs and you just want a few hundred books, ask them to recommend another printer.

Paper comes in 'weights'; the pages of most paperback books are printed on paper that weighs from 60 gsm to 100 gsm. The lighter the paper, the flimsier and cheaper it feels. Heavier paper, obviously, weighs more; while this makes the book feel more expensive, it costs more and should be a consideration if you are going to be posting your book.

The cover of a book, called a 'coverboard', is coated on one side only and usually weighs around 220 gsm to 240 gsm.

> **Tips on choosing paper**
> ▶ *Ask for paper samples (both pages and cover) and see which ones you like the feel of.*
> ▶ *Always get a written quote.*

Think about where you will store your books once they have been printed. Your printer may be prepared to store your books for you if you do not have the space yourself. You will be responsible for distributing them as well. Some printers offer print on demand (POD) and have links to wholesalers and distributors like Gardners.

Before the book goes to print, you should see a set of proofs and 'sign them off'; that means, you have said you are happy with the proofs and that the book is ready for printing. If you miss any errors then that is your responsibility. If, when your books are printed, there is a fault and it is found that the printer is to blame, you can get the books reprinted free.

Typesetting
Some printers offer typesetting as part of their service. Otherwise, you could typeset it yourself or you could use a professional typesetter.

There are publishing consultancies, such as Amolibros (www.amolibros.co.uk), who offer services such as typesetting and have a list of contacts for printing, design and websites.

Typesetting your book allows you to work out the number of pages you will end up with. POD uses single sheets of paper in the production process so that is very straightforward. Conventional printing uses large sheets of paper which make up 32 pages; these are folded and trimmed into 32-page sections. A paperback is therefore made up of any number of 32-page sections. Each 32-page section increases the print cost.

What if, having laid out your text, you find that your total number of pages is 180? You can either opt for another 32-page section (which would give you 192 pages) or do a bit of judicious editing and get the page count down to 160. Editing does not just mean cutting out text; you can reduce the point size, cut down the front matter pages or change the margins, the leading or the tracking.

Vanity publishing

As we are looking at using 'specialists' to produce your book, this is a good point to consider vanity publishing. Vanity publishing has a bad name. The 'vanity' bit came from the effusive reports sent by many of these firms, praising the work of the authors for their wonderful manuscripts (regardless of whether those manuscripts had merit or not).

Not surprisingly, firms offering this service do not call themselves vanity publishers; they use terms like 'subsidy', 'self-publishing', 'joint venture', 'shared responsibility' or 'co-operative publishing'.

If you sign up with a vanity publisher, you will be asked to grant them an exclusive licence to exploit your work. What you are paying for is the actual publication of the book. An unreliable and dishonest vanity publisher will print as few books as possible.

In *most* cases, vanity publishing is where a publisher advertises for writers ('Authors wanted') and charges them a lot of money (often thousands of pounds – up to £10,000 in some cases) to print a number of books. The vanity publisher takes the money from the author so has no need to print any books to make money. Royalties may be promised but are seldom paid. The author pays a vanity publisher to print their book but they do not own the books; they are the property of the publisher. Vanity publishers sometimes claim to have a special relationship with some booksellers, implying that they will get your books stocked there. That is unlikely. Production values are not always very good.

> **Tips on vanity publishing**
> - Read the fine print of the agreement; a clause which says they will print 'up to 1,000 copies' or send out 'up to 20 flyers to reviewers' doesn't really mean anything; they could technically just send out one copy.
> - Be wary of references to storing and warehousing; subsidy publishers tend to use print on demand.
> - If they retain the rights to exploit a book and charge thousands of pounds – avoid them; they are vanity publishers.

However, not *all* subsidy publishing involves being ripped off and exploited. Many print on demand firms are subsidy printers. The publisher provides a service (laying out and producing copies of a book) for a reasonable price. A good subsidy publisher will:

- *explain the services on offer*
- *allow you to retain all the rights to your work*
- *tell you that you can order more copies after the first run*
- *allow you to have your own imprint/publishing house name on the book*
- *not promise to get great press coverage*
- *not tell you how brilliantly written your book is*
- *not promise that your book will make money*
- *happily send you examples of other books they have produced for clients*
- *allow you to terminate the relationship at any time and with no penalty.*

The Society of Authors has useful advice on vanity publishing and self-publishing.

Print on demand (POD)

Print on demand means, quite simply, printing a book (and it can be just one book) only when an order is placed; it is not another term for 'self-publishing', nor is it a form of vanity publishing. Storing and distributing books are expensive parts of the publishing process, so being able to order books as and when you need them (often in very small quantities) is an attractive prospect for some authors. Many of the big publishing houses use POD for some of their backlist. Print on demand is a form of digital printing, as opposed to lithographic, which makes it a cheaper option for shorter print runs.

This also means that practically any book can be bought even if the publisher does not hold any stock. If the book is listed on Amazon or in a retailer's catalogue, when an order comes in, it will be sent on to a POD printer (as long as that printer has EDI – electronic data interchange) who holds the digital file for the book; they will produce and print one copy to meet that order on your behalf.

USING A COMPANY TO SELF-PUBLISH

There are many companies that offer POD to self-publishing authors. They are a form of subsidy publishing in that an author pays some money to get their book into print. Author Solutions (which has six self-publishing imprints, including AuthorHouse), iUniverse, Xlibris, Lightning Source, Lulu, Pen Press, CreateSpace, Blurb and many others offer self-publishing print on demand in various formats. In many cases, they are also epublishers (more about epublishing in Chapter 7).

POD packages will be slightly different with each company. An advantage of using a self-publishing company like Matador, Xlibris or Pen Press is that the books can be ordered on Amazon and via other bookshop sites so you do not have to be part of the distribution process. Anyone visiting that company's site will also be able to buy your book.

Companies like Lulu will keep accounts for you and organize the production of print on demand. Profits are paid into a bank account or a PayPal account. You set the selling price and the epublisher will tell you how much each will cost to print. After printing costs are deducted, you receive an agreed percentage of the profits.

Tips on choosing a POD publisher/printer

There are a lot of companies advertising POD with some services as an added extra (such as marketing, getting ISBNs and so on). Get all the details and compare and contrast; what do they offer and what do you need?

- *Read writers' magazines and forums and see which companies are getting the good (or bad) press.*
- *Ask to see some samples; there should be guarantees about the quality of paper and the binding.*
- *Ask for contact details of authors who have used their services more than once; you want to make sure the company is well-established and reliable. Were they happy with royalties and contracts? Were there any unexpected costs, loss of rights, poor quality product?*
- *Ask how quickly orders will be met.*
- *Find out how you can terminate the publishing agreement if you change your mind (the Society of Authors/Authors Guild will check through contracts before signing); a non-exclusive contract with no yearly commitment is best.*
- *Check ISBN numbers are included if you want them provided.*
- *Ask whether they will let you use your own ISBN and imprint name; not all POD companies are flexible in this way so that can be one way of narrowing down your choice.*
- *Check the licence and what you are granting to the POD publisher; you want to be able to keep the rights to your book.*
- *Make sure nothing is being licensed to a third party without your agreement.*

Insight

Do not go with a company that requires 'grant of rights' – you are signing away your exclusive rights to publish, reproduce and distribute your work for the full term of copyright (i.e. your lifetime plus 70 years).

Websites such as Lulu and Blurb offer free software so you can lay out your book yourself. Only when you order a printed copy (or copies) do you pay. You upload your manuscript and photos, use the formatting tools to choose the size, binding, cover, page layout and so on. You can play around with the format until you are happy with the finished product. As John Richardson explains in the case study at the end of the chapter, the costs are so reasonable that it is worth getting one copy printed, just to see if you are happy with the finished product; if not, you can go back and play around with the formatting some more until you are satisfied it is what you want. The other advantage of using POD is that printing can be done very quickly. You can have your book in your hand in a matter of weeks.

Marketing and promotion

As a self-publisher, your success in selling your book lies with how motivated you are and whether you have the time and desire to market your 'product' (i.e. your book).

Every book needs the marketing efforts of its author behind it, but more so when it has been self-published. You do not have the muscle and know-how of a publisher's publicity and marketing department behind you, nor do you have their budget (although marketing budgets are not very big unless you have a proven track record of success). Although some self-publishing POD companies offer marketing (usually at an extra cost), this cannot really match the efforts of a committed author.

> *Self-publishing can be a route to getting taken on by a mainstream publisher. If you sell a few hundred books, you've shown that you have got a market. It's telling the publishers something about your motivation and your profile; that you're prepared to put time in on marketing. On the downside there does still seem to be some stigma around being self-published. Publishers may assume that you only take that route because you have done the rounds and been*

> *rejected. It is the number of sales that will persuade them otherwise.*
>
> Katherine T. Owen, self-published author, *It's OK to Believe*

It can be a way of proving yourself to a publisher before they take you on. If you have a finished product *that is successful*, this is an attractive prospect to a publisher. A traditionally published mass-market book, even if it sells poorly, should sell between 5,000 and 10,000. If you can start to match those figures, you may just find agents and publishers sitting up and taking notice.

What you do have, though, is the self-belief that the book was worth printing in the first place. You know the story behind how it was written and what it is about better than anybody. You know the audience a lot better than a publicity professional does. Unlike the professional publicity people, you do not have to promote anyone else's book but your own.

> *Just when I thought everyone had forgotten* The Lazy Cook, *out of the blue I received an email from the publishing house, Allison & Busby, saying they'd seen my recipes in a magazine and that they'd love to publish a book. The contract I've signed with them means that I can no longer sell my first four self-published cookery books because some of the recipes will be used in a new book,* The Lazy Cook's Family Favourites. *However, I can still sell and promote* The Purple Spoon.
>
> *Although I have had a good relationship with A&B the difference in self-publishing and handing over to a publisher was evident from the start. They choose the recipes to be included, the layout, the title, the cover, the price and the date of publication, which was planned for October 2009 to catch the Christmas market but was deferred until March 2010. I had to rewrite most of the recipes to their specification and always to a deadline date. They will listen to me but the final decision comes from them. The advantages, I hope, are that they will be the ones doing the promotion and marketing and I will sit back and collect the royalties!*

It must always be remembered that as a self-publisher, as the books roll off the printing press there is only one person to sell them – you! Once you have written your book you must stop thinking like a writer. Publishers have got staff experienced in marketing and promoting books; as a 'self-publisher you have to fill those roles. It is hard work but exciting and rewarding.

Mo Smith, author
www.lazycookmosmith.co.uk

Other information

The **Arts Council of England** supports a website for new writers, helping them to develop their writing: www.youwriteon.com. Members upload opening chapters or short stories and the YouWriteOn system randomly assigns these to another member to review. You then review another member's story excerpt – assigned to you at random – each time you want to receive a new review back in return. After five reviews a story enters the chart system and the highest-rated writers receive free feedback each month from editors for the leading publishers Orion and Random House.

Booktrust (www.booktrust.org.uk) is an independent educational charity that aims to bring books and people together. The website has useful information, including a fact sheet for authors looking for a publisher or authors who are thinking of self-publishing.

Case study

John Richardson, self-published poet

A lot of the great poets have self-published; William Blake, for example, produced and published almost all his work himself. It was a recognized way of publishing poetry. So now that self-publishing is becoming popular again, it's gone full circle.

(Contd)

The self-publishing route I have taken is easy; you don't have to be that technically literate and people pick it up readily. There are several sites on the internet [such as Lulu, Blurb] that offer free, downloadable, book-layout software which you use to create your own books. You compose your pages and you can build a book in about an hour. You then upload your document to the web server and the company turns them into books; I've used Blurb for my poetry. I have an artist friend who put a lot of photographs in her self-published book which worked well. The hardback ones, in particular, are lovely.

It does have some drawbacks; it's not as sophisticated as Word. I did a paperback version successfully and thought it would also work as a hardback but when it came out in hardback the text had run to one side. But this is a minor problem and I can send it back to have it done again. You can literally move a word one space and it can throw the whole book out because it can shift text around and the formatting can bleed from one page to another so if you change something at the bottom of one page, you have to check all the following pages which probably means it isn't ideal for novels. Also it doesn't do automatic indexing. But for something like poetry it is perfect because with poems, you usually do a page at a time.

Colour can be a problem, too. With a traditional printer, they colour match what they print carefully. When you're doing it from a computer screen yourself, it isn't always quite the colour that it appears on the printed version. And if you're very particular, like an artist, that's going to be important for you. For other self-published writers, it's unlikely to matter to them.

There is an element of to-ing and fro-ing, of experimentation, to check that the final reproduction is right; one book I did had a photo on the front which was a bit too dark at first. So my advice is have one book printed, to see how it looks, before you decide to do an actual print run of several copies. That is the other thing that makes this so practical – the cost. I've done one book for £2.95. It can cost very little to produce a book. For example, I had a budget of £300 to produce a book for one of our poetry societies. I got 76 copies, plus postage, for something like £275. There are about half a dozen formats to choose from so the size of the book is physically limited by those formats. There's a price calculator to help you work out the cost and if you buy more than ten books, a discount kicks in.

I'm not interested in making a living; all I want to do is cover my costs. With my first book, I set myself a budget of £100, worked out how much it would cost and then said to myself, 'Right, I've got to sell at least eighteen of these to cover my costs' and I did that easily. For me, this is a hobby. So putting in £100 on my hobby is fine.

I did choose to do one book in a seven inch square format. It took me about four days to get it laid out but I'd made the mistake of doing the design before checking how much it was going to cost. When I did that, I realized that the book would work out at £10 a copy. I couldn't do it that way on the budget I had so I went back, found another design, checked the price and laid it out again.

From bitter experience, I've learned that you should get feedback from other people. I strongly recommend that. I thought my first book was perfect when I put it together. I sent it to friends, one of whom told me that the poems were in the wrong order. I replied they didn't need to be in any order; they were just separate poems but she insisted that there was an order. And she had a point, I realized. I didn't think it mattered but in fact it does. I've read a lot of poetry books since then and if you look, you can see that there is a structure to them.

There is a great deal to do in terms of putting a book together. Simply choosing the right cover, getting the right image, the right type font and all the rest of it, how to lay it out...I had a commission from a friend to produce one book, a book of love poems. I gave it to a friend who was an artist and she pointed out
(Contd)

that I couldn't publish it with the design I had chosen because it was too stark; it was bright white shiny paper and black text. So she suggested toning it down, making it less shiny and using grey instead of black which softened it, making it much more appropriate for love poems. It would never have occurred to me to do it that way.

I wanted to use a copy of a William Blake painting on the front of one of my books and I thought there wouldn't be a copyright problem because Blake was dead. I found the painting, which is in the Birmingham Art Gallery, and thought I'd just better check it would be ok. Could I use it? No, they said, you've got to pay us. Even though it's on the wall of a public art gallery and the image is all over the internet, the photographic copyright is owned by the Art Gallery and that's what I'd be using. I was able to use it in the end because I did pay them some money but if I hadn't, I could have been sued. And people do come after you now because it's very easy to search on the internet to see whether you've infringed copyright. The best advice is take a picture yourself; then it's yours. Or get official permission from the owner.

I hadn't realized at first that every book has an inside cover, with the name, the publisher, the title on it. You have to have a page with the ISBN, references, copyright and so on. Even something simple like where to put the name of the poet in an anthology of poems has to be considered. I put the names on the bottom left because some poems extend over more than one page. So you know if a person's name is at the bottom, you've come to the end of the poem. It's not a right or wrong; it's just my decision to have it laid out that way but it has to be consistent.

The one thing I've learned, particularly about self-publishing poetry, is that the words are important. With poetry, you have to be conscious of the odd word hanging off the end of a line which looks wrong. Whatever else you do, you have to facilitate the reader reading the book and finding the poems. So everything you do has to be aimed at that; the font has to be clear, the title has to be clear; you give indications of where poems begin and end, particularly if there are different people's poems in the book. As long as when a person opens the book, they don't get any unexpected surprises, like a sudden change of font. The easiest thing to do is to go and read other poetry books and see how they are done. They are the professional people; they know how it works and what doesn't. I think this is particularly important with poetry.

A big poetry book sells in the thousands; contrast that with a successful novel that sells in hundreds of thousands. I know I can sell 20 books a year, that's no problem. I do readings; that's where the market is for self-published poets. All I'm interested in is selling one or two books after a reading. That's the easy way to test the market. You can also test the poems in your poetry group. Sometimes, I publish work that I like and I'm not too bothered whether other people like it or not because I have the freedom to do that.

It definitely does something when you have a book in your hand. There's a world of difference between an electronic book and a physical book – a book you can put in your pocket. There's something almost organic about having the words on the paper and they're your words; it does something to your spirit.

I never considered trying to get taken on by a publishing house. The route for that, while it is practicable, is a long one for a poet. You've got to establish a track record, which means being published in magazines for several years; ideally, you've got to win a reasonably prestigious competition; you have to do readings; in other words, you need a 'poetry presence'. When you do, you could start to approach publishers. And it would probably be a small printing press that might take you on and they'd probably only print several hundred of your books. If you sell a thousand
(Contd)

poetry books, you're in the top league! I can publish 50 and it costs me less than £200 so why should I bother trying to get a publishing house to take my books? I'm not interested in trying to be in the top flight; I just want my books on my shelf and for friends to be able to have copies of my books.

10 THINGS TO REMEMBER

1 *Self-publishing allows you to be in control; you can make all the decisions, you control the pace of the project.*

2 *Self-publishers must be publisher, editor, agent, salesman and publicist if they want to sell their books.*

3 *Self-publishing can help you to develop your writing. You can get a book out of your system before moving on to your next project.*

4 *Make sure that the ISBN is registered in your name (or the name that you have given your publishing house).*

5 *You need to avoid underestimating your costs, overestimating demand and underpricing your book.*

6 *You can use a freelance editor and/or proofreader to look over your work and give it a professional finish.*

7 *Vanity publishers should be approached with caution; some charge a lot of money and make promises that they do not keep.*

8 *When you are producing your book, you will be judged against the quality and production values of professionally published books.*

9 *Short sentences can be effective when you write your blurb.*

10 *Print on demand (POD) means you pay for books only when you actually put in an order for a print run.*

7

Ebooks and epublishing

In this chapter you will learn:
- *what an ebook is*
- *about the changing face of epublishing*
- *about digital rights management.*

> *This paperback is very interesting, but I find it will never replace a hardcover book – it makes a very poor doorstop.*
> Alfred Hitchcock, film director

> *The changing face of the book marketplace occupies publishers' minds greatly…I don't think an author should worry about this. If the general public knew what we knew, no books would get published!*
> Trevor Dolby, publisher, Preface Publishing, an imprint of Random House
> www.prefacepublishing.co.uk

Epublishing produces ebooks. One hesitates to write any chapter about epublishing and ebooks because information becomes out of date almost before this gets to the typesetters. Nevertheless, it is a subject that is exercising the minds of the publishing industry. In fact, one publisher speculated that more paper has been used discussing ebooks than there have been ebooks published.

However, there is clearly a market for ebooks and it is one that is going to grow. One example of a successful transition to epublishing has been science journals. Ninety per cent of *Nature*, a journal that covers a variety of scientific disciplines, is digital. Scientists, it seems, have been quicker than most to circulate their work within their community in a digital fashion. That is in marked contrast to the world of fiction, which has had a much slower uptake.

How many people will read ebooks? It seems that, at the moment, nobody is really sure. It was a slow start but momentum is growing. Whether you will see 20 per cent or 50 per cent of readers in 20 years' time preferring a digital format, ebooks are certainly here to stay in some shape or form.

Initially, many ebooks were non-fiction. Now, all publishers have been adding to their ebook lists and more titles, both fiction and non-fiction, are becoming available. Books that were once out of print are coming back into circulation and, thanks to Project Gutenberg (www.gutenberg.org), you can download a huge number of out-of-copyright ebooks free.

Travel book publishers, such as Lonely Planet and Rough Guides, are experimenting with how they show their content. Other companies are creating ebooks with enhancements, such as author profiles, behind-the-scenes features, hyperlinks to other websites and mini documentaries. Certainly that is one way that ebooks can develop and evolve. Another is by creating content (such as video, sound) that is designed specifically for an electronic platform.

Publishers of children's books are also exploring ways of using ebooks. Ebooks on mobile phones are ideal for very young children because:

- *there are only six lines per page so they are easy to take in*
- *they are in a landscape format, similar to a computer game format and therefore familiar and approachable*
- *interactive quizzes make the experience more enjoyable*
- *they would suit dads who like using the latest technology with their children.*

Ebooks are already established in China; with 'novel' the most searched-for term on Chinese search engines. Japan's mobile phone novels are hugely popular; some novels are being downloaded over 200,000 times a day.

Ebooks can either be downloaded and read on a PC, ebook reader or mobile phone or be printed off and read on hard copy. Some ebooks are tied to a specific device; others can be read on various devices. Amazon's Kindle, Sony's Reader, Barnes & Nobles' nook are just some of the ebook readers currently available. Other downloads are able to be read on mobile devices such as iPhone and Palm Pre.

At the moment, ereaders like the Kindle and the nook are relatively expensive. So they are currently being bought by the older generation because they have the disposable income. Yet it is the young people with iPhones who will be accessing apps ('apps' = 'applications' = 'computer programmes') like eReader and Stanza to read ebooks.

> **Insight**
> Ebooks can automatically open at the last read page. The text can be searched.

Ebooks can also be bought from book retailers, such as Amazon, Waterstone's and Barnes & Noble, and there are dedicated online book retailers, such as Kobo in the UK. Kobo, for example, has support from UK publishers including Random House, Penguin Group, Bloomsbury, Simon & Schuster and Faber. The store has a catalogue of 2 million titles. The majority of them come from the Internet Archive and are free, while Kobo's bestsellers will be on offer for just £8.99. It offers titles in EPUB and PDF formats – which, unlike Amazon's Kindle, are non-proprietary. Once downloaded, Kobo's ebooks may be moved to other devices, including ereaders and smartphones. Digital Rights Management (DRM) protection, installed at publishers' discretion, will prevent file-sharing.

An advantage of having an ebook version of your work is that it could encourage people to buy it who might not have bought your traditional paper version. American writer Boyd Morrison began selling his first book via Amazon's Kindle, priced at $0.99, and by making his work available for free on his website. After three months, along with a big push on the message boards of Kindleboard, MobileRead and Amazon (online forums) he had sold over 7,500 books.

> *There are a lot of different platforms out there (Cybook, Sony Reader, nook, Kindle and so on); you can read on a variety of devices. My iPhone can hook into my Amazon account and I can download ebooks onto that. Project Gutenberg [full texts of public domain books] is great too; I can read all the works of Shakespeare for free by downloading them onto my phone. I am really surprised at how I like the ereaders. Why buy a book for $25 when I can get it for $9.99? And read it on my phone, in the cinema while I'm waiting for the movie to start. I thought I would miss the tactile feeling of turning the pages but I don't. I was really surprised.*
>
> Todd Armstrong, Senior Acquisitions Editor, Communications and Media Studies, SAGE Publications www.sagepub.com

Scribd

Scribd is currently the largest social publisher in the world. You can turn a file into a web document and share it with everyone. It is free to use and most of the documents uploaded by members are free to view and download. The website claims more than 50 million people a month are finding and sharing writings and documents on Scribd.

Documents can be shared on other websites, including Twitter and Facebook. Publishers like Simon & Schuster, Random House and Harvard University Press already distribute content on Scribd.

You can charge as much as you like if you want people to pay; it must be at least US$1. Scribd takes 20 per cent of the earnings as a consignment fee. It then deducts a 25c transaction fee from your net revenue for every document purchased.

Obviously, the content you sell must be original. As the author, you retain all rights to the original content uploaded to the website and you can remove your work at any time.

> **Did you know?**
> In 2009, Governor of California Arnold Schwarzenegger said that all students in the state should switch to ebooks to help cut public spending on school textbooks. California had spent £322 million on school books the year before.

Epublishers

> *The next big thing which is going to affect traditional publishing is the emergence of epublishing. Why does an author need an agent or publisher these days? Why does an agent need a publisher? And does a publisher even need a bookshop? An author can go online and self-publish and potentially accrue better royalties with faster returns. And, the book goes straight to the consumer. There are huge possibilities for writers. Up until now, internet publishing, POD, was a new industry. It was considered the poor man's choice, the 'you've not made it as an author' option and the quality of the product isn't guaranteed. But some writers are doing it because it makes money sense, especially if they've got a niche market. I say why not? It could even be seen as a savvy decision. As long as they market and edit professionally and aim to at least cover their costs.*
>
> Helen Corner, Cornerstones Literary Consultancy
> www.cornerstones.co.uk

There are also dedicated online publishers who take on authors' works in much the same way that a traditional publishing house would and produce their work as ebooks. In other words, they pay to license your book. Their submission guidelines tend to be similar: a query letter which includes a brief synopsis and the book's genre.

Do not send your manuscript unless asked to do so and follow the submission guidelines – unsurprisingly, these will be electronic submissions. Epublishers tend not to pay advances but do often pay much higher royalties than traditional publishers. When your book starts to sell, you will receive royalties on those sales. Royalty rates vary from epublisher to epublisher so do check what their rates are.

A word of caution: epublishing is popular with vanity publishers. Be careful about agreeing to pay an epublisher for services. Even if no money has changed hands, some epublishers make their money from taking advertising on their websites or by buying the rights to an author's work. *Not* all epublishers are suspect but do some homework before you sign up with anyone. Ask yourself if the epublisher's website is the right place to sell your work.

Tips on epublishers

If you are considering using an epublisher, do check out what they offer carefully:

- ▶ *Ask what other authors and titles they produce.*
- ▶ *Do they have quality standards? Or can anyone place a book on their website, regardless of style, content matter and quality?*
- ▶ *How do they make money? Is it by advertising or by commissioning authors?*
- ▶ *How long have they been operating?*
- ▶ *Look at their contract and terms and conditions.*
- ▶ *Is their site secure?*

If you do decide to go with an epublisher, *only* sign over English ebook rights; retain all the other rights, especially all electronic rights. And make sure you can end the contract within a reasonable period of time (two years, for example).

SUBSIDY EPUBLISHERS

We have established that epublishers will publish your book for you on demand. They offer a range of services (editing, marketing, etc.), for which you pay an additional fee. Either you can buy your books yourself from these companies (as discussed in Chapter 6) or they are available to buy to anyone browsing the site.

Print on demand is becoming a popular way not only of writers having their books published but also of readers buying ebooks. Lightning Source, for example, is one of the biggest POD printers in the US; it has over 100,000 titles available to order in its digital library.

> **Insight**
> Ebooks, unlike print books, are subject to VAT.

Self-epublishing

As a self-publisher, you could take a leaf out of Boyd Morrison's book and make your work available on your website, either free or by charging for it.

Your Word document can be converted into an ebook format. There are several available, with more coming on line all the time (MobiPocket, Libris, PDF, EPUB are just some of them). Certain versions will suit a particular application.

If you do want to charge for your ebook, either you can sell it as a CD and post it to the buyer or, if you want to offer it as a downloadable file, you must try to ensure that it is downloaded by only one person and not shared with all and sundry for free.

You need to use software that has security features that prevent buyers from sharing your book: for example, the latest professional version of Adobe Acrobat.

If you are offering downloads, use an application like www.e-junkie.com, which provides you with a shopping cart and buy now button. Depending on how much material you upload, it can cost as little as $5 a month. For example, when a buyer clicks on the PayPal 'buy it now' button and pays for the goods, PayPal notifies the application provider, which sends an email to the customer with the download.

AMAZON

If your book is listed on Amazon, you can add your book to programmes like 'Search Inside' and Kindle (only the book's rights holder can apply for 'Search Inside'). 'Search Inside' digitizes your book which means that the Amazon computer can search and analyse the content as well as the book's name, the author's name and the ISBN. The book will pop up when people enter applicable search terms when looking for a book.

Amazon Upgrade sells a digital version of your book to people who have already bought your hard-copy version. For a fee (10 per cent of the retail price, which is then doubled for non-trade titles, e.g. a £10 book would cost £2 to have the digital version; 5 per cent of the retail price for trade books). The upgrade fee is then split 50/50 between the author and Amazon. You need to have added your book to 'Search Inside'. For more information, go to Amazon and look at the Amazon Upgrade information.

Did you know?
Text Book Torrents, a site allowing people to exchange scanned copies of textbooks, had over 20,000 people swapping files at any given time. Publishers and rights holders finally succeeded in shutting the site down in 2008.

Digital Rights Management (DRM)

There is a worry that digital publishing will go the way of the music industry and be rife with illegal downloads. Will it also be dominated by one or two devices? Or will there be several platforms which people can use to access and read ebooks? Maybe the fact that lessons have been learned from the music industry means that there will not be overall domination by one download service or device. The digital piracy issue has not yet been fully resolved.

DRM is the technical means of controlling usage on the internet. It enables rights owners to identify their intellectual property via metadata and gives the opportunity to describe the rights on offer, fees and access conditions for potential users in a reliable licensing environment. It can also track usage and collect appropriate revenues.

It is not ideal yet, though. DRM software has got problems; it can be broken into by hackers. It can also be simply sidestepped by the user scanning in a printed book and posting it for free on the internet.

The difficulty is keeping track of any material that might have been posted illegally. It is proving something of a headache to publishing houses that have thousands of titles; it is helpful if authors (whether published or self-published) keep an eye out on the internet for any pirate copies. If you find a pirate copy and you are published by a publishing house, contact them and they will take the appropriate action. Don't take the matter into your own hands if you have a publisher because it can complicate matters; the publisher can use the Publishers' Association anti-piracy portal.

If you are self-published and think that your copyright is being infringed, contact the website operator and ask them to remove it because it infringes your rights; alternatively, contact the internet service provider (ISP) to close down the website.

ELECTRONIC RIGHTS

> **Insight**
>
> Mark Le Fanu, General Secretary of the Society of Authors, has said that the phrase 'digital rights' in a contract is too vague ('Don't Get Diddled in the Digital Age', ALCS Spring 2010 newsletter) and that authors should make sure that every contract deals separately with all the different ways and contexts in which a book can be exploited.

Electronic rights cover the right to make use of the book in its digital format. This is new territory with developments occurring almost weekly and no one really sure what will happen in the future. That can be a concern when preparing to sign a contract. As Mark Le Fanu has pointed out, clauses can be rather vague. If you are concerned, it might be worth asking that the electronic rights clause be reviewed in the future. The publisher usually has the right to sell an electronic edition within two years of the first UK publication of the book.

Electronic rights can mean:

- *making the book available online*
- *interactive (with audio or video)*
- *print on demand.*

Pricing

When ebooks and ejournals started becoming popular in the scientific community, it used to be that you could buy a print journal for £100 and you could get the digital version for £10 extra.

There is concern in the publishing industry that digital or electronic means 'cheaper'; after all, as far as the consumer is concerned, if you buy house insurance online, you usually get a discount. Ebooks do not have to be printed on paper, stored in a warehouse or distributed. So, to the potential buyer, they are obviously not as expensive in that sense. Yet, the author's creative input was just the same as if it were a paper book and that creativity needs to be rewarded (financially).

The pricing of ebooks has not settled down yet. When Dan Brown's *The Lost Symbol* was published, you could buy a print version in many shops at the discounted price of £10. Yet it was selling as an ebook for £15.19. At the other end of the scale, Amazon is currently buying ebooks from the publisher at the same price as the paper book but selling it at $9.99. That is at a huge loss but it is a strategic move to capture the market. It seems unlikely that they will continue to offer such low prices indefinitely.

> **Insight**
> If you are producing your work on your website and want it available as a download, use PDF files because they will work on a variety of devices (e.g. PC, Mac, PDA). PDFs do not work for mobile phones because the pages are too large.

10 THINGS TO REMEMBER

1 *Giving your reader a choice of format, ebook as well as paperback, helps to drive sales.*

2 *If you are producing your own ebook, have it as a PDF file because that can be read on a variety of devices.*

3 *If your book is published by an epublisher, only sign over the ebook rights.*

4 *Ebooks are becoming popular in certain genres: science, travel, children's.*

5 *Ebooks can encourage people who might not have bought a paper book to look at your work.*

6 *Epublishers do not always pay advances but their royalty rate can be higher than traditional publishing houses.*

7 *Epublishing is also popular with vanity publishers; do your homework before you sign up with anyone.*

8 *Keep an eye out for illegal publication of your work on the internet; if you are a published author, let your publishing house know immediately you find anything.*

9 *If you think your copyright is being infringed, contact the website operator and ask them to remove the item.*

10 *If that does not work, you can contact the ISP (internet service provider) and ask them to close the website down.*

8

Promotion and publicity

In this chapter you will learn:
- *how to promote your book once it is published*
- *what a publisher's publicist will do for you*
- *how to be your own publicist.*

Without publicity, there can be no public support.
Benjamin Disraeli, politician

If a book is on quite a broad topic or it is a general fiction book, how are people going to distinguish between your book and all the others out there? It can be the author that makes the difference. In radio, even TV, they want the personality. You wouldn't get an author on the radio who couldn't talk passionately about their book or subject area. You want someone who is interesting, who will respond, who will come back with interesting angles and ideas – showing the personality behind the book.
Suzi Williamson, publicity, A & C Black
www.acblack.com

The book is finished; it has been typeset, proofed and printed. Copies of your book are ready to be sold but if you want people to buy and read your book, you have to let them know about it.

In this chapter, we will look at how you can promote your book. In the past, the writer was an almost anonymous, shadowy figure. It was all about the book, rather than the person. Nowadays, the writer is an integral part of the package and they must do more of the work of publicity than writers in the past would ever have done. A successful writer becomes a brand on which promotional expenditure can be based.

The days of authors sitting at their desks, waiting for calls from their publisher's publicity department are long gone. Once the book has been commissioned, I will bring an author in and ask them to keep a note of everything that occurs to them while they're writing the book in terms of where they can sell it; people they can tap into, contacts they know, just write them down. So when we come to the point, three to five months before publication, the author can come back to us with a list of things we might be able to use to help us sell the book. And I expect them to come along with stacks of ideas; three quarters of which we hope we've already thought of and a quarter which will be fantastic new ideas.

Trevor Dolby, publisher, Preface Publishing, an imprint of Random House
www.prefacepublishing.co.uk

You are unlikely to have a reputation that will sell your book for you. You need to market yourself as well as your book; the writing alone is not enough. Shy authors do not sell many books. The reward is that the more you promote your book, the more copies you will sell.

I had no experience of marketing but I began by cold-calling local shops, both independent and national chains. I never telephoned first because I didn't want to give the buyer or manager the opportunity to say 'No thank you' before they'd seen the book. I was offered a book signing at my local W. H. Smith. I approached Ottakars in Cirencester. The manager was so enthusiastic about my books and always displayed them front-facing on a stand of their own. But if you really want to get anywhere, if you're really serious about your book, you need to promote it beyond your local area. That's when you start to write to national newspapers and magazines. When I look back at my letters from that time, I do laugh. Some of them are two pages long! My daughter intervened, 'You've got to email them, then follow it up with a phone call and actually speak to them.' I found it really hard getting to

8. Promotion and publicity

speak to the right person; tracking down the correct phone number was an art in itself and you could immediately tell from the tone of their voice whether they were interested or not. The reply I mostly received was, 'We only feature celebrities.' My local Waitrose directed me to their head office. After many phone calls, the buyer said she would take my book. I couldn't believe it! It wasn't just my local store, it was countrywide.

Mo Smith, author
www.lazycookmosmith.co.uk

Maeve Binchy is a recognizable brand, even if most people would be hard pressed to name all the books she has written. Mo Smith chose her brand, the Lazy Cook, early on in her writing career and has maintained it throughout. When you are not writing, you need to think of yourself as the 'product'.

Think about these questions:

- *What do you want your brand to say about you?*
- *Do you want to brand yourself as a writer in a particular genre or keep the branding as broad as possible?*
- *Do you need a pseudonym? (You might confuse people if you start as a poet, write a romantic fiction novel and then turn your hand to literary fiction.)*
- *Will your website represent your brand? (Make sure that style is also reflected in your stationery: A1 sheets, flyers, business cards, headed notepaper, etc.)*
- *How can you enhance the brand? (e.g. You could become an expert in your field; give talks, workshops, etc.)*

Publishing house marketing department

This is responsible for:

- *originating all sales material (catalogues, 'blads' – book layout and design, samples, etc.) which the sales team will use*

- *working with the sales team and big bookshops/supermarkets on special promotions*
- *preparing advertising for trade (post-published press advertising, along with reviews, other publicity)*
- *organizing the company's sales conference where the new season's publishing is presented to sales reps and overseas agents.*

Publishing house publicity department

This works with media on 'free' publicity, i.e. reviews, features, author interviews, bookshop readings and signings, festival appearances, book tours, radio/television interviews. Each author/book gets a publicity campaign that plays to the book or author's strengths.

The timescale for planning book publicity is different depending on the type of book. For a lead fiction title at one of the major publishing houses, they might be planning 18 months to two years in advance of publication; particularly if it is for a bestselling author. For general fiction, a medium-sized publishing house would generally plan marketing and PR around 12 months in advance and they would start to firm up their plans maybe six months in advance of publication. That would include making sure that journalists and researchers were aware of the book and have features or interviews in their schedule.

Even if your book has been picked up by a publishing house, it does not follow that the publicity department will put its muscle – and its money – behind your book to promote it. Bestselling authors will get that level of interest and finance because there is more of a guarantee that the money will be recouped. It is a fact that publishers spend money on books that are going to do well. But you can help by working hard at your own publicity; whether it is supporting the publicity department or being your own PR agent.

What makes you interesting?

Some authors are really good self-publicists; they know instinctively what they should be doing and they don't expect help from publicists. If that's the case, we would still need to know what they were up to (in terms of PR) because it can clash with what we're doing, so it's about keeping in touch with your publicist. For example, I may send a book to someone you have approached several times; perhaps they weren't interested or you've already got a reading arranged. Then I ask if they'd like to do an interview/event with my author... it can look unprofessional.

Suzi Williamson, publicity, A & C Black
www.acblack.com

If you are with a publishing house, you will be asked to fill in an author's questionnaire or publicity form. Remember that publicity people do not know the detail; you do as the author of the book. So fill in the details.

The author publicity questionnaire contains the following:

- *brief biographical sketch (include anything relevant to the writing of the book or that is newsworthy)*
- *any competing titles? How does your book differ from them?*
- *are there any academic or professional courses that could use your book?*
- *professional bodies, organizations, clubs which you belong to: would any of these be useful in promoting sales of your book?*
- *would you be prepared to visit schools, libraries? Will you be attending any events to promote your book?*
- *are you prepared to give media interviews? If so, are you happy for your contact details to be passed to the press?*
- *do you have any press contacts?*
- *are there any journalists you think should be approached about your book?*

- *do you have your own website? Are there any websites that would link to yours?*
- *possibly your date of birth; this is needed for eligibility if your book is being put forward for an award.*

If you are doing your own publicity (or having to fill out a publisher's publicity form and need a bit of help to formulate your answers), ask yourself the following:

- *what is your USP (unique selling point)?*
- *what would make you stand out to the press?*
- *why would a journalist want to write about you?*
- *are you prepared to answer questions about yourself as well as your book?*

Even if you have been picked up by a publishing house, it is still worth driving your own publicity. It proves to your agent and publisher that you are making an effort to be read by others.

Promotional material

As a published author, you can buy your book from the publishing house at a reduced rate. The rate is usually about 40% discount for the author. If one of our authors came to me and asked for five copies to send out to publicity contacts, then I would probably supply them from my review copy allocation. Gratis copies are at the publisher's discretion; they may not be so accommodating if you asked for 100 copies to send to your friends!

Suzi Williamson, publicity, A & C Black
www.acblack.com

Publicists for traditional publishers produce an AI (advance information – also known as an advance notice or forthcoming title) sheet, to show the booksellers what the book is about.

It is produced about six to nine months ahead of publication and contains:

- a picture of the jacket
- a description including hardback or paperback
- the number of pages
- format
- classification details
- blurb/summary
- ISBN
- price
- information on the author
- any publicity/promotion
- sales of author's last title
- contact details.

If you are a self-publisher, there is no reason why you should not produce your own AI and send it to booksellers, wholesalers and library suppliers. You can have an order form at the bottom or on the back. An A5 sheet of paper will be perfectly adequate for this.

> **Insight**
> Try to send out any promotional literature as far ahead of publication date as possible.

When publishers print books, they have a certain number of free copies that they can give out that have been built into the overall budget at the very beginning. If you are self-publishing, you will have to be careful how many books you choose to give away as review copies. Those are books you have paid for and you will not get the money back on them if you give them away. There is also no guarantee that a book reviewer will feature your book even if you do send them a copy.

The book itself is a form of promotional material. Many authors supplement their free copies given on publication with ones bought from the publisher at a reduced rate. These can be given away (to friends, colleagues, interested parties) as you see fit. Mills & Boon were quick to spot a potential market when the Berlin Wall came down in 1989; the publisher had members of staff handing out 750,000 free copies of their romances to people in the street. While you probably don't want to operate on the scale that Mills & Boon did, free copies can help promote you and your book.

> **Insight**
> Before you send out a review book or give one as a gift, check through for any errors (pages not trimmed properly, binding inadequate). Mistakes do happen but you should be the one to discover them, not a potential reviewer.

If you are working with a publisher, ask them for leaflets or flyers of your book so you can leave them in relevant places (bookshops, libraries, or, if it's on a particular subject, somewhere relevant: for example, in a gym or leisure centre for a healthy eating book). The publicity department should also be able to supply you with a .jpeg file of the cover of your book that you can use on your website and own publicity material.

> **Tips on promotional material**
> ▶ *Use your book cover image for promotional material. It helps fix the image of the book in a potential buyer's mind.*
> ▶ *Bookmarks are relatively cheap to produce, useful and don't cost the earth to mail out; if you do use them when you send out your books, don't put them inside the book where they could get missed.*
> ▶ *You could use other items (T-shirts, mugs, stickers, badges, posters) as promotional items.*

Publicity in the media

Self-published authors can often achieve good PR; if a publicist contacts a journalist, they know immediately that you've got a book to plug and can very quickly say 'no'. Authors can get a better response than we would get, because they are the authority and have passion for their subject. Don't be afraid of approaching journalists yourself. Think of all those pieces in the national press with author interviews, background stories and profiles; there will be a short byline at the end of the piece with details about the book. The book gets a mention but the journalists are often interested in the author.

Suzi Williamson, publicity, A & C Black
www.acblack.com

Read newspapers, look at television programmes, listen to the radio; make a note of where books are mentioned and work out where you could promote yourself; national prime time morning radio programme or local radio station afternoon programme? Style magazine or business newspaper?

As Trevor Dolby suggests on p. 183, it is worth keeping a list of potential contacts as you work on your manuscript, anything from the local newspaper to national radio and magazines. As when approaching agents and editors, make sure you have the right person and that you spell their name correctly.

Pulling together your own author questionnaire will help formulate some ideas for your self-promotion. It can also provide information for your press release.

The media is interested in the author, rather than the book itself, so you need to take this slant when producing your press release. What makes you special? What makes you stand out to the press? Remember the following:

- *Local reporters are always interested in local published authors (if your story or subject can be linked to a place, the local media in that area should be contacted).*
- *There are several publications for the over 50s; contact them if you are a 'mature' writer.*
- *Consider your gender; can you tie into publications aimed specifically at men or women?*

Other ways to promote yourself:

- *Enter writing competitions; if you become a finalist or, even better, win, you are newsworthy.*
- *Write a regular column in a local newspaper or magazine.*
- *Offer to write reviews for newspapers/magazines.*
- *Add yourself to Wikipedia.*

NEWSPAPERS AND MAGAZINES

Marketing yourself is a big job. I would love a publisher to do that for me. But when I discovered that you really have to do it yourself anyway, it made me look at self-publishing as an option. It's going to be you building up your profile and looking for and doing interviews; the publishers are not going to do it all for you. Some publishers now even want evidence that you will do this work before they take you on.

Katherine T. Owen, self-published author, *It's OK to Believe*

The role of the literary editor in the book pages of a newspaper or magazine is not to sell books. Their function is to entertain and be informative.

Getting publicity here depends on the lead times of magazines and newspapers; some monthly publications have quite lengthy lead times and they would want to plan their seasonal and major features or interviews six to nine months in advance so you have to get the information to them then.

Publicizing a book can be quite time-critical, particularly with the news media or 'newsy' magazines. They won't touch it if it's been around for the last six weeks. That's the same with the monthly magazines. You need to plan ahead. If your book links in with the Christmas market, it would be sensible to start thinking about approaching some publications in April. For the specialist market, publications don't mind waiting and reviewing a book after publication. Journals, for example, may come out only every three or six months so would happily review a book 18 months after publication (certainly if it was an important title).

Journalists and broadcasters generally prefer to be approached initially by email (a short email with two or three paragraphs; get to the point straight away and explain why your story would be suitable for their publication or programme). Don't just send an email to a group of people at the same time; they want to feel that careful thought has gone into the approach and that your pitch is relevant. If you say that you feel your story is perfect for a particular section or page or on a particular date, you imply you know what their publication is all about.

If your work is in a specialist area subscribe to magazines that cover those subjects. They will often review books and interview authors. If you think that they will be interested in you and your work, get in touch with them.

Pass on the details of your local or specialist press to your publicist (if you are working with a publisher) and ask them to send out review books for you or do it yourself if you are self-publishing.

The Writers' & Artists' Yearbook, *The Writer's Handbook* and the *Writer's Market* all have a list of national, regional and local newspapers as well as weekly and monthly magazines.

If you do get (good) reviews:

- *keep copies*
- *post them on your website*
- *ask if you can post the review on Amazon*
- *send copies of the review to bookshops and libraries.*

Insight

Offering your book as a prize in a competition or as part of a reader's offer in a magazine or newspaper is a good way of getting your book cover in front of people and is a lot cheaper than having an advert.

Books that are on a niche, specialist topic often stand out on their own. You don't need to be able to talk to the media if you've published on a specialist or newsworthy topic, such as climate change or politics, birdwatching or crafts, because readers in your specialist area, or in the press, will be talking about it anyway; the content of the book is what is important here. But I think if you've written a fiction book, for example, it's more about knowing your market. So go along to literary events and listen to interviews with authors; make sure you read articles. Media training can be useful, but you don't need to pay for media training to become media savvy; it's about being aware of what's going on and how other people respond and get news for their books. It's all about common sense really; where could you see your book being featured? In which paper or magazine? It also might be a good idea to role-play questions and answers with a friend before any interview, making sure that you're well prepared for any difficult topics.

Suzi Williamson, publicity, A & C Black

www.acblack.com

TELEVISION & RADIO

Relatively obscure and unknown books and authors have enjoyed success after being featured on programmes like Oprah's Book Club, Richard & Judy's Book Club and the TV Book Club. *The Bookseller* looked at the effect of the Richard & Judy Book Club and estimated that in the six years the club was running, over 30.8 million copies of the 100 books featured were sold.

Getting a title onto a show like this is *not* easy and, rather like the initial submission process, a book is up against stiff competition. For the TV Book Club, publishers do not pay to have their books featured. Each publishing house can submit up to six books, which can be around 800 titles to be considered. The final list is then whittled down by a group of readers made up of staff from Cactus TV, the company that makes the programme.

The odds are against a book getting through. However, nothing ventured, nothing gained. By all means, send out a review copy but more in hope than certainty.

A list of regional and national television and radio stations can be found in *The Writers' & Artists' Yearbook* and *The Writer's Handbook*.

> *AA – We're not very good at self-publicity; it's not in our nature. I would rather die than go out and say 'Hello, here I am.' The author, Jill Fraser, talks to Women Institutes, three a week sometimes, which is fantastic.*
>
> *MS – We should do that.*
>
> *AA – I know we should. It helps to have someone with you. I was in a bookshop in a motorway service station which had copies of our books on display. My partner went in and said, 'This is the author, do you want her to sign them?' So I signed six and that's six sold. I wouldn't have done it on my own though; I would have walked straight past.*
>
> *MS – I think you have to be really brazen at times. The more you do, the better you become. You have to be more proactive than you would probably feel comfortable being.*
>
> *AA – My absolute is that you have got to keep your dignity and credibility. There are areas I won't discuss or write about just to flog books; why should I? It's my private life and I think Meg feels the same way.*
>
> *MS – I think it's a very, very short-term gain. You might shift some more books [if you do reveal things about your private life] but the damage that it you could do to your relationships is much more lasting.*

Annie Ashworth and Meg Sanders, authors who write as Annie Sanders
www.anniesanders.co.uk

THE INTERNET

Research has found that the web is currently the most popular source for finding out about the latest books, followed by browsing in shops.

A website and/or a blog help define your identity and give you a presence on the internet. And if you are a rather shy person, who shudders at the thought of knocking on doors to raise awareness of your book, websites and email can help with promotion.

Amazon
Once your book is listed on Amazon, you can join Amazon's Author Central, a free service which allows you to promote yourself and your books to users of the website. You can have a photo, biography, upload missing book cover images, blog with readers, list all your books and give notice about any talks or signings you may be doing. You can add your books to programmes like 'Search Inside the Book' and Kindle so that they are available for customers to buy (only the book's rights holder can add the book to 'Search Inside'). For more information, go to https://authorcentral.amazon.com.

If you feel particularly confident, you could post a video book trailer on your Amazon author page (as well as on YouTube) introducing yourself and your book. Amazon uses short author videos of authors talking about their books. Professor Stanley Wells did a three-minute video piece, off the cuff, for his book *Shakespeare, Sex & Love* (OUP) as pre-publicity.

Amazon allows authors to have one video at a time on their author page. They ask that the video focus on specific features of the book and your experiences as a writer. Instructions on how to upload the video can be found on Amazon's Author Central page.

Tips on Amazon
Many authors check their sales rankings on Amazon regularly. No one is exactly sure how the calculations are
(Contd)

made but any book that is sold on Amazon gets a ranking: from 1 to the millions. Fiction is a tough genre to get high rankings in; it is easier if your book belongs to a more niche genre (gardening, cooking, military history, etc). If you get it into Amazon's top 100, you have a bestseller on your hands.

Average ranking on Amazon – what it means:
   2,000,000+ – *one consignment copy has been sold*
   1,000,000+ – *around 50 copies of the book have been sold*
   100,000+ – *up to 200 copies sold*
   10,000+ – *anything from 1–50 copies sold per week*
   1,000+ – *10–100 copies sold per week*
   100+ – *between 1 and 100 copies sold per day*
   10+ – *100–500 copies of the book sold per day*
   Under 10 – *around 500 copies sold each day*

Things you can do to help raise your ranking:

▶ *Get your friends and family to buy your book from Amazon on the same day. A spike of sales affects the sales rankings; Amazon re-ranks books every hour so a big sale in one hour can have an effect.*
▶ *If you can keep your ranking in the top 10,000 (a couple of sales a day) that is considered to be a solid, commercially viable book.*
▶ *Seasonal timing can affect ranking, i.e. if your book is popular at a certain time of the year.*
▶ *If you know people with websites that have a database of clients, get them to promote your book...on the same day.*
▶ *Get friends to rate your book; one that receives five-star reviews that are rated helpful by others will be promoted by Amazon; it is programmed to recommend books that have positive activity.*

There is only a limited amount of work an editor can do on a book, at some point they have to get it published and earning money. It's the same with publicity. You might think that you should be going on a world tour and being interviewed on Oprah but you have to be realistic about the amount of time a publicist can spend on your book.

Publicists will grade your book and allocate time to it depending on their expectations of sales and PR opportunities; and they may be working on many books each month, so it's useful to be aware that they can't always drop everything to work on a last-minute idea.

From September to December, it's the run-up to Christmas. September is the month when the most books are published, closely followed by October, because that's when people want to get them out for the Christmas market. This means it's a difficult time to get press coverage for books, unless you are a famous author or celebrity. January is a good time for certain types of books: sports, diet, New Year's resolution kind of thing. Mother's Day is good for books for women; Father's Day for men. If it's books for schools, we publish them from April to August so they're ready for the new term. So it's just thinking about those seasonal opportunities which can help publicize your book.

Suzi Williamson, publicity, A & C Black
www.acblack.com

Your own website

One of the most important things you can do for yourself as a writer is to get yourself a website. Definitely, everybody should have a website – because if journalists want to get in touch with you, it's so much easier if they can just Google you and have your website pop up. I did, it cost me £300 and has been worth every penny. A website helps to raise awareness of yourself and your book and act as a point of contact.

Maria McCarthy, author
www.mariamccarthy.co.uk

All the authors interviewed for this book would not be without their websites. For them, it is a way of promoting their work and having a point of contact with their readership. A website does not have to be complicated; in fact, the simpler the better because if it is too complicated, it takes too long to load. The aim is to show your work and, ultimately, sell your books. Make sure that the style and feel of your website fits your image and brand.

- *Have a photograph of yourself and of the cover of your book/s.*
- *If you have a strapline use that as your domain name; otherwise, just use your writing name.*
- *Useful links should be just that – useful – and relevant; don't include your favourite shopping sites. Give some thought to the links and your website could become a useful resource for other authors.*
- *Have a page for reviews.*
- *Advertise any talks or appearances you are giving.*
- *Use Google keywords to see what people are searching for. What words and phrases are people typing in to search engines? Make a list and use them in your website (or when you are planning the contents of your book).*
- *AdWords: set a budget (a certain amount each month), choose keywords that you feel people would type in and drive traffic to your website this way.*
- *Set up a link to Facebook, Twitter, etc. on your website so visitors can access more information on you.*
- *Check if your work is being discussed anywhere on the web and join in the discussions. Point people to your website.*
- *Reward people who go to your website; run a competition and have your book as a prize.*
- *Link in with local companies and offer your book as part of a sponsorship deal; for example, if someone buys your book on getting fit and running a marathon, they get a percentage off a purchase from a local sports shop.*
- *Put a website link on any promotional material you send out; ask if they would like regular updates about your book/appearances/blog. (NB Make sure you say that you are keeping your contacts list confidential and not sharing it with others or handing it on to a listing agency.)*

Did you know?
As a marketing ploy, author Christopher Fowler left signed, customized first editions of his books in locations in London. He posted clues to their whereabouts in his blog on his website.

> One of the first books was left in a pub in Kentish Town; Fowler put the clue up on Sunday morning at 8am. At 8.10am, the pub landlord phoned him, complaining that there was a queue of people outside demanding to be let in!

I think self-marketing is becoming increasingly important for authors. Anything such as having your own website, a blog, a presence, they're all grist to the publicity/marketing mill. Given that the print media are increasingly hard to get any presence in, because there are fewer journalists, fewer book reviewers and fewer everything, the more authors can grab that particular bull by the horns and start to get their name out there by any means, the better. We always like it if an author comes along with dedicated website followers – that's an automatic plus from a book marketing point of view.

Doug Young, Publishing Director, Sport & Entertainment, Transworld
www.transworld-publishers.co.uk

A website shows that you are prepared to engage with your readership and push sales of your books. That is something a publisher likes to see.

If you have a publisher and are planning to have a website built, ask if they will supply images, logos and reciprocal links. The Society of Authors has a list of website designers recommended by members.

Insight

If you are writing for children or young adults, you really should have a website. These are the readers who are online a lot of the time. If they want to find out more about you, they will go looking for your website, rather than go to the library.

Blogging

It's not just about writing a book now; authors have to be open and helpful about 'spreading the word'. They have their own websites, their own platforms, blogs, twitters, etc. I think authors recognize the fact that that is something they need to invest in. Obviously, there are people who don't do this and they can still be very successful, but I think it helps any new author if they are open to being visible and contactable; if they're not shy about having a website or a platform where people (members of the public that is) can contact them, rather than just writing the book.

Camilla Goslett, literary agent, Curtis Brown
www.curtisbrown.co.uk

Blog – the word comes from web-log (hence 'blog'). It's a kind of online diary that you add 'posts' to. Blogs can be topical, personal, or about the craft of writing. The advantage of blogging is that it is free and requires very little technical proficiency. But, if you are embarking on a blog, you need to keep them updated...and well written.

A blog doesn't necessarily lead to a book deal; editors are not glued to their computer screens searching for the next big thing in blogging. Blogs are like books – they are successful if people want to read them. However, some 'blooks' (books based on a blog or website) can do well.

Judith O'Reilly started *Wife in the North*, a blog about downshifting from London to the north of England; it became a big hit in Britain and America. Her blog was mentioned on the website of an MP whom she had asked for advice. That was picked up by another blogger and linked to his site and so it went on. Less than six weeks after starting her blog, she landed a £70,000 publishing deal.

Julie and Julia won the inaugural Blooker Prize awarded to blogs that had been turned into books. Written by Julie Powell, it was turned into a book by Little, Brown & Co and a film by Nora Ephron and starring Meryl Streep.

The website One Red Paperclip was created by Kyle MacDonald, a Canadian blogger who traded his way from a red paperclip to a house in a series of online trades over a year. *One Red*

Paperclip: How a Small Piece of Stationery Turned into a Great Big Adventure became a book, published by Ebury.

The Intimate Adventures of a London Call Girl by Belle de Jour sold over 250,000 copies and was made into a successful television series.

These are exceptions to the rule; there is no guarantee that book buyers, or more to the point, literary agents and publishers, will read the blog and be inspired to publish it in book form. So don't feel you have to have one if you are an aspiring author. However, the discipline of writing a blog regularly *can* help improve your writing.

Tips on blogging
- *Check out other bloggers who write on a similar subject (as you did when you were writing your book).*
- *Participate in other blogs; comments you leave can link back to your site which can lead to more people visiting it.*
- *There are several websites that offer web or blog templates for free (e.g. blogger.com, blogspot.com or wordpress.com).*
- *Amazon allows you to blog through your Author Central account; each posting gets 'attached' to all the books you have published and featured on Amazon; the more books you have, therefore, the more exposure you get when you blog here.*
- *If you are blogging, give as much attention to the quality of your writing as you would to your book.*
- *Don't share written work that you value on a blog; keep it for your book.*
- *Ration the amount of time you spend blogging; it might be a better use of your time if you actually worked on a book rather than a blog.*

Insight
Increasingly, bloggers are writing reviews about books so it may be worth sending them a book.

Sometimes, I've had authors who have been very good at getting media coverage themselves; often it is because they have brilliant contacts in their particular area of expertise, especially if it's a very niche area. For example, one of my authors researched all the science fiction sites on the web, made contact and, as a result, was interviewed by several of them, gaining valuable coverage for his book in the process.

Suzi Williamson, publicity, A & C Black

www.acblack.com

> **Insight**
> Blogs and tweets are only relevant if your target readers are bloggers and tweeters as well. They will not work for everyone.

Our website is the hub of our business. We post interviews with our authors and we now have a YouTube channel where we post video clips of our authors so that anyone from foreign publishers and scouts to ordinary people can drop in and see our authors in action. I am also very interested in building a sense of community among our authors in various ways.

A lot of authors don't know where to start when it comes to having a website; some are very web savvy and others not. Personally, I think there's a bit too much emphasis on social networks but anything that helps to build a fan base is a good thing. I have a long-term dream that we could provide more structured information to help writers in terms of their self-promotion. We do what we can to help promote our writers – and this is something I'd like to enhance in the future – but, by and large, marketing and promotion is still mainly the province of the publisher.

Sarah Davies, literary agent, The Greenhouse Literary Agency

www.greenhouseliterary.com

Social networking sites

One advantage of using social networking sites is that they are global so you could be attracting a worldwide audience and network with likeminded people (either readers, other authors, or both).

And writers are not the only ones who have spotted the potential. Random House, for example, launched a Facebook application called Random Reads, which allows users to read extracts from over 7,000 Random House books and share them on their Facebook profile. Lulu has We Read – a social book club linked to Facebook, MySpace and others.

Philippa Gregory tweeted a serialization of her novel *The White Queen* for Simon & Schuster, as did R.N. Morris for his crime novel *A Gentle Axe* (Faber). Stephen King's book *Under the Dome* (Hodder) was promoted with a Twitter campaign and internet marketing that used 5,000 bits of text hidden in websites, which could be found by following a set of clues. Even publishers have been getting in on the act, with Penguin, HarperCollins, Faber, Profile and Random House all tweeting regularly. When Stephen Fry commented on *Sum: Forty Tales from the Afterlives* by Canongate author David Eagleman, it shot up Amazon's Movers & Shakers list by 250,000 per cent.

Social networking sites should not be the main plank in your publicity and marketing strategy. There have been several successful campaigns but, while they seem to work best if you want to connect with a particular group or community, book buyers are currently not turning to Facebook and Twitter for suggestions on what to read and buy. Indeed, this approach would not suit every book. Over half of children and young adults in the UK have a profile on a social networking site; for adult users of the internet that figure drops to over a fifth. This is important if you want to connect with an older audience. Promoting on Twitter a book that is aimed at a more mature readership may not be the best way to target your audience.

Insight
Make sure that you have a line under the signature of your outgoing emails that gives the name of your latest book or where you will be appearing to promote your book. Ensure you keep it up to date.

If you embrace the social networking sites as a way to publicize yourself and your work, don't waste all your writing time. There are ways of updating all your sites in one go, for free, using websites such as www.8hands.com or http://ping.fm.

> **Insight**
> In order to see your book on a library shelf, get friends and family to order copies through the libraries.

Publicity in bookshops

The books that you see in the windows of the large bookshop chains are not there because of their artistic merit. They are there because the publishing house paid for them to be there. Retailers charge publishers for including their titles in special promotions or placing them at the front of the store.

If you are being promoted by a publishing house, you might be one of the lucky authors who gets this kind of money put behind their book. For the majority, though, their best bet will be targeting independent and local bookshops and offering to do events in their shop as a local author.

> *We're very happy for authors to suggest doing a launch or a signing. If it's someone who isn't very well-known, we explain to them then and there that in order for it to work, they will have to do a lot of the pushing, the marketing, themselves and to make sure they have people they can bring along to it. Obviously, we have a mailing list and we let people on it know about events; we also advertise what we're doing. However, an unknown author won't pull people in off the street on the strength of their name so if they can bring along a crowd, then that's great.*
>
> *You don't have to pay the bookshop for this. Any money we make out of the event is from sales of the book. We'll*

sell tickets because if you don't, you never know how many people are coming or people will say they'll come and then don't bother to turn up. If they buy a ticket, they will usually make the effort to attend. And if someone buys a ticket, we tend to then give them back the money off the price of a book bought on the night.

Even if you are an author published by a publishing house, I would still encourage you to approach your local bookshop yourself and not expect the publicity department to do it for you. A lot of the best events we've had are from authors actually coming into the shop, rather than us going through their publicist. For instance, my wife tried to get Julian Fellowes [novelist, Snobs, Past Imperfect, Phoenix*], for a signing but found it hard work to get a response from the publicist. And then one day, Julian Fellowes just popped into the shop and we asked him if he'd like to do an event, 'I'd love to do an event,' he replied, 'It's just the right sort of town for me.' And we had a very successful evening. Sometimes, it seems that publicists' jobs are to actually deflect attention away from their authors rather than organize events for them.*

Alex Milne-White, proprietor, Hungerford Bookshop
www.hungerfordbooks.co.uk

In order to survive nowadays, independent bookshops need to keep in tune with what their customers want. They have to be proactive and creative. Events are a popular way of giving customers something extra, bringing people into the bookshop. They also benefit authors too.

Even authors who sell a respectable number of books do not automatically get a book launch by their publishers. However, whether you self-publish or have a publisher, there is nothing to stop you organizing one yourself. You *could* ask your publisher for a contribution to the launch but it is not guaranteed that you will get anything. You are not restricted to holding the launch in a bookshop; that has just been a traditional venue in the past.

Whether you have linked up with a bookshop (independent or part of a chain) or have decided to do your own launch, you need to offer:

- *a pleasant venue – it could be a bookshop, somewhere relevant to the subject of your book, a café, an art gallery, a museum or a library. If you are paying for the launch, don't use anywhere too expensive. Cheap or free would be better. The advantage of holding the event in a public place is that you might be able to draw in passers-by; a low turnout in a private room offers no opportunities to increase the numbers. Avoid using outdoor locations unless you can guarantee that the weather is going to be good.*
- *a suitable time – generally, launches take place in the early evening but you do not have to stick to that time. If, for example, your book has a strong business theme, you could consider having a breakfast launch; alternatively, you could have a launch after lunch. Avoid Friday and Saturday evenings.*
- *drinks – you need a reasonable quantity but you are not running a bar. Someone needs to be in charge of filling glasses.*
- *food – not always necessary (unless you are launching a cookery book) but nice to have a few bits and pieces to nibble. A few biscuits with cheese goes well with wine.*
- *readings – the author should consider reading some short passages from their book. Don't go on too long.*
- *selling and signing – give people the opportunity to buy the book and make sure you sign it.*
- *attendees – make sure your friends and family attend, even if they are not going to buy your book; you need to create a good atmosphere and for that, you need people. Send out invitations to make sure they know when and where it is. Family and friends will form the bulk of the audience; you also need influential people to attend. Invite local journalists, radio presenters, bookshop managers, even your solicitor, bank manager and accountant. The more people you can get talking about your book, the better.*

Make sure that you publicize your event in advance. The invitations should go out in good time and you should have posters up to advertise the event (in the window of the venue, in the local bookshop, school, library).

As the event gets nearer, contact your key people to ensure that they will turn up. You should also leave enough time to get a few extra people if you think numbers are looking low.

On the day:

- *arrive early and make sure the room is set up for the event*
- *get a table ready where you can sign books*
- *prepare the food and drink*
- *check that you have enough change if you are planning to sell your book*
- *make sure that the toilets are presentable and usable*
- *have bin bags so you can clear up afterwards*
- *write a 'thank you' note to the manager of the venue afterwards.*

If you wish to claim your expenses as tax-deductible, be careful about labelling them as 'party'. Expenditure on 'entertainment' is not allowed. However, a book launch *is* part of promoting and selling books.

Insight
If you are going to be signing books, prepare three or four key phrases that you can write in the book rather than just writing your name. It looks like you've made more of an effort, which will be appreciated by the buyer.

What is more important: the author or the book? It totally depends on the type of book. It's great if the author is known and has an existing platform on which to help promote and publicize the book. Obviously this is a big factor with fiction, where fans will always buy a favourite author's new release. But if the book is poor, that doesn't help anyone. Plenty of first-time authors have hit huge success because their books tapped into a current trend or timely topic in a captivating way. With publicity budgets what they are (shrinking), more and more responsibility is given to the author to get his/her book out there and seen/heard, which is why an existing platform helps.

Amy Vinchesi, editor, Watson-Guptill, an imprint of Random House
www.randomhouse.com

Literary festivals

There are growing numbers of regular literary festivals, which need an endless supply of authors. They bring readers and writers together and create a wonderful creative buzz. If you get the chance to appear at a literary festival:

- *research the festival before you get there. Find out who else is appearing and what they will be talking about. If you can, attend one or two other events to get the feel for the festival and the sorts of questions people are asking.*
- *if it is taking place in a town or village that you don't know very well, do some research on the place, which you can then relate to your talk.*
- *what format will your event take? Is it a small, cosy chat with an interviewer or are you expected to stand up in front of hundreds and give a talk?*
- *don't be offended if people don't buy your book after your talk; think of it as an investment in future sales.*
- *remember that people will be observing you when you are giving your talk and when you are chatting with people so make sure you act as if you are delighted to be there.*

It is always worth approaching the organizers of literary festivals directly and asking them if they would like you to appear. This probably works best at some of the smaller festivals and especially ones that are local to you; they like to promote local authors. You could consider doing a double act with another writer.

Some festivals pay authors to speak but it is not a given and, even if they do, it is not a huge amount of money. Be grateful if they offer to pay travel expenses.

The advantage of literary festivals is that people are attending because they want to and, if they've signed up to your talk, because they want to hear *you* speak.

For more information on festivals around the country, go to the British Arts Festivals Association website (www.artsfestivals.co.uk).

> **Insight**
> Volunteer to help out at your local literary festival. You will learn an awful lot about what makes a successful event and you will build up goodwill with the organizers, who may look more kindly on you as a prospective speaker because of your help.

Launch parties, book signings, literary festivals, conferences, panel discussions...these events are all about seeing you and your book. There may be only 20 or 30 people at an event but they can pass the word to friends about your book.

Remember that events like these are not purely for you to stand up and exhort listeners to buy your book. Look at how chat shows on television deal with authors who have books to plug; there is a brief mention but then the author is there to entertain. If they do that well enough, listeners are more likely to go out and buy their book.

> *I'm thinking of putting a DVD in one of my poetry books. Bloodaxe Books did it; they recorded poets reading their work. I've got a computer at home, a camera; I could burn off a DVD, put it in a pocket in the back of the book. It would be easy. Listening to a poet is fascinating. There's a transformative process; the written word read is different from the spoken word and a good reader can bring a bad poem to life and a bad reader can kill a good poem. It's one way of publishing. Have you noticed on Amazon, when they*

sell books, there's often a little video to go along with it? I bought a Chinese cookery book for my son for Christmas. And I was quite surprised to see the little video on Amazon of the author, promoting her book. It's an example of the author selling it.

John Richardson, self-published poet

Giving readings and talks

Offer to give readings at bookshops, libraries, schools and colleges. Visits to libraries, schools and colleges are particularly important for children's authors. If you are with a publishing house, they will support you at these events; either by sending out books for you to sell at the event or even (sometimes) providing drinks, etc.

If you give a reading, make sure you collect the names and email addresses of the people who attended the event. You should be planning to build a list of people who are interested in you and your work; these are the people who will potentially be buying your books.

Leave flyers on seats, giving information on your website and also saying that if people would like updates on your books, any other readings, etc., to leave their contact details. Offering an incentive, like an author newsletter, a chapter from your forthcoming book or a competition with a prize, is even better.

Data protection rules state that you must give people the opportunity to refuse the option of further information from you, e.g. 'If you do not wish to receive further information from John Author, please tick the box.'

Organizations such as the Rotary Club, the local Chamber of Commerce, the Women's Institute and so on are always looking for interesting and entertaining speakers. You will not get paid for your talk (although you may get travel expenses). It is an opportunity to spread the word about your book and you can always take along copies to sell and sign afterwards.

Whether talking to adults or to children, it is worthwhile finding out about your audience before you give your talk. You should ask:

- how many people will be attending
- what the room format will be
- who will be introducing you – offer to give them some information or have a quick chat over the phone. Remember to get them to say that your book is for sale after the talk.
- how long they want you to talk
- if there will be a microphone. Will there be somebody there who knows what to do if it is not working?

TALKS TO CHILDREN

Think about the size of the group you are happy to talk to and how many sessions you will do in a day. Think about the form your 'talk' will take; will the children be interacting or do you prefer to read to them and then answer questions?

If you have a website, you can advertise your willingness to give talks and encourage schools and libraries to contact you to fix up a visit. Alternatively, there are several websites and publications that list authors who are willing to undertake visits; some may charge a fee:

www.literacytrust.org.uk
www.ncll.org.uk
www.artscape.org.uk
www.nawe.co.uk
www.classactagency.co.uk

Public libraries and School Library Services also have lists of visiting authors, as do organizations such the Arts Council.

Some schools and local authorities are insisting that individuals/ groups who visit schools and libraries have some form of public liability insurance. The Society of Authors has details on this, as does the Arts Council.

Some places also request vetting and clearance from the Criminal Records Bureau. If you have not got clearance, consider getting it. Until you do, make sure that you are always accompanied by a teacher or librarian; partly to cover yourself and partly so you do not end up having to act as a substitute teacher keeping order!

> **Insight**
> Take your book on the bus or tube and read it. If anyone asks you about it, don't admit to being the author. Just tell them it's brilliant and that they should buy it.

Marketing and publicity are not something that should happen only for the month after publication. It is an ongoing process if you want to continue to sell your book. Getting your manuscript accepted demands persistence – and so does promoting your book: you have to be able to sell it. Someone said writing was a quiet business but promoting a book was a loud business.

> **Insight**
> If you can get your book sold in bulk, let the publishers know. For example, some businesses will ask for 1,000 copies to sell on themselves.

Case study

Angela Waller, author, *The Snows of Yorkshire, Before There Were Trolley Dollies* (Pen Press) www.angelawaller.co.uk

I had the first book, The Snows of Yorkshire, *rattling around my head for about 25 years. Places I went, I would see things, a piece of furniture, a chair, or I'd hear a story about someone... they all slotted into this story. I had never told anyone, except my husband, that I wanted to write it because the world's full of people saying 'I could write a novel' until something tripped me up at a dinner party one evening. The host came over and said, 'So what's this about a book?' I replied that it was just an idea I'd had about a family saga, covering 600 years but divided into five parts so you get the interesting bits and don't have to slog through the dreary bits. He was a retired professor of English Literature and said, 'You should do it.' So the next day, I sat down and started. And I wrote every day until I'd done 110,000 words knowing I was going to edit bits out.*

I started writing magazine articles in my 60s when we moved back to England, having lived abroad for many years. Doing the articles has helped my writing because I have learned the discipline of moving things along, of editing my work. No matter how much I might think, 'That's a really lovely phrase', if I've only got 1,500 words to play with I may have to cut it out.

Despite the fact that the Writers' & Artists' Yearbook *tells you that every literary agent receives an average of 19 unsolicited manuscripts every day, I went through the list and cut out the ones who only handled crime or children's fiction and so on, and looked for the agencies that dealt in women's fiction, family fiction or history. I think I'd only tried about seven or eight agencies but the same big envelopes came dropping back through the letterbox, along with a polite note saying, 'No, thank you. We wish you luck' and so on. It's no good telling yourself that Frederick Forsyth had his first book,* The Day of the Jackal, *returned by 18 agents and was only accepted by the nineteenth. You pick up this big brown envelope and you think, 'I don't give a damn about Frederick Forsyth; this is me being rejected again.'*

Then a cousin of mine, whom I trusted, said she knew someone who had self-published his book using a company called Pen Press. So I made contact with them. I didn't have a budget in mind at first; in the end, I paid £3,300 in total. That is £1,100 up front and then the rest at designated stages. You can opt for different 'packages', from just having five books printed to a full partnership package. I sent them my book's synopsis and the first
(Contd)

few chapters. They then wanted to see the whole manuscript. After that, they said they'd like to go the full partnership route with me because they liked the book so much.

For this, a reader went through my manuscript and came up with suggestions on parts that should be edited. I didn't like taking out some of my favourite bits but it did help move the story along. So I sent the amended, edited manuscript back to them. I then got a proof copy which I was told to read very, very carefully because any mistakes that were missed at that stage would be expensive to change afterwards.

I had an idea of what I wanted on the cover. The publishers came back with a layout but it wasn't quite what I wanted, the house wasn't right, so my husband and I found a picture of a house which he doctored up on the computer and we used that. I had final approval of the cover design. From there, they went to print and I think the first print run was 300 copies.

I was given 20 copies which I sent out as review copies and Pen also sent out review copies. The full partnership package includes marketing the book and they obtained several magazine reviews and I got some more, including one in Saga magazine. Pen also arranged an interview on a local BBC radio programme. I took the bit between my teeth and contacted other local radio stations. Only one got back to me but they've had me on three times. When my second book came out, I contacted them all again and I was asked back and did additional radio interviews. You have to be pushy. Perhaps 'pro-active' is a better word! Well, you don't have to be pushy but you're not going to sell as many books if you don't try to do all you can to promote it.

You have to promote the book yourself. Nobody will know about it unless you do. There's no magic publicity fairy going round at night leaving notes on people's pillows, saying 'Buy The Snows of Yorkshire *because Angela Waller wrote it.' Marketing and networking are very important for self-published authors. Nothing ventured, nothing gained. I contacted a couple of authors about whom I'd written articles, reminding them who I was and offering to send a copy of the book. Rosalind Laker (the romantic novelist) agreed to read the book and said she'd give me her honest opinion. Two weeks later she rang and said she loved it, would I like a comment from her that I could use on reprints? And so that was quoted on the cover.*

Pen Press sent me and about ten other authors on a one-day marketing seminar which was quite useful. They teach you that if you ever get hold of a features editor or someone who reviews books, first of all flatter them. Tell them you know how busy they are and get their email address so you can tell them about the book there. Practise explaining what your book is about. I've got it down to under 15 seconds. If they're interested, they'll ask you more. What they'll probably do is ask you to send them a copy of the book and get off the phone! You have to practise so you can get across the bits you need to say.

It doesn't matter how old you are, it's never too late, which is what I said to the people at Saga *magazine. I wrote to them: 'Your readership is 50+. I've just had my first novel published at the age of 76; would it be of any interest for a small article?' The Features Editor said they didn't think it would interest their readers but if I would like to send a review copy they'd pass it on to the person who reviews the books. I was thrilled and started to thank him profusely but he stopped me and pointed out that the book reviewer receives hundreds of review copies every month and will only review three or four. I sent it off nevertheless. About three months later, the magazine arrived and there, on page XX, was a photograph of the book and a review! I was thrilled.*

The publishers put the book on Amazon. A friend, who lives in Thailand, bought it on another website (www.historydirect.co.uk). I've no idea how it got there but I wrote to them, explaining that my book had been bought through their website and people had been very pleased with the service and I was happy to recommend them. That establishes a little friendly link. So when the next book
(Contd)

came out, I contacted them again and asked if they'd carry this book as well and they do, as they consider it is 'social history'.

When I lived in America, I went to a couple of British–American clubs which are all over America. So I went on Google, found out where there were branches and sent out 40-odd emails. I told the truth which is that I wrote the book because I love England and have a love of English history. I suggested that any of their members who were feeling a little bit homesick for England might enjoy reading it and it could be bought on Amazon. That resulted in quite a few sales in America.

When my first book was about to come out, I went to my local branch of Waterstone's in Chichester and asked to see the manager. I hadn't got a copy of the book yet but said it was coming out shortly, gave my 15-second description and asked if they would consider having me in the store to do a book signing. 'Yes,' she said. I then asked if they thought any of the Waterstone's branches in Yorkshire would be interested and I went to Leeds, Hull and Sheffield three weekends in a row (wondering why I hadn't set the book closer to home!). After the book signing in Leeds, the manager came up and asked me how I thought it had gone. I told her I wasn't too impressed because we'd only sold 13 copies. 'Well, you outsold Michael Parkinson when he did a book signing here.' Now that made me feel better; I outsold Parky! You only have to ask a bookshop. It's in their interests to promote and sell books. The library also asked me to go and talk to a reading group; they ended up ordering six copies for the library, which is very good.

I also do a lot of talks about being an air hostess in the 50s and 60s which is how my second book came about. The publishers said, 'Look, this talk is so popular, why not make it into a book?' I wasn't keen at first because I thought it would be too short but my husband said, 'We've been married over 40 years and I'm still listening to your airline stories, so why not give it a go?' So, I did, self-publishing again, using the same company as before.

I contacted W. H. Smith's sales and marketing people, told them about the book and sent them a review copy. I felt the ideal place to launch it would be at an airport and I suggested doing a book signing for them there. They got back to me, saying it would be too difficult to arrange from a security point of view, which was disappointing. Then Pen, the publishers, got involved and W.H. Smith ordered 250 copies and put them in their airport bookshops, which was very nice.

If you're going to self-publish, think about the subject matter of your book and contact every magazine that might possibly review your book. For the air hostess book, I contacted publications like Aviation Weekly *and several other serious aviation magazines and they reviewed my book. The Royal Aeronautical Society also reviewed it. You can get details of all magazines from the* Writers' & Artists' Yearbook.

I was at a party where someone asked me what my second book was about and I replied, 'Oh, it's all about what went on when I was flying.' A retired BOAC captain was standing opposite me and I saw his jaw drop, and he asked 'Not all *about what went on?' I just beamed at him and said, 'You'll have to read it when it comes out, won't you?' whereupon he asked for a free copy. It's a common misconception that authors get their books free, they don't. I was given just 20. I do buy copies of my book so I can send them out. If I buy 100 myself, I get a percentage off the full price.*

To help promote your book, consider giving talks to the Women's Institute or similar groups. You have to do an audition for the WI, which they hold once a year. I went along thinking I was a bit old for this caper but they had about 200 people from all the West Sussex WI groups there as an audience. There were seven or eight speakers; you were given 20 minutes to speak and five minutes for questions. The WI have a directory for each local area and it is a great coup to get into it. The directories have the address and contact details of speakers, information on what
(Contd)

they charge for mileage, their fee and so on. For anyone who has self-published a book and who wants, likes or is able to give talks, this is a good audience.

When I give a talk, I get there early and put one of my bookmarks (which has details about my books on them) on every seat. Bookmarks are very, very useful sales tools. If I chat to people in the supermarket queue, I'll mention my books and I'll hand them a bookmark. Never go anywhere without a copy of your book and bookmarks.

There are also lots of free magazines, parish magazines, anything like that in your area so get a picture of you and your book and get a write-up in there. They may not have the biggest circulation compared to national magazines but they do have a readership. Out of one little magazine, with a circulation of 3,000, I've sold 16 books, which isn't going to make my fortune but it is nice to think, 'There's another cheque being paid into the bank.' And anyone you talk to, anyone who reads your book, is potentially going to talk to someone else about it.

Maeve Binchy said that, in publishing, promotion is as important as the prose. And recently, someone sent me a little paragraph about John Grisham who said that when his first book was published, he discovered it's a lot harder to sell a book than it is to write one. And I thought 'Ain't that true?!'

10 THINGS TO REMEMBER

1. *Be available and well-prepared for events.*

2. *Keep a list of media contacts.*

3. *Be prepared to do some of your own legwork; the publicist is not your PA.*

4. *Fill in your author questionnaire; if you don't, it is hard for the publisher to get you any publicity or support you.*

5. *Think about your USP, your hook or angle. How can you comment or contribute to an article that can promote you and your book?*

6. *Set yourself a budget if you intend to produce your own flyers/ bookmarks, advertise, etc. and stick to it.*

7. *If you are blogging, give as much attention to the quality of your writing as you would your book.*

8. *Check if your work is being discussed anywhere on the web and join in the discussions. Point people to your website.*

9. *Blogs and tweets are only relevant if your target readers are bloggers and tweeters as well.*

10. *Get friends and family to review your book online and order copies from the library.*

9

Selling the book

In this chapter you will learn how:
- *books are sold*
- *to get your books into bookshops*
- *to manage your sales.*

> *If you want to get rich from writing, write the sort of thing that's read by persons who move their lips when they're reading to themselves.*
>
> Don Marquis, author and journalist

At the beginning of this guide, we looked at how the publishing industry had changed dramatically over the years. Just as the publishing world changed, so did the booksellers. Those changes have had a major impact on how books are sold.

From small independent booksellers, university bookstores and independently owned chains, such as W.H. Smith, the high street began to acquire new players. Barnes & Noble, in the US, expanded in the 1970s and 1980s; in the UK, Waterstone's and Dillons appeared, offering a huge choice of titles. As the chains grew, so did the discounting. In 1975, Barnes & Noble was the first bookseller in the US to offer *New York Times* bestsellers at a 40 per cent discount on the publisher's list price. Waterstone's was one of the first in the UK.

Discounting is the percentage margin between the retail price of a book and the price at which it is bought from the publisher. Book retailers pushed for higher discounts, the right to return unsold books and longer credit periods. Since the chains were providing professional bookselling of the publishers' titles, in well-stocked shops that were proving popular with consumers, the publishers agreed. The book wholesalers, who supplied the independent bookshops, also demanded a discount from the publishers to match that of the discounts the chains had won. In the 1990s, the supermarkets began to add books to their stocklist, especially the bestsellers, at extremely competitive prices and now one in five books bought in the UK come from supermarkets. Alongside these sellers are the online retailers, with Amazon being the most successful; it is the largest bookseller in both the UK and the US. The bookselling market is highly competitive.

AA – We had a gripe one day, didn't we, and we were reminded very smartly how much money they were spending on our behalf. Publishers have to pay to get you in a good position in Waterstone's, they pay to get you in a good position in supermarkets...they have got money to pay out on top of everything. You have got to be realistic; it's like any business. They're selling a product and your creation is suddenly that product, like a tin of baked beans. As 'Annie Sanders' we are now a product; they are making us into a brand and you have to go with it. It's the nature of the beast. Let's face it, people buy Maeve Binchy now without reading the blurb. People buy what they know.

MS – We once had an idea for a radically different book and the response from the publishers was 'No, we don't want that' because once you've become a successful, saleable product they don't want you to change. There are some well-established writers who write very different books. Susan Hill, for example, has written non-fiction, ghost stories, crime; Robert Harris has gone from writing books like Enigma *to books on Ancient Rome that have done fantastically well. Generally, though, once you're known for writing one type of genre, publishers are very uncomfortable with you changing.*

Annie Ashworth and Meg Sanders, authors who write as Annie Sanders

www.anniesanders.co.uk

Publishing a book does not automatically mean that it is stocked by a retailer. Some of the biggest publishers negotiate long and hard with the booksellers, having to agree to substantial discounts, just to get their books on the shelves. On some of the bestselling trade books, it is not unusual for the big retailers to get a 60 per cent discount off the price of a book; that is in addition to what a publisher has to pay to promote the book (for example, paying for it to be at the front of the shop). Even small and self-publishers will be expected to give a discount off their books. In that respect, they are no different from a traditional large publishing house.

Authors never like the idea of discounting their books but if you are dealing with retailers and wholesalers (we will look at wholesalers in more detail later on in the chapter), you will have to offer a discount. Most wholesalers expect between 55 and 60 per cent, which is fairly standard for any new publisher. At that level of discount, a wholesaler such as Gardners can give all their customers their normal trade terms. If they get less than that, they will cap the discount to the customers. The more the publisher gives (in discount terms) the more the wholesaler can pass on to their customers and, therefore, the more attractive the offer is.

So if you give only 20 per cent discount, the wholesaler (who works roughly on a 15 per cent margin) is going to give their customers 5 per cent discount. If a bookseller looks on their system and sees that they are not going to make much, if any, money on the book sale, they will not bother to stock it. It is in the publisher's interests to give the best discount they can.

If you (as a self-published author) do any direct business, you can charge what you like for your book (via your website, for example). Offset what you are having to give the wholesaler for a small number of orders against the direct orders, where you are going to get your full money. And maybe you will have to do it as a loss leader if you want to get across the door of Waterstone's or somewhere similar. Think where else you could get your full recommended retail price.

Sales

If you decide to sell and distribute your books yourself, you will need to handle all the orders. This will involve generating invoices, sending the books to the customer and dealing with any returns. If you use a distributor, you will have to pay them a fee for their services.

You will have to make sure that books are packaged so that they do not get damaged and you will have to remember to add the postage costs into your overall budget. If there are returns, you will need to issue credit notes or refunds.

The advantage of selling your own books is that you set your own rules. If you use a wholesaler or bookshop, you have to abide by theirs.

RETURNS POLICY

Wholesalers and most retailers will take your book on a sale or return basis; in other words, if they do not sell your book, they can return it to you. This will be part of your agreement. A return might be due to a damaged book or if the buyer simply changes their mind.

If you are selling direct to members of the public, offer a refund or to replace the book. Don't quibble with them and put them off buying from you again.

GETTING PAID

If you are selling books yourself, you can accept payment by cheque or credit card or, if selling online, you can use PayPal.

If you want to accept credit card payments, you should shop around and find out what the costs of accepting card payments will be. You will be charged differently for credit card and debit card transactions (credit card and charge card charges can be anything from 2 to 6 per cent of the value of each sale). There will also be a monthly fee if you rent the card terminal. Talk to your bank to find out the costs. It may work out that the amount of use would not cover your costs.

If you are starting out selling online, using a service like PayPal probably makes more sense. PayPal gets you a free shopping cart on your website. It accepts secure payment by credit card. You pay a set amount per transaction (currently 20p), plus a percentage of the cost of the transaction (between 1.4 and 3.4%). Got to www.paypal.com for more information.

KEEPING RECORDS

If you are selling your books, you must keep accurate records so that you know when orders came in, how many books were ordered, what the payment was, when the books were sent out and if there were any returns. This system should apply to all sales: to wholesalers, bookshops, members of the public. Update this system regularly.

Draw up some order forms. They should have your contact details, the book title, ISBN and price. There should be space for a date and an order reference. The buyer will need somewhere to put their contact details and the quantity they are ordering. You can put the order form on the back of your AI/flyer if you wish.

You will need a sales book in which to list:

- *customer's name*
- *date of order*
- *order reference*
- *quantity*
- *type of order (online, phone, by post)*
- *date order dispatched*
- *date of invoice*
- *date of payment.*

When you send out your orders, add a delivery note. This is basically the same as the order form except you should have a line for a signature (plus printed name) and date that says 'Received by...'

PAYMENT AND BAD DEBT

It is worth stating what your terms are for payment of invoices; many companies have 30 days. At the end of each month, go through your invoices and check that they have been entered into your system. If there are any unpaid invoices that are now outstanding (i.e. unpaid after 30 days), you should first send a reminder. If you have the customer's contact details that can involve a quick (polite) phone call, email or fax. Non-payment is often due to forgetfulness so a gentle reminder can solve the matter.

If, despite the polite reminder, the invoice is still unpaid, you can either write it off as a bad debt (especially if it is a small amount of money) or you can threaten to take them to the small claims court. If you chose to go down the latter route, you need to send a letter stating quite clearly that if payment is not received within a set time, legal action will be taken.

The small claims court deals with disputes involving sums of under £5000. Hearings are informal and you do not need to use a solicitor or barrister. You will need:

- *a standard claim form which is available from www.hmcourts-service.gov.uk*
- *guidance notes (also available from the website)*
- *copies of all written documents relating to your case.*

The court serves your claim on the person who owes you money; they have 14 days to reply. If they dispute your claim, you will both be asked to attend the court. Both sides will be asked to give their evidence. You should be brief and state your case clearly. A judge will hear both sides of the argument and then make a ruling.

The price of a book – where the money goes

When a book is sold, the author will get only a percentage of that money, as will the publisher. The price of a book has to cover:

- *manufacturing costs*
- *royalties*
- *distribution and marketing*
- *publisher's overheads*
- *trade discount*
- *publisher's net profit.*

Even if you are self-publishing, you should take into account costs such as distribution and marketing (review copies, postage, driving to a talk and selling books afterwards) and overheads if you want to get a true picture of how much profit you are making.

> **Did you know?**
> Bestselling books tend to be by authors who have healthy backlists, year after year. They don't even need to be alive; Enid Blyton was 12th and Tolkien came in at 23rd in Nielsen BookScan Data's list of bestselling authors of the 1990s (Shakespeare was 57th and Charles Dickens was 93rd).

When publishers are pricing a book, they will calculate the likely orders from their various customers. We looked at setting the price of your self-published book in Chapter 6. If you have been taken on by a publishing house, they will set the price of your book and you will have no input on this.

> *With literary fiction there isn't the expectation that an author will turn a book out every year on a strict timetable, but we don't like to have long gaps between books either because people's memories are short. In the past it was easier for writers to start modestly, with the idea that their career would develop over several books. Although that does still happen, I think it is much more difficult nowadays.*

Apart from anything else, publishers find it a great deal harder with each successive book to change perceptions if the previous ones haven't really sold well. Booksellers can now look at precisely what they sold of the last one and, generally (though not in every case), will take a huge amount of persuasion to support a new one if the last one didn't do very well. Literary editors also become progressively less interested, so it just gets harder each time. Unless an author writes a very different book (by different I mean on a different level) and then we can go to the booksellers and say 'We know the last one only sold x but, believe us, this is a huge leap forward, read it and you'll see.'

Carole Welch, Publishing Director, Sceptre
www.hodder.co.uk

Timing

Certain books do well at particular times of the year so if you want your book to do well and you can tie it into a season that could dictate the timing of when you make your book available for sale. Publishers are very aware that timing the publication of their author's work can be critical to it selling successfully.

A lot of new books are brought out in October and November, ready for the Christmas market. That means there are a lot of new titles competing for attention – new titles that have the backing of large publishing houses. Conversely, fewer new books come out in the New Year, apart from the 'traditional' New Year's resolution titles of health, diet, travel and personal development. You could, therefore, consider bringing out your book when there is less competition; that's what Heinemann did in 1998 with their then new author, Kathy Reichs. Her first book, *Déjà Dead*, got to number one.

Timing is also important if your book is tied into the academic year. Schools will be looking at their budgets at the beginning of the year and deciding what to buy.

The trade will be working about six months in advance. So buyers will be looking at the December market in May/June. If you are selling your books, you will have to work ahead as well. To get an idea of the timings, get hold of wholesalers' catalogues.

Getting your book stocked in a bookshop chain or supermarket

All major supermarkets and book chains buy through companies who store and dispatch the orders. I had to open an account with Gardners, the people who supply books to Waitrose and other major stores. They dictate the discount (at that time 52.5 per cent), and all orders are placed on a 'sale or return' basis. So you could get an order for 1,000 copies but get 999 unsold copies returned and you've got to take them. I also had to cover cost of carriage, and settlement was made 90 days following the date of my invoice. But I needed these people, they were my introduction into many stores countrywide, they were always so helpful and surprised at the success of a self-published book.

Mo Smith, author
www.lazycookmosmith.co.uk

For the big booksellers, there are usually five key points they look at when considering whether to take a book on:

- *track record*
- *support from the publisher*
- *market context*
- *pricing*
- *the cover.*

The actual contents and quality of the writing is not a key consideration.

The big chains and supermarkets have buying departments who specialize in particular categories and genres. The buyers, based at head office, are the ones who make the decisions as to what books are taken on and sold in the high street stores. Buyers will specialize in particular genres (children's fiction, cookery, etc.). With the large numbers of books being printed each year, it is impossible for the chains to take on every book that is published so do not expect to walk into a bookstore or supermarket and see that they stock your book.

Discounts, as discussed, are expected. The big promotions, such as having books at the front of the store, are paid for by the publishers. It is unlikely that a self-publisher will be able to afford to participate in a similar promotion.

Insight
There are certain areas in a bookshop that are regarded as prime areas: the window, the front of the shop and by the till.

As a self-publisher, you may not be able to get your book into a bookshop chain or supermarket as a *stock* item but you can hope to make it available on special order or on the store's core stock catalogue. In the US, Barnes & Noble review over 100,000 submissions from publishers each year. Most of those books are added to the chain's database and a small order placed for their warehouse. The Small Press Department of Barnes & Noble will consider books from small presses (i.e. small publishers and self-publishers); they like to see a finished copy with marketing and promotion plans, trade reviews, suggested retail price and information on what makes the book unique and different from the competition.

At Waterstone's, the buyers will decide which books to take centrally and how to promote them (for example, as Book of the Month, 3 for 2, or a window promotion). Waterstone's has a central buying system. Like Barnes & Noble, Waterstone's has a department that deals with independent and small (self-) publishers and advises them on how to get books into the Waterstone's system. That can result in a book being ordered centrally to any number of stores or to a select few with a particular strength in one area.

Local Waterstone's stores can also select and buy titles themselves, so it is a good idea to make friends with your local store managers. Send them your AI or flyer, explaining why you think it would be suitable for their store and whether you are prepared to do signing events. You can get a full list of Waterstone's stores from the Independent Publisher Coordinator (details below).

If you would like your book to be considered for central buying/core stock in Waterstone's, send a copy with a covering letter to: Peter North, Independent Publisher Coordinator at Waterstone's (full contact details are in the Appendix).

If you go to the websites of the big bookshop chains, there will be a link for independent publishers with information on what is required to stock your books. Most bookshop chains expect you to have an ISBN, a recognized book distributor and details of your book on Nielsen BookData (or Books in Print for the US).

Even when your book is taken on by a major chain, they can still return unsold books (around a fifth of all books are returned to publishers). The terms can state that you have to accept returns 90 days after the shops received your books.

> **Insight**
> Bookshops do not have unlimited storage space; they will have spare stock of the big sellers but not much else. Do not be surprised if your book is not stocked in every bookshop you go into; they don't have the space. They need convincing that they should stock your book.

Getting your book stocked in an independent bookshop

The large chains can be quite hard to get a book into because a lot of it is about central buying. It's not impossible but it's not that easy. The advantage of independent bookshops is that you'll meet the manager, probably straight away, who will be able to make a decision, probably on the spot, and hopefully it will all work out fine for both parties.

We have to know our market – the sort of books that are likely to sell, that will be good for our area, our customers and our shop. We see some reps from the publishing houses, like Penguin and HarperCollins. Other than that, we look at the catalogues of new titles from our wholesalers which come out each month; most of our backlist comes from Gardners. We'll go through the catalogues and pick out the books that will suit our market.

With an independent shop like ours, an author could approach us and ask us to stock their book. We do our best for either local authors or authors writing about the local area we're in. We'll generally stock those...unless they're complete rubbish! As long as they have some relevance, it's worth it for us.

If the books are about the local area, they are quite likely to sell. There's an important distinction between a local author and local subject. We'll try local authors but possibly on a sale or return basis because you just don't know how it will go at first. It does depend on the individual book; they only tend to sell if the author is quite good at promoting themselves. For example, we have one local author, a lady in her 80s called Iris Lloyd, who is writing a series of novels that are self-published. Her friends and people she's given talks to come in and buy them and those do very well.

We do quite a lot of events ourselves – readings, sometimes just a signing or the occasional launch. We're a very small shop so we use lots of other venues. For instance, Iris Lloyd did a talk for us; about 20 people turned up but that still made it worth doing, especially if they all tell a friend about the book.

Alex Milne-White, proprietor, Hungerford Bookshop

www.hungerfordbooks.co.uk

Around 100,000 books are published each year in the UK. There are around 2 million books in print. Bookshops need to stock a range of backlist titles and new frontlist titles. Choosing which books to stock can be quite a balancing act. In Chapter 8, we mentioned AI (advance information) sheets, which publishing houses send out to bookshops, libraries and wholesalers. It is a good idea to produce your own if you are self-publishing and send them out.

Independent bookshops may buy their stock directly from you; many of them will also use the big wholesalers and distributors (see below).

The Booksellers Association represents all booksellers in the UK, including the independent stores. They have a database of over 3,000 shops. You can buy mailing lists (either as a printed list or in the form of labels) from them. The printed list includes telephone and fax numbers. You can choose from a number of categories (such as geographical location, subject, and so on).

Currently, the cost is, for one-off use, £15 per 100 + VAT. Excel electronic versions of the printed lists are available from £25 + VAT per 100. The complete list in Excel is £650 + VAT. For all details, go to the Booksellers Association website (www.booksellers.org.uk).

> **Insight**
> Make sure you are a customer at your local bookshop; they are more likely to want to support you if you support them.

Distribution and wholesalers

Many bookshops will not buy direct from authors or small publishing houses (which is what you effectively are as a self-publisher). It would be a nightmare for a bookseller to have to process thousands of purchase orders from publishers, both small and large, so they prefer to source their books from one place. You will have to open an account with a wholesaler – and offer them discounts – if you want your books distributed in this way.

You will see references to wholesalers and distributors and there is a difference between the two.

BOOK DISTRIBUTORS

These:

- *buy books from the publisher and sell them on*
- *take orders from both bookshops and wholesalers*
- *will also hold all of the publisher's stock*
- *have sales reps who visit retailers and actively 'sell' books*
- *expect a percentage of the revenue received from the retailer.*

Many of the big publishing groups own distributors (for example, the distributor, The Book Service (TBS), is owned by Random House) and bookshop chains like Barnes & Noble have their own warehouse and distribution systems. Book distributors in the US include: Ingram Book Company, Small Press United and Consortium; distributors in the UK include: TBS, Bookpoint Ltd, GBS, Littlehampton Book Services. It is unlikely that a distributor will take on a sole book from a publisher.

Doing it yourself

Distribution is just another name for posting your books out to customers. The advantage of selling your books yourself is that you can sell them for the full price and not at the discount demanded by the retailers. Encourage these sales! Give some added value by signing every book you send out.

If you decide to do this yourself, you will need:

- *somewhere to store your books*
- *stationery (Jiffy bags, envelopes, parcel tape, address labels)*
- *promotional material – to include with the book*

- *postage – stamps*
- *a filing system – to process orders; check names and addresses; take payment against orders.*

If you are sending out one or two books, now and again, the distribution should not be a problem. It can get complicated when orders flood in. You have to process the orders accurately, parcel them up and then get them to the Post Office.

If you think you are going to be sending out a lot of parcels, look at the services offered by the parcel companies; they often offer a discount for large numbers of parcels.

BOOK WHOLESALERS

These:

- *offer a service for publishers by taking orders from retailers, whether that is an independent bookshop, library, a national chain of bookstores or a supermarket*
- *stock books that are in demand*
- *agree terms with retailers, take orders and ship those orders to the retailers*
- *handle the returns and manage any disputes with bookstores, etc.*
- *expect a discount on the cover price for supplying a book (around 55 per cent); publishers have to pay postage to deliver copies to them.*

Books are listed online on the wholesaler's website and in their printed matter. They will either stock the book physically in their warehouses or just list them in their sales catalogue. Some wholesalers in the US will cover only a specific region (e.g. Southern California or the Tri-state area) so be aware of that if you wish to use one, especially if your book has a regional focus.

The big wholesalers in the UK are Gardners, Marston Book Services and Bertram Books; in the US, they are Baker & Taylor

(B&T) and Ingram. Around 30 per cent of their sales come from independent bookshops. Wholesalers can also act as distributors for small publishers and they are increasingly offering POD as an additional service.

Advantages of using a wholesaler:

- *You lower the cost per book by cutting out the distributor.*
- *You know what you ship out and what condition the returns are in.*

Disadvantages of using a wholesaler:

- *If the orders add up to just a few per month, it will not take up too much time of your time but if sales start to increase, you can spend a lot of time shipping books out to the wholesaler.*
- *You have to chase up invoices/payment.*
- *You may have to store your books somewhere yourself, especially if they are only listed rather than stock items.*

Wholesalers do not just take on any book. For the big publishers, such as Penguin, wholesalers will usually buy anything they publish; that includes the high-end, education/higher education academic books that go for hundreds of pounds or dollars. The big, well-known publishing houses are 'stock publishers'.

Some wholesalers will deal with a new publisher/author only if they place four or more titles with them or if they have a strong track record of previous sales. Companies like Baker & Taylor and Gardners are more open to smaller publishers but they will not *stock* your book unless there is proven sales activity.

Gardners currently *stocks* nearly one million titles (including print on demand lines, listed not stocked lines and 50,000+ DVDs) even though there are far more books in print. In the US, Ingram works with over 25,000 publishers and imprints.

Wholesalers will physically stock a book only if they think it has 'got legs', i.e. that they can sell it because they have a customer or an outlet that would take it. One buying manager estimated that around 98 per cent of what they are shown from the small or one-man-band publishers are turned down. They do not stock a book just because it has been physically published; they only stock books to customer order. In other words, they stock books that are selling.

Wholesalers will agree how many copies they are going to take (for example, 50 or 100 copies) from the publisher but they remain the property of the publisher. At the end of every month, the wholesaler sends a statement showing any copies sold to the publisher who then invoices them for those books.

If you are a self-publisher and a wholesaler agrees to stock your book and asks for 500 copies, do not assume that you have 'sold' them. They can be returned to you at any time if they are not bought up by any of the retailers. And you have to take them back (the publisher pays for carriage/postage on returns).

A self-published book of memoirs written by Joe Bloggs would most likely be a non-stock item. In other words, a wholesaler will not physically have the book in their warehouse but they will have it listed – as long as that title is registered with Nielsen BookData and has an ISBN. So if anyone (a bookshop or Amazon, for example) places an order for that book, the wholesaler will pass the order on to Nielsen, which in turn sends the order to the publisher; the publisher then sends the book to the wholesaler who sends it on to the customer. That is a special order service (SOS). For the majority of self-published authors, that is what happens to their books.

If you wish to try to get your book onto a wholesaler's list, check before you send a sample copy of your book for consideration. *Very* few wholesalers will take copies and, in many cases, actively discourage authors/publishers from sending them in. If you contact Gardners, for example, you will be asked to email them the details of your book. Every book they don't have in stock but they have ordered to customer demand is recorded. You will then get a response that says they will monitor the book's sales. Wholesalers will regularly check their SOS bestseller list. If they see a sales increase over the next three to six months, they will contact that author again to discuss the possibility of being listed and/or stocked.

Tips on dealing with wholesalers
- *Don't hound wholesalers if you have sent in a sample copy; reading books is not their job.*
- *If they order four copies from you, four copies is what they want because they've had four orders – no more than that.*
- *Don't send 50 extra copies 'just in case'; they have nowhere to keep them.*
- *Wholesalers deal with enormous amounts of stock all the time (Gardners get 300+ pallets of stock a day). Don't expect someone to go rifling through them to find one Jiffy bag or envelope with your submission in it.*
- *November and December are the busiest months for wholesalers and distributors; warehouses are a hive of activity as books are loaded into boxes and shipped out. Avoid this time of the year if you are trying to get a response.*
- *Wholesalers order books to customer demand.*

Insight
If you do manage to get your book stocked by a wholesaler, you still have to keep up the publicity and marketing pressure, otherwise an awful lot of your books will come back to you. Wholesalers (like retailers) won't hold on to them forever and you still own those books, even when they are sitting in the wholesaler's warehouse.

However, wholesalers are always on the lookout for possible good sellers. Before Christmas, for example, a wholesaler picked up on a halogen oven cookbook. Even though it was not produced to the highest standard (it was black and white, the photos were unappetizing), it was the only one of its kind on the market so the wholesaler stocked it and sold thousands. That was at the beginning of November; by the end of December, 4,000 copies had been sold. The wholesaler spoke to the publisher, told them it was selling well but that it was being let down by its poor quality. They suggested adding some extra colour and an additional £1 on the price; the publisher took that advice, gave the book a new ISBN and they sold a further 6,000 copies in January.

The same thing happened when the *Pass The Citizenship Test* book came out; it was the only book of its kind so a wholesaler went straight in, ordered thousands and did extremely well. The book flew off the shelves. There is always a chance that a book might get picked up in that way but they are few and far between. The wholesalers know the market and what can sell. They also know what doesn't sell.

If you work hard at pushing your sales, people like Gardners, B&T, Bertrams *will* notice. They cannot take a book from scratch and do the sales and marketing for you. When you've proved that your book will sell and that people want to buy it, you can then approach the wholesalers.

If you are accepted by a wholesaler, you will

- *need to open an account with them*
- *offer a large discount*
- *cover the cost of postage yourself*
- *accept any returns.*

Insight
Authors should visit local retail outlets where books are sold (both independent, national, supermarkets, etc.) and find out which distributors they use.

A friend passed the new book to the editor of YOU *magazine. I was delighted and thought it would be a wonderful way to promote the book. As a distraction from the excitement of waiting for the feature to appear, my husband and I went off for a short holiday. On return, the first thing I found was an email from the Sainsbury's distributor – subject: 'Book Returns'. They requested the return of 1,500 of the 4,000 books originally ordered. I didn't know what I was going to do with all those books. I rang the distributor but was reminded of the terms of 'sale or return'. Even so, I was a bit confused because the supermarket buyer had been so positive and confident about sales. I rang her but she'd moved on to another area and the fellow who'd taken over wasn't the slightest bit interested in my books. This is what happens so many times. You just get in touch with the person you need and they move on.*

I didn't have the nerve to ask my printer to take these returns so cleared a space in the garage for them. My heart sank, but was lifted when I received an unexpected call from The Book People who said, 'We understand your book is being featured in YOU magazine; would you like us to handle your sales?' I asked how many they thought would sell 'It just depends on the subject and the feature,' they replied. 'We've handled Nigella's latest book and she sold 1,000 copies.' I thought that I might sell about 50, a hundred if I was lucky.

The magazine came out with three pages of copy and photographs of me and my food. I was delighted. The following Monday I received my first order by email; by the end of the week, I'd sold 3,000 books. It was going so well that titles were beginning to run out and it was now my turn to contact anyone who might have unsold copies to return them and I also managed to empty the garage of the Sainsbury's returned books. That one magazine feature resulted in sales of 6,000 books.

Mo Smith, author
www.lazycookmosmith.co.uk

Selling to libraries

Libraries do not buy directly from the publisher; they use specialized library suppliers. Like wholesalers and retailers, the library suppliers will want information well in advance of publication. Send your AI and a covering letter (asking if they will stock your book and on what terms); do not send a copy of your book.

Library suppliers in the UK (some of which are also in the US) are:

Askews Library Services
Blackwell
Coutts Library Services
Peters Library Services

The Chartered Institute of Library & Information Professionals (CILIP) have mailing lists of all the libraries in the UK which you can purchase and use to send out your AI sheets to librarians round the country (contact details are in the Appendix).

> *We market to professors who we hope will adopt a book for a course. Sales reps go around and knock on doors and try and catch professors in their office, saying 'Let me tell you about this* Principles of Economics *book; you're using the McGraw Hill one – here's why mine is better.' It's exactly like drug companies; you're not selling to the end user, you're selling to the person who 'prescribes' the book.*
>
> Todd Armstrong, Senior Acquisitions Editor,
> Communications and Media Studies, SAGE Publications
> www.sagepub.com

Selling online

Amazon is the leading online bookseller in both the UK and the US. In this section, we will look at Amazon in detail. All books that have an ISBN will appear on Amazon. When an order comes through Amazon, the information linked to the ISBN will be checked and the order passed on either to you directly or to a wholesaler.

If you are the publisher, you can contact Amazon and get an enhanced listing. The more information a book has on Amazon, the more it sells. If you are not a major publisher, your book will be listed but shown with a delivery time of one to two weeks. Joining the Amazon Advantage programme means that they will hold a few copies of your book in stock and make it available for next-day delivery. However, like other book retailers, you will have to give a considerable discount (around 55–60 per cent) on the cover price. You will need to ship enough copies to Amazon so that they can meet the orders and you will have to accept returns (paying for their shipping). They will contact you via email when you need to send them more books. Information on Advantage can be found on the Amazon website.

Amazon will pay after the book has been bought and shipped to its customer. As the publisher, you are paid on a monthly basis, 30 days after the end of the month in which the book is sold. You can access sales and inventory reports for your book online.

Joining the Advantage programme currently costs around £23.50 (inc VAT)/$29.95 for annual membership.

In the US, although not in the UK, Amazon currently says that any POD books sold on its US site would have to be produced by BookSurge, its in-house POD printer. One way round this would be to have a print run done (even if it is a very short one) and keep the stock at home.

Alternatively, register yourself as a Marketplace seller which means you send out the books to customers yourself. Amazon charge a listing fee (only if the item is sold) plus a percentage of the sale price (currently 15 per cent). If you are selling online, get a PayPal account (which is free). If you are selling abroad, you can leave your money in this account until the exchange rate is favourable.

Join the Amazon Associates programme and you will get 5 per cent of anything that anyone buys after following a link from your website. The percentage increases after 21 items.

Make sure you:

- *review your own book on Amazon*
- *get your friends and family to review your book*
- *get friends to buy a bestseller **and** your book*
- *feature your book on Listmania; don't put your book first on your list. Get friends to list your book on their Listmania; frequency builds presence online.*
- *add your book to your wish list*
- *add your book to 'Search Inside' because books that have this facility sell better on Amazon.*

Amazon is the dominant book retailer online. There are other players but they are not yet challenging Amazon for first spot. If, however, your book has a niche market, a particular specialism, you could contact websites that deal with the same subject and see if they will feature your book.

Independent Publishers Guild (UK)

The Guild (www.ipg.uk.com) runs seminars, a spring conference and, most importantly, has a stand at the leading book fairs (London, Frankfurt). You would have to pay money to be featured on their stand but it is considerably cheaper than having to buy a space of your own at such prestigious book fairs.

There are different categories of membership. As a self-publisher, you would be interested in full membership (publishers who have published three or more titles) or non-voting membership (publishers who have published fewer than three titles). Price of membership is based on turnover; for example, if your turnover is less than £100,000 a year, membership currently costs £201.72 (inc VAT).

In the US, the Independent Publishers Group (IPG) fulfils much of the same function. For more information, go to www.ipgbook.com.

Left-over books

Publishing houses, usually because they want to clear storage space in the warehouse, regularly sell off large quantities of their unsold books at heavily discounted prices; this is called 'remaindering'. They will only do this if they feel that the books are no longer being bought, i.e. the cost of storing them outweighs any income they might be bringing in.

There are various companies that buy up remaindered stock at very low prices and sell them on in discount book shops. If no one buys the stock, the books are pulped.

If you have a garage or spare room full of books that you need to clear (in order to store copies of your next book perhaps), you could consider remaindering your books. Only do this is you really do not want to put the effort into publicity and sales or your book is seriously out of date.

Rather than trying to sell them off, consider donating them to a charity. For example:

BookPower (www.bookpower.org)
Book Aid International (www.bookaid.org)
Book Trust (www.booktrust.org.uk)
BTBS The Book Trade Charity
    (www.booktradecharity.wordpress.com)
The Paul Hamlyn Foundation (www.phf.org.uk)

Case study

Sally Bee, author, *The Secret Ingredient* (HarperCollins)
www.sally-bee.com

I had a personal reason for doing my first book. Out of the blue, I suffered three massive heart attacks at a relatively young age. Having survived, I became a spokesperson for the British Heart Foundation and gave counselling sessions to other heart patients. What struck me very quickly was that people were not being given the right help when it came to diet and recipes. So I started handing out a few recipes to people and the results were coming back that they were working for them. So I wrote more and more.

At the same time, I was looking to get back to work in television. I was going to be on a series for Channel 4, but along came the credit crunch and the plug got pulled on it. I'd done a lot of work on a book of recipes that was to have accompanied the series so my husband suggested that I should go ahead and publish the book anyway.

Now, my mum had self-published a book; she'd written a story about my life, about the heart attacks. She raised some funds to publish the book herself, took them to the British Heart Foundation (BHF) and they sold them, making about £12,000 for the charity.

I needed something positive at that point so I got on with self-publishing my book. I did the layout myself and went to the same printers my mum had used and sat with their designers for a few days. I did look at the other books for ideas but there are so many different recipe books out there. As a self-publisher, it's important to have the courage of your convictions. A lot of what people will tell you is their opinion, and opinions differ. You can't listen to everyone. I had so many different mock-ups of the front cover; I'd lay them out and I asked everyone who came to my house which one they liked. Well, they all chose something different. You have to go with what you like best at the end of the day.

I didn't have a clue how many I should have had printed. In the end, 1,000 was the best value at the price I could afford. We brought the books home and I put a few in my shopping bag but I was really embarrassed to get them out. Nobody judges you when you are writing the book. Once you print your book and put it out into the world, you are open to everybody's opinion. What if they didn't like it? But then someone asked me if my book had been printed, I pulled one out and they just started selling.

This was initially to people I knew but my stock of a thousand books was going down which gave me the confidence to create some publicity about it. I did local papers at first and it just grew from there. I had a website built and I continued with my talks to medical and patient groups.

I had a very strong conviction that I was writing something that people needed. I suppose that conviction made it much easier to promote the book. Every mouthful I eat has to nourish me because I have a very poorly heart and nourishment is the only thing that keeps me healthy. Yet I have three small children at home and I want them to grow up loving food as I always have. The book is very marketable because it's something everybody wants to know – how they can eat well but be healthy. I am proof that it works. I have chronic heart failure but I have no symptoms at all. Journalists know that it's a story that people want to read.

I soon realized that when I did some PR, I'd sell books. I'd stop the PR, the sales would stop. It's that black and white. If I do a radio interview, the counter thing showing hits on my website will be racking up; then it will slow down and by day four, it will have finished if I haven't done any more PR. And whether you're selling on Amazon or through your own website, you can see immediately the response that you are having to different campaigns.

I had to be very pro-active keeping up to date with my press releases. I'd look at the number of books I had in stock, see there were only a few hundred and think that I should slow down on the
(Contd)

publicity front a bit until I got some more printed. And then, when there were enough in the garage, I'd do another news item.

That's the other thing that people don't always realize. People who self-publish and need to promote their book mustn't feel embarrassed about getting in touch with the media. Remember that journalists need stories; so just give them what they want! There's nothing to be embarrassed about at all. That's one thing I learned – to be pro-active on your publicity. Constantly.

I wanted to get the book in Waterstone's so I phoned their head office and spoke to the person who deals with independent publishers, which is what you are if you self-publish. He told me they couldn't even consider it, let alone stock it, unless I went through their supplier, Gardners. So I phoned up Gardners, sent my contact there the book, kept badgering him but couldn't get anywhere. Then I found out he was going to be at the London Book Fair so I told him I'd find him and prod him in the back with a pink fluffy pen to make sure he would remember me. Sure enough, I went to London, went to the Book Fair, found him and prodded him with the pen. The next week, I rang him and yes, he remembered me! However you have to do it, you have to make proper contact with these people. There's a whole host of books out there. They will only know about yours if they listen to you and in order for them to listen to you, you have to get in under their skin. They were now listening to me. I then got back in touch with the man at Waterstone's, told him the fluffy pen story and said Gardners wanted to stock my book. I then told Gardners that Waterstone's wanted to stock my book...finally, Gardners said I could send 50 of my books.

I went into my local Waterstone's, and said I wanted to do a book signing event which they agreed to. So immediately, Gardners had an order for those 50 books. Gardners came back to me and said they'd need another 50. Make it a 100, I said, I'm doing a book signing in Nottingham where I grew up. OK. Next phone call, send 200 because I've got a news item coming out. So I just kept chipping away at it until it got put into the Waterstone's system;

not because they wanted it, they didn't, but because there was a demand for it. As a self-publisher, you are in charge of creating your own demand and the booksellers and distributors will look at it because they have to.

Bookshops love events. When I did the signing in my local Waterstone's, I took in a few bits of food and we made quite an event of it. I just invited all my friends because I didn't know if anyone would turn up! We sold a few but, more importantly, it meant that I was able to have a poster in the shop window for a few days leading up to the event which increased people's awareness of the book. They also put the book at the front of the shop so shoppers could see what was being talked about. Booksellers are very open and they love anything local. So authors must go into their local bookshop and ask if they can do an event. Then it's a case of contacting local radio, local newspapers, making sure they cover it when it comes out and just create as much hoo-ha as possible. It's all about building a story. You write a book; you know you want to sell it. A journalist doesn't want to help you sell a book; they want a human interest story. So, if you've got a book that you want to sell, it helps that if alongside it you've got a story that the journalist can write about.

I didn't make money myself from the first book (the proceeds went to the BHF charity) but then that wasn't my intention. I covered my expenses, such as cost of the book, the postage; I wasn't out of pocket or anything. I did intend, however, to use the book as a stepping stone to get back to work. I decided early on to concentrate on the food and I wanted to do something cheery and positive because all people ever wanted to talk about were my heart attacks and I wanted to move on. So it wasn't completely selfless because I was using it as a vehicle to help me move on. And it's worked.

Someone I know told me her sister's friend, who lives in Austria, has my book. I don't know the sister or the friend so I have no idea how the book got there. Another friend was in New Zealand and found himself talking to someone who was trying to order a Sally
(Contd)

Bee book. The book is definitely out there! It's amazing where your books end up.

The order from the White House came out of the blue. At first, I thought it was the White House café in Keyworth where my mum lived. But it was the *White House in Washington DC. I immediately sent a press release out saying 12 books had been ordered by the White House. I am now in touch with the First Lady's office about going over so it has worked brilliantly.*

I put the press release out and the newspapers picked it up big time. I was quite happily tootling along with the story and having a bit of fun. Then I started to get phone calls and emails from publishers and agents, asking me to meet with them. I found out that my book had reached number one on Amazon in the cookery section; I knew I was selling lots of books but I thought you had to sell something like 50,000 for it to be considered a success. You don't. If an unknown first book sells 3,000, it's deemed a success. I had no idea. I thought I was doing small fry but I was up to eight or nine thousand by this stage.

When I first had the idea for the book, I'd gone round agents and publishers to see if they were interested but nobody was. I'm so stubborn. I felt that if they didn't want to talk to me before, why should I talk to them now? I'd done very well, thank you, and I'd just go and publish my next book on my own again. But then I had a call from this one literary agent. I was really busy when she rang but she promised to be quick. She had three children like me; she didn't mess about; she understood I was busy and got to the point. She asked to represent me and find me and my books a really good home. She said she wouldn't get me the biggest advance but that if I wanted a career out of this, she could really help. I really liked her and got on with her. And so, over the phone, before even meeting her, I said 'OK, let's do it.'

I was in the enviable position then of people chasing me and I think that's the position you have to be in, to be able to pick and choose. I was in a very different position now. In the past, when

I'd been knocking on the doors of agents and publishers with ideas for books I wanted to write, it was impossible. Now, they invited me in; they wanted to see me. Clare, my agent, got a meeting with HarperCollins. I was very cool at first because I knew I had a proven sales record. I had the attitude that I didn't need them; they needed me. Actually, since then I have realized that I do need them but at that time, I was quite happy with the way things were.

HarperCollins is definitely the best home for me. They identified with me about building a brand, which I'm very interested in. I have a very clearly defined idea of how I want my next five years to be. I know that I don't want to work for years and years because I won't be able to. Now is my time. My twenties were spent having fun and working; my thirties were spent having babies and heart attacks; now in my forties, I'm in the best health that I'm ever going to be, my children are old enough; who knows what the future holds for me healthwise so I know I've got a five-year window where I want to work.

What HarperCollins offered me was support for that plan. They would take this book on, relaunch it and make it better. Then we would do another book after that. They promised me that as long as the book was successful I would have a home with them for five years and we'd build the brand together.

I love working with an editor because I've become a better writer. She makes me justify and quantify everything. I love the fact that she hasn't messed with any of my creative writing but she has asked questions of me about what I had written ('Why did you finish it that way? I felt I was left hanging at this part' that kind of thing). I haven't necessarily changed those things but it has made me think about how I write. My editor is a person whose opinions I do listen to because I trust her judgement.

Also, as far as recipe writing goes, I have full support from the publisher. So I write my recipes and other people come along and do all the technical stuff; for instance, the book has had to be

(Contd)

Americanized because it's going to be sold there, they've done all that. They paid a fantastic photographer to do the food pictures, the family pictures and the cover shot. They didn't give a huge advance but they have invested a lot of time and money in the project which my agent says is the best way. I've had input on the design and I've enjoyed everything they've thrown at me. So, I love having the support, having worked on my own for so long.

But I am also glad that I self-published first. I had a very clear idea of how I want to appear and present myself and my book. I've been able to prove that it works because I self-published. The good bits about self-publishing are that I have been able to have the courage of my convictions and it was under my control. I haven't waited for anyone else; I've done things when it's been right for me to do them. It's a great achievement, I feel. I've published my own book.

10 THINGS TO REMEMBER

1. Retailers and wholesalers get high discounts (up to 60 per cent) off books from publishers.

2. Books are taken on a sale or return policy.

3. Most books tend to sell well in their first year of publication. Sales of adult hardback fiction and paperback titles have peaked by around three months. Sales for non-fiction hardback and paperback fiction written by well-known authors last longer.

4. A lot of new titles come out in October–November; the New Year is relatively quiet for book sales so it can be a good time for new authors and self-publishers to bring out a book. There is less competition.

5. The big bookstores look at an author's track record, support from the publisher, the market context, pricing and the cover. A book's actual contents and quality of writing are not key considerations when deciding whether to stock a book or not.

6. While it is hard to get your book physically stocked by a wholesaler or retailer, you can get it added to their catalogues if your book is listed on Nielsen's BookData.

7. November and December are the busiest months for wholesalers and distributors so avoid this time of the year if you are trying to get a response about getting your book stocked.

8. All books that have an ISBN will appear on Amazon.

9. Joining the Amazon Advantage programme means that they will hold your book in stock and make it available for next-day delivery.

10. If your publisher wants to remainder your books or you need to clear storage space and you want to get rid of some of your self-published books, consider giving them to charity rather than throwing them away.

10
Being a writer

In this chapter you will learn:
- *about earning money*
- *the discipline of writing*
- *about writing as a business.*

> *I never had any doubts about my abilities. I knew I could write. I just had to figure out how to eat while doing this.*
>
> Cormac McCarthy, author

Being able to sustain yourself as a writer is just as important as being able to write well. In this chapter, we will look at what you need to help you keep writing and publishing books.

Should you give up your day job when you successfully publish a book? Writing is not well paid so if you want to do it again, you will need an income and be able to pay the bills while you write. While publishers and agents would love you to devote all your time to writing your next work for them, they are not keen on the idea of needy authors. You need to be self-sustaining and practical in your approach to your writing career.

> *I think authors like J.K. Rowling and Dan Brown have done us all a disservice in some ways because people do perceive book sales in huge terms. Someone who works with my partner saw* The Xmas Factor *for sale in a supermarket and commented that the royalties must be rolling in. A lot of people have this belief that it's an easy way of making money. Book-writing has never been a*

guarantee of making money. It's like acting; there are a handful of people who are making a living out of it.

Annie Ashworth, author
www.anniesanders.co.uk

You need a substantial financial cushion behind you if you want to do this full-time. Forget the articles in newspapers and magazines about six- and seven-figure advances for books; the majority of writers do *not* make huge amounts of money. The top 10 per cent of authors earn more than 50 per cent of the total income earned by authors. In 2007, a survey by the Authors' Licensing and Collecting Society found that a UK author's average earnings were around £16,500 a year but typical earnings were more likely to be £4,000.

Even if you are paid a handsome advance for your book, you will not receive that amount as a lump sum. It will be paid out over a period of time (minus any agent's commission and income tax) and, as you must always remind yourself, is not a grant but an advance against any royalties earned on the book. There is always the chance that the book will not go on to earn its advance and that will be the only amount of money earned from that title.

Ideally, you should not go into this for the money. The main reward should come from creating something and then seeing your work in print. At least to start with, regard it as a part-time job.

Contrary to what you read in the newspapers, the vast majority of authors don't earn big advances and it can be hard for writers to earn a living just from writing. Some do, of course, from literary novelists such as Ian McEwan to John Grisham, but people seem to get the impression that it's more common than it actually is. What people also don't realize is that even if the advance is relatively modest, say £5,000, publishers can still lose on that. Even if the book sells a decent amount of hardbacks and paperbacks and earns that advance, by the time you have taken off overheads and the cost of distribution, marketing, production and returns, the publisher could well have lost a great deal more than that. Most publishers will also have big unearned advances – i.e. books they have overpaid for. That's partly the nature of the business; it is a gamble and sometimes you get it wrong, sometimes you get it right.

Carole Welch, Publishing Director, Sceptre
www.hodder.co.uk

Income and expenditure records

You need to declare everything you earn; even if it isn't much to start with. Initially, your outgoings may exceed your income as a writer. If you do not need to have a full- or part-time job to support your writing, you could register as self-employed and claim tax rebates against certain expenses. If that is the case, keep a record of transactions and receipts so you can claim; estimates will not be acceptable. It will be up to you to declare your income and expenses.

Allowable expenses are those incurred wholly and exclusively for business purposes. Revenue & Customs makes a distinction between 'capital allowances' and 'expenses'.

Capital allowances include:

- *computers*
- *fax machines*
- *photocopiers, etc.*

Expenses (i.e. the outlay involved in the day-to-day running of your writing business) include:

- *proofreading, typing, researching*
- *stationery*
- *printing*
- *postage*
- *telephone calls, faxes*
- *subscriptions to societies and associations (e.g. Society of Authors)*

- *advertising*
- *travel (meeting with agent, publisher, interviews, research, etc.); use of car/taxis for your writing*
- *accountancy*
- *working from home: a percentage of heating, lighting, etc. (but do take advice on this as it could affect your home's exemption from certain tax liabilities).*

Ideally what you'd like for non-fiction is for the book to go into a second or third edition because it's a nice revenue stream; and revising books for second and third editions isn't nearly as onerous as writing the book in the first place.

Todd Armstrong Senior Acquisitions Editor, Communications and Media Studies,
SAGE Publications www.sagepub.com

Royalty statements

Royalty statements are not easy to read, let alone understand. Even the publishers admit that. It does not help that they are linked to computer programmes that produce the information. It is high time that someone came up with a programme, used by all the major publishers, that produced straightforward, clear and easy-to-read statements. No one is trying to hide information from you deliberately, but do not be surprised when you struggle to make sense of what it is telling you.

If there are figures that you do not understand, contact the royalty department of your publisher and ask them to clarify things. If you have an agent, you can ask them to explain what the figures mean.

Send a query (email is probably best) clearly stating what points you would like clarified. Keep to the point and be polite.

An author is paid when a retailer buys a book. However, if that book is returned (because the bookshop did not manage to sell it to a customer) it will affect the next royalty statement. If the returns are greater than the sales, the royalty statement could show a negative. It does not mean that the author has to return the money from the previous statement.

Royalty statements are sent out either every six months or once a year. Payments are usually made within three months of the statement date. Make sure that the payments are received; if not, contact the royalty department.

If you have a literary agent, you will receive your royalty cheque from them. They will also list any charges that they have incurred as your representative; it may be that the agreement with the agency states that the author will cover the cost of postage for the manuscript. This should be agreed when you are taken on by an agent. If there is anything on the list of fees that you do not understand or feel should not have been charged to you, discuss it with your agent immediately.

> *Luckily, I am not the main breadwinner; otherwise I would still be doing my job as a research professional and writing in the spare time that it allowed, which is what I did the year before I had my first child. I worked three or four days a week and then wrote the other days of the week. I'm hoping that the writing will bring in enough money to let us have luxuries; you know, pay for a holiday or two, maybe get the downstairs toilet redecorated, buy a new oven, that sort of thing. I'm not expecting to be able to buy a castle in the Scottish Highlands.*
>
> Bryony Pearce, author
www.bryonypearce.co.uk

ALCS (UK)/Authors Registry (US)

The ALCS/Authors Registry manages the collective rights for writers, making sure that they are compensated if their work is copied, broadcast or recorded either at home or abroad.

You need to register with the ALCS/Authors Registry to get a share of royalties that relate to any scanning/photocopying or use of your (copyrighted) printed words.

These organizations collect payments for photocopying and other similar uses of copyrighted works, carried out under national blanket licensing systems. Each organization charges a commission for payments distributed (currently 9.5 per cent for members for ALCS and 5 per cent for the Authors Registry).

Go to www.alcs.co.uk or www.authorsregistry.org for further information.

For photography and artwork, register with DACS (www.dacs.co.uk).

Writers' unions

The two main organizations in the UK are the Society of Authors and the Writers' Guild. They describe themselves as trade unions for writers. The Society is specifically for writers while the Guild represents writers who work in broadcast media.

For a relatively inexpensive subscription, the Society offers a lot to the writer. You can join the Society only if you are a published author (including self-published for profit) or have an offer of a publishing contract. They will read through a contract and provide free advice on negotiating any changes; they produce a quarterly publication, *The Author*, full of useful articles and updates on the publishing world. They also produce a range of *Quick Guides* (covering a range of subjects: copyright, moral rights, permissions, literary agents, etc.), which members can download for free and they hold different events and seminars throughout the year. For more details, go to www.societyofauthors.org. The Authors Guild in the US (www.authorsguild.org) performs the same function as the Society.

Be versatile

The main source of new books is a publishing house's existing authors. A reliable writer who has a proven track record of titles that sell is a valuable asset to both agent and publisher. It is only when you become really successful as an author that you become a recognizable brand; in other words, readers know exactly what they are getting when a new book by Dan Brown or Clive Cussler comes out. Fans of writers like that probably don't even bother to read the blurb on the back of the book; they know the brand, they know they like it and so they will buy it.

Until you get to that level, try to be versatile with your writing. You have successfully published one book but be open to experimenting with your ideas and style. Continue to read widely and expose yourself to new writers and new genres. It may open up new avenues for you to try.

Discipline

Waiting for inspiration to strike is not the road to getting published. You need to have a discipline and structure in place to help you write. Set aside time to write and regard it not as a hobby, but as a job of work. You have to be ruthless with yourself and your available time.

Tips on maintaining discipline
- ▶ *Avoid procrastination, answering emails, buying things from internet sites that you don't really need.*
- ▶ *Practise self-discipline – don't answer the phone or the doorbell when you are writing.*
- ▶ *Set yourself a target of a certain number of words before you can either get up and have a cup of tea or stop work for the day. Like exercise, you can start with a modest goal, perhaps a few hundred words, and gradually increase the number.*

- *Find a place to write. Harriet Goodwin, for example, has a rather nice shed in the garden as her writing space. J.K. Rowling famously wrote the first Harry Potter book in a café. It does not matter where you choose to write – the space in your head is what counts – but you need to feel comfortable in order to get to that place.*
- *Work out **when** you can write – most writers have an optimum time of day when they can write. Make sure you take advantage of that time. If you cannot choose a time, experiment to find out when you are at your most creative and can concentrate (the hour before everyone else in the house gets up; the hour after they've gone to bed; during school hours). Get the time right and you can be most productive in a short space of time, rather than staring at a computer screen or sharpening pencils.*
- *Practise – and aim to get your words into print, even if it is just in the local church newsletter.*

Writer's block

You don't hear about 'nurse's block' or 'accountant's block' so why should writers be any different? If writing is your business, you cannot afford the luxury of 'writer's block'.

Writer's block is often all about having a bad day rather than not being creative. So don't think of it as a 'block'; think of it as a challenge that you will overcome. You may need to experiment to find a strategy that will help you remove that block.

Tips on writer's block
- *Consider the problem, write down a few questions – then leave it alone overnight or for a couple of days. Don't think about it. Then, look at the questions and write down the first thing that comes into your head. Very often this can produce the answers you were looking for.*
- *Rewrite your last page to pick up the momentum again.*

(Contd)

- ▶ Don't stare at a blank screen or page; write anything down – you can always delete it the next day.
- ▶ If you have an agent/editor, talk to them; if you don't, talk to a friend.
- ▶ Go for a walk or do something mindless and let your mind wander while you do it.
- ▶ It can be important to stop at the right place; picking up the narrative the next day or whenever you get back to your work can be made easy or difficult depending on where you leave it.

Tools of the trade

Carpenters have their chisels, planes and rasps, chefs have their favourite knives. Whatever the profession, we all have tools of the trade that help us to do our job. Writers are no different.

Always have something to write on wherever you are so you can scribble down a thought or an observation when it strikes you.

Jacqueline Wilson writes her books in longhand into notebooks, only typing them up on the computer when she's finished. Frederick Forsyth reputedly bought the whole stock of a certain type of paper he favoured when the company that produced it went out of business.

Whether you have embraced the computer age or prefer to write longhand at first, make sure you are comfortable with what you write on. If you are working on a computer:

- ▶ *back up your work*
- ▶ *keep up to date with anti-virus/anti-spam protection*
- ▶ *and...back up your work!*

Insight
Don't share the computer with anyone. A rearranged desktop can throw you and there is a danger that you could lose your

work to an accidental delete or virus. One writer writes on a laptop without internet or email to minimize the risk.

A writer's tools also include a desk or table and something to sit on. Unless you can happily write on the bus or in a café, you need to make sure that your work station is set up to help protect your back, neck and arms. Even if you work from home, set up your work area professionally and be comfortable at the same time.

If you are using a computer:

- *make sure your arms are at a relaxed 90-degree angle*
- *the top of the monitor screen should be at eye level*
- *the monitor should be at arm's length*
- *feet should be flat on the floor.*

Support network

AA – I always think it's quite funny when you email an author how quickly you get a response. Every writer is just dying for someone to divert them. When that little symbol pops up on your computer, you just have to deal with it!

MS – Yes, they're all on Twitter wasting the day. You do have to ring-fence some time and make it your job – even if you are doing another job as so many authors have to.

Annie Ashworth and Meg Sanders, authors who write as Annie Sanders

www.anniesanders.co.uk

Family and friends are important for a writer. They are your support network but they also need to know when to leave you alone. Draw up some guidelines as to when you can or cannot be disturbed when you are writing.

Writing is a solitary business so it is good to have a network of people around you that you can talk to, interact with and bounce ideas off. Friends are especially useful if you are having a hard time with your writing; everyone needs buoying up and encouraging.

Age

At a publishing workshop, there were a couple of questions from writers worried that they were no longer young and therefore concerned that publishers might think they were too old and not worth investing in.

The answers from agents and editors were encouraging. They felt that it is hard to write about a range of people and their emotions when you are very young; it is much easier when you are 60. Mary Wesley had her first adult novel published when she was 71; she went on to have 10 bestsellers and sold over 3 million copies of her books. Angela Waller and Mo Smith, interviewed for this book, would be the first to admit that they were not in the first flush of youth when they self-published their books. Readers enjoy good books, regardless of the age of the writer. Publishers are looking for authors who can say something and be promoted – age does not come into that.

> *My motivation has never come from how much money I might make; as long as I had sufficient funds to pay for the printing costs that was all that mattered. For me, it is a hobby that I love and an opportunity to promote my recipes to the public at large. But you've got to enjoy it, otherwise you'd give up. Sometimes I think I must be mad, as I make my way to give a talk with heavy boxes of books to transport, it's pouring with rain and I've got to find my way down dark country lanes, but after my talk follows a grateful and enthusiastic vote of thanks and a round of applause. My spirits are lifted and I'm eager for the next assignment. Take it from me, if you have complete confidence in your work, give self-publishing a go.*
>
> Mo Smith, author
> www.lazycookmosmith.co.uk

Conclusion

You are a writer because you write, not because you have been published. Nigel Watts, author of *Write a Novel And Get it Published*, talks about the importance of writing for love, not money: 'If your first goal is to be published, such ambition will likely taint what you are writing and ironically reduce your chances of a sale.'

So write for yourself first and foremost; write because you have to. Mastering the techniques of that craft and improving your writing talent should be the goal of every writer. If you do that, then you can think about getting your book published. In order to see your book in print, you will need hard work, determination, perseverance and a dose of good luck. Sometimes it seems that the odds are stacked against you. The only sensible thing you can do is to write because you love writing. Write the kind of book you would pay good money for.

Case study

Harriet Goodwin, author, *The Boy Who Fell Down Exit 43*; *The Extraordinary Legacy of Elvira Phoenix* (2011); *The Hex Factor* (Stripes) www.harrietgoodwinbooks.com

I think I had always known that I could write – but up until a few years ago I didn't have the spark of a fantastic premise. I have four children and am also a professional singer, so I had my work cut out juggling things as it was.

Then, just two weeks after having my fourth child, I had a dream. I dreamt that a boy crashed through the surface of the earth and fell down a tunnel into a ghostly Underworld populated by a colourful collection of spirits. The tunnel (which I somehow knew was called an 'Exit' – a connecting place between the worlds of the Living and the Dead) was ringed with golden ladders and peppered with

(Contd)

luminous green algae. In the morning I remembered the dream and scribbled the gist of it down on a piece of paper.

Dreams usually fade – but this one didn't. It wasn't in the least bit bothered that I had a new baby and that time and energy were in very short supply. It seemed to be telling me, 'Here you are – here's your idea. Sit down and write!' And so I did!

At first I managed only ten minutes each day. I didn't know how to use a computer back then, so wrote in longhand. I still have the A4 notebooks in which I wrote the first draft, and very much enjoy showing these off when I go on school visits.

After about eight months of writing, which I did completely in secret, I decided to find out whether or not what I had written was any good – so I sent the manuscript to Cornerstones, the London-based literary consultancy.

I got back a nine-page report; they had read it really thoroughly. The first thing they said in the accompanying letter was that I shouldn't leap straight into revision, that I should put the manuscript away for six weeks and let things mulch around in my head. There were also some suggested areas of reading at the end of the report, including Teach Yourself How to Write a Blockbuster *(the only 'how to' book I actually read).* This book explained all sorts of techniques which I had never come across by name before (e.g. 'show don't tell') and learning about them was extremely useful.*

The report was positive but I am immensely self-critical, and once I started the revision process I set about ripping my manuscript to shreds! I rewrote whole chapters and let nothing slip through the net. The characters were developed; the plot became more streamlined; wherever I found a 'was' or a 'were', I tried to replace it with a strong verb. Suddenly the writing was springing off the page – and it was incredibly exciting.

*Now called *Write a Blockbuster And Get it Published*

I spent four or five months revising and then thought 'What next?' I knew that one option was to send the manuscript back to Cornerstones for another report, but decided to put the whole thing on hold over the summer holidays. Towards the end of the summer an email came through from Cornerstones about a fiction competition that was being run by the SCBWI. The sensible part of my brain told me that I couldn't possibly be ready for a writing competition yet and that I shouldn't leap into things too quickly. But a nagging little voice in the back of my mind said, 'Just put it in the post and forget about it!' And that is exactly what I did.

It turned out to be one of the best decisions I ever made – because six weeks later I had a phone call telling me I had been chosen as one of the winners of the competition. In the days that followed I received interest from several literary agents and remember having a conversation about the possibility of one of them representing me, with my two younger children having a major Lego fight in the background. In the end, I signed with Sarah Davies of the Greenhouse Literary Agency: I liked her immediately when we met up in London and felt she really clicked with my book.

Sarah wanted revisions – many of which were going to take a lot of thought. But it all came together gradually and I began to see that the book that was now emerging was a hundred times stronger than the old one.

Once I had revised it, The Boy Who Fell Down Exit 43 *was submitted to various publishers and Stripes bought it in a two-book deal.*

So far, I have found the editing process to be pretty relaxed. I know it's not like this for all authors – but it yields fantastic results for me, since I never have the sense that a knife is being held to my throat. I am now revising the second book and have just got a deal for a third, The Hex Factor, *also with Stripes. I receive my advances in parts: on signature of contract, on delivery of manuscript and upon publication.*

(Contd)

All my own children are now at school, so I write in my shed at the top of the garden between 9 and 3 when there's a bit of peace and quiet. And as well as that there's all the publicity...

When I met the Stripes team for the first time, I had to fill out a questionnaire so that they could find out whether or not I was willing to talk to schools and do interviews on the radio and TV, etc. Writing can be a very solitary occupation – so I'm always more than happy to come out of my shed and publicize my books in whatever way I can. In the beginning, my publishing team sorted me out with an intensive launch week, during which I went round six or seven schools. Now I organize the school visits myself and thoroughly enjoy them. I make sure that a letter goes out to parents before my visits, so that children have the chance to buy a book and have it signed. I am also responsible for bringing in a stock of books myself. There's a lot of organizing involved!

I've been in touch with the media too. Because I live on the border of Staffordshire and Shropshire I have been featured in both counties' magazines – and was also recently interviewed by the Guardian. Since The Boy Who Fell Down Exit 43 *was shortlisted for the Blue Peter Book Awards 2010, I have had a great deal of other media interest, and will be speaking on a panel at the Oxford Literary Festival.*

I'm really glad that I invested in a website. Someone else designed it for me and I sorted out the text. It's a great tool: it means that children can leave messages on the site and that I can reply to them. I run frequent competitions and have a page of Exit Numbers Around The World which has really excited my readers' imaginations (I bet you didn't know that Exit 35,006 is behind the biggest rollercoaster in Blackpool – or that there is an Exit in the middle of Dubai?!) The website also means that schools and libraries can get in touch with me quickly and efficiently.

I didn't write to get published. I wrote because I had a dream that just wouldn't let me go. And what a dream it turned out to be!

10 THINGS TO REMEMBER

1 *If you are planning to claim writing expenses against tax, keep all your receipts.*

2 *Royalty statements are issued either every six months or once a year; payments are usually made within three months of the statement date.*

3 *The ALCS/Authors Registry collects payments for photocopying and other use of an author's written work.*

4 *Join a writer's union (Society of Authors, Writers' Guild).*

5 *No other profession suffers from a 'block' so why should writers? Just call it having a bad day.*

6 *Be comfortable with what you write on (paper or computer).*

7 *Always back up your work on computer; never have just one copy of your work.*

8 *Your work station (table, chair) should be comfortable: arms should be at a 90-degree angle; top of the monitor should be at eye level.*

9 *Have a support network of family and friends around you; but make sure they know when to leave you alone if you're working.*

10 *Publishers want authors who write well and have got something to say; it's never too late to start writing.*

Appendix

A & C Black
www.acblack.com
36 Soho Square
London W1D 3QY
t: 020 7758 0200

Agency for the Legal Deposit Libraries
www.legaldeposit.org.uk
161 Causewayside
Edinburgh
Operates on behalf of the Bodleian Library, Cambridge University Library, National Library of Scotland, Library of Trinity College, Dublin and National Library of Wales

ALCS (Authors' Licensing and Collecting Society)
www.alcs.co.uk
The Writers' House
13 Haydon Street
London
EC3N 1DB
t: 020 7264 5700
f: 020 7264 5755
e: alcs@alcs.co.uk

Alliance of Literary Societies
www.sndc.demon.co.uk/als.htm

Amazon
www.amazon.co.uk/www.amazon.com

Author Central –
authorcentral.amazon.co.uk/authorcentral.amazon.com
Amazon Advantage –
advantage.amazon.co.uk/advantage.amazon.com

American Booksellers Association (ABA)
www.bookweb.org
200 White Plains Road
Suite 600
Tarrytown, NY 10591
t: 800 637 0037
e: info@bookweb.org

American Society for Indexing
www.asindexing.org

The American Society of Picture Professionals
www.aspp.com
117 S Saint Asaph Street
Alexandria, VA 22314
t: 703 299 0219
f: 703 299 9910

Arts Council (England)
www.artscouncil.org.uk
14 Great Peter Street
London SW1P 3NQ
t: 0845 300 6200
f: 01619 344426

Askews Library Services (UK)
www.askews.co.uk
218–222 North Road
Preston PR1 1SY
t: 01772 555947

Association of American Publishers (AAP)
Washington DC Office
Association of American Publishers, Inc.
50 F Street, NW
4th Floor
Washington, DC 20001
t: 202 347 3375
f: 202 347 3690

New York Office
Association of American
  Publishers, Inc.
71 Fifth Avenue, 2nd floor
New York, NY 10003
t: 212 255 0200
f: 212 255 7007

Association of Authors' Agents
www.agentsassoc.co.uk
David Higham Associates Ltd
5–8 Lower John Street
Golden Square
London W1F 9HA
t: 020 7434 5900

Association of Authors' Representatives (US)
www.aaronline.org
676-A 9th Ave, Suite 312
New York, NY 10036
t: 212 840 5770

Association of Illustrators
www.theaoi.com
2nd Floor, Back Building
150 Curtain Road
London EC2A 3AT
t: 020 7613 4328
e: info@theaoi.com

Authors Guild (US)
www.authorsguild.org
31 East 32nd Street, 7th Floor
New York, NY 10016
t: 212 563 5904
f: 212 564 5363
e: staff@authorsguild.org

Authors Registry (US)
www.authorsregistry.org
e: staff@authorsregistry.org

Baker & Taylor (US)
www.baker-taylor.com

Barnes & Noble (US)
www.barnesandnoble.com
The Small Press Department
Barnes & Noble, Inc.
122 Fifth Ave
New York, NY 10011

Bertram Books (UK)
www.bertrams.com
t: (new publisher enquiries) 0871 803 6666

Bibliographic Data Services Ltd
www.bibliographicdata.com
Publisher Liaison Department
Annadale House
The Crichton
Bankend Road
Dumfries DG1 4TA
t: 01387 702251

Blackwell – library services (UK/US)
www.blackwell.com
Beaver House
Hythe Bridge St
Oxford OX1 2ET
t: 01865 333000
100 University Court
Blackwood, N J 08012
t: 800 257 7341

Book fairs
Beijing   www.bibf.net
Bologna (children's book fair)   www.bookfair.bolognafiere.it/en
Frankfurt   www.frankfurt-book-fair.com
London   www.londonbookfair.co.uk
US   www.bookexpoamerica.com

Bookbrunch (UK)
www.bookbrunch.co.uk
e: subscriptions@bookbrunch.co.uk

Bookpoint Ltd (distributor)
www.bookpoint.hachette-livreuk.com
130 Milton Park
Abingdon OX14 4SB
t: 01235 400400

The Bookseller (UK)
www.thebookseller.com

Booksellers Association (BA)
www.booksellers.org.uk
t: 020 7802 0802
e: mail@booksellers.org.uk

Bowker
www.bowker.com
121 Chanion Road
New Providence, NJ 07974
t: 908 665 6770
toll free: 877 310 7333
To register your title in Books in Print, go to www.bowkerlink.com.
You will need an ISBN before you can register your details.

British Association of Picture Libraries and Agencies (BAPLA)
www.bapla.org.uk

British Fantasy Society
www.britishfantasysociety.org.uk

British Library
Legal Deposit Office
Boston Spa
Wetherby
West Yorkshire LS23 7BY
t: 01937 546268 (monographs)
01937 546267 (serials)
f: 01937 546176
e: legal-deposit-books@bl.uk

Chartered Institute of Library & Information Professionals – CILIP (UK)
www.cilip.org.uk
7 Ridgmount Street
London WC1E 7AE
t: 020 7255 0500
e: info@cilip.org.uk

Chevron Publishing (UK)
www.chevronpublishing.co.uk
PO Box 2240
Pulborough
West Sussex RH20 9AL
t: 01903 744333
e: info@chevronpublishing.co.uk

The Children's Writers & Illustrators Group (CWIG)
c/o The Society of Authors (address below)

Cornerstones Literary Agency (UK)
www.cornerstones.co.uk
Milk Studios
34 Southern Row
London W10 5AN
t: 020 8968 0777
e: helen@cornerstones.co.uk/kathryn@cornerstones.co.uk

The Copyright Libraries Agency
100 Euston Street
London NW1 2HQ
t: 020 7388 5061

Copyright Licensing Agency Ltd (CLA)
www.cla.co.uk
Saffron House
6–10 Kirby Street
London EC1N 8TS
t: 020 7400 3100
f: 020 7400 3101
e: cla@cla.co.uk

Coutts Library Services (UK/US)
www.couttsinfo.com
Avon House
Headlands Business Park
Ringwood
Hampshire BH24 3PB
t: 01425 471160
e: salesuk@couttsinfo.com
1823 Maryland Avenue
PO Box 1000
Niagara Falls, NY 14302-1000
t: 800 263 1686
e: salesus@couttsinfo.com

Crime Writers' Association
www.thecwa.co.uk
e: info@thecwa.co.uk

Curtis Brown (UK/US)
www.curtisbrown.co.uk/www.curtisbrown.com
Haymarket House
28–29 Haymarket
London SW1Y 4SP
t: 020 7393 4400
f: 020 7393 4401

10 Astor Place
New York, NY 10003
t: 212 473 5400
f: 212 598 0917

Federation of Children's Book Groups (UK)
www.fcbg.org.uk
t: 01132 588910
e: info@fcbg.org.uk

Gardners
www.gardners.com
1 Whittle Drive
Eastbourne
East Sussex BN23 6QH
e: (small publisher helpline) sph@gardners.com

GBS – Grantham Book Services (distributors)
www.granthambookservices.co.uk
Trent Road
Grantham NG31 7WQ
t: 01476 541000

The Greenhouse Literary Agency
www.greenhouseliterary.com
t: Sarah Davies (US) 703 865 4990
t: Julia Churchill (UK) 020 7841 3959
e: submissions@greenhouseliterary.com

GS1 (UK)
www.gs1uk.org
Staple Court
11 Staple Inn Buildings
London WC1V 7QH
t: 020 7092 3500
f: 020 7681 2290
e: support@gs1uk.org

hhb agency (UK)
www.hhbagency.com
6 Warwick Court
London WC1R 5DJ
t: 020 7405 5525

HarperCollins Children's Books (US)
www.harpercollinschildrens.com
10 East 53rd St
New York, NY 10022
t: 212 207 7000

Hilary Johnson Authors' Advisory Service
www.hilaryjohnson.demon.co.uk
1 Beechwood Court
Syderstone
Norfolk PE31 8TR
t: 01485 578594
e: enquiries@hilaryjohnson.com

Hodder
www.hodder.co.uk
338 Euston Road
London NW1 3BH
t: 020 7873 6000

Holt Jackson Book Company Ltd – library services (UK)
www.holtjackson.co.uk
Park Mill
Great George Street
Preston PR1 1TJ
t: 01772 298000
e: info@holtjackson.co.uk

The Hungerford Bookshop
www.hungerfordbooks.co.uk
24 High Street
Hungerford

Berkshire
RG17 0NF
t: 01488 683480

Independent Publishers Guild (UK)
www.ipg.uk.com
PO Box 12
Llain
Login SA34 0WU
t: 01437 563335
f: 01437 562071
e: info@ipg.uk.com

Ingram Book Company
www.ingrambook.com
One Ingram Blvd
La Vergne, TN 37086
t: 800 937 8200
e: customer.service@ingrambook.com

International Standard Book Numbers (ISBNs)
www.isbn.nielsenbookdata.co.uk (UK)
3rd Floor
Midas House
62 Goldsworth Road
Woking
GU21 6LQ
t: 0870 777 8712
f: 0870 777 8714
e: isbn.agency@nielsen.com

ISBN Agency (US)
www.ISBN.org
630 Central Avenue
New Providence, NJ 07974
t: 877 310 7333

IPG – Independent Publishers Group (US)
www.ipgbook.com
814 N Franklin St
Chicago, IL 60610
t: 312 227 0747 (trade or publisher enquiries)
e: mlozano@ipgbook.com
The IPG are linked to Small Press United, a distributor for start-up publishers and publishers with fewer than five titles.

John Murray Publishers (UK)
www.johnmurray.co.uk
338 Euston Road
London NW 3BH
t: 020 7873 6000
f: 020 7873 6446

Library of Congress Cataloguing in Publication
http://cip.loc.gov/cip/ecipp14.html
Registers your book for access by libraries and government archives.

The Literary Consultancy
www.literaryconsultancy.co.uk
Free Word Centre
60 Farringdon Road
London EC1R 3GA
t: 020 7324 2563
e: info@literaryconsultancy.co.uk

The Literary Market Place
www.literarymarketplace.com
Lists contact information for publishers, editors, literary agents.

Littlehampton Book Services
www.lbsltd.co.uk
Faraday Close
Worthing BN13 3RB
t: 01903 828500

National Association of Writers' Groups
www.nawg.co.uk
PO Box 3266
Stoke-on-Trent ST10 9BD
e: nawg@live.co.uk

National Union of Journalists – NUJ (UK)
www.nuj.org.uk
e: info@nuj.org.uk

National Writers Union (US)
www.nwu.org
113 University Place
6th Floor
New York, NY 10003
t: 212 254 0279
e: nwu@wu.org

Nielsen BookData (UK)
www.nielsenbookdata.co.uk
t: Publisher help desk – 0845 450 0016
e: pubhelp.book@nielsen.com

Nielsen BookScan (US)
Author enquiries – contact Brianna Buckley:
t: 646 654 4778
e: brianna.buckley@nielsen.com
Publisher enquiries – contact Dennis Halby:
t: 646 654 4765
e: dennis.halby@nielsen.com

Peters Bookselling Service (UK) – specializes in children's books
120 Bromsgrove Street
Birmingham B5 6RJ
t: 01216 666646
e: sales@peters-books.co.uk

The Picture Research Association
www.picture-research.org.uk
Box 105 Hampstead House
176 Finchley Road
London NW3
t: 07771 982308

Preface Publishing
www.prefacepublishing.co.uk
e: info@prefacepublishing.co.uk

Public Lending Right (PLR)
www.plr.co.uk
Richard House
Sorbonne Close
Stockton-on-Tees TS17 6DA
t: 01642 604699
f: 01642 615641

Publishing News
www.publishingnews.co.uk
39 Store Street
London WC1E 7DS

Romance Writers of America
www.rwanational.org

Romantic Novelists Association
www.rna-uk.org

SAGE
www.sagepub.com
SAGE Publications USA
2455 Teller road
Thousand Oaks, CA 91320
t: 805 499 0721
SAGE Publications UK
1 Oliver's Yard

55 City Road
London EC1Y 1SP
e: info@sagepub.com

Science Fiction & Fantasy Writers of America (US)
www.sfwa.org
5 Winding Brook Drive, #1B
Guilderland, NY 12084
t: 518 869 5361

Small Publishers of North America
www.spannet.org

Society of Authors (UK)
www.societyofauthors.org
84 Drayton Gardens
London SW10 9SB
t: 020 7373 6642

Society of Children's Book Writers and Illustrators (UK/US)
www.britishscbwi.org/www.scbwi.org
8271 Beverley Blvd
Los Angeles, CA 90048
t: 323 782 1010
f: 323 782 1892
e: scbwi@scbwi.org

Society for Editors & Proofreaders (UK)
www.sfep.org.uk
Erico House
93–99 Upper Richmond Road
Putney
London SW15 2TG
t: 020 8785 5617
f: 020 8785 5618
e: administration@sfep.org.uk

Society of Indexers
www.indexers.org.uk
Woodbourn Business Centre
10 Jessell Street
Sheffield S9 3HY
t: 0114 2 449561 or 0845 872 6807
f: 0114 2 449563
e: info@indexers.org.uk

Society of Women Writers & Journalists (SWWJ)
www.swwj.co.uk
27 Braycourt Avenue
Walton on Thames
Surrey KT12 2AZ
e: wendy@stickler.org.uk

TBS – The Book Service (distributors)
www.thebookservice.co.uk
Distribution Centre
Colchester Road
Frating Green
Colchester CO7 7DW
t: 01206 256000

Transworld Publishers
www.transworld-publishers.co.uk
61–63 Uxbridge Road
London W5 5SA
t: 020 8579 2653
f: 020 8579 5479
e: info@transworld-publishers.co.uk

UK Children's Books Directory
www.ukchildrensbooks.co.uk

US Copyright Office
www.copyright.gov
t: 202 707 5959

Waterstone's
www.waterstones.co.uk
Capital Court
Capital Interchange Way
Brentford TW8 0EX
t: 020 8742 3800
Peter North – Independent Publisher Coordinator
e: peter.north@waterstones.com

Watson-Guptill Publishers (US)
www.randomhouse.com/crown/watsonguptill
The Crown Publishing Group
1745 Broadway
New York, NY 10019
t: 212 782 9000

Western Writers of America
www.westernwriters.org
MSC06 3770
1 University of New Mexico
Albuquerque, NM 87131-0001
t: 505 277 5234

WordCounter
www.wordcounter.com
Highlights the most frequently used words in a given text.

The Word Pool
www.wordpool.co.uk
Children's book site with information on writing for children and a thriving discussion group for children's writers.

Working Partners (book packager)
www.workingpartnersltd.co.uk
Stanley House
St Chad's Place
London, WC1X 9HH

t: 020 7841 3939
f: 020 7841 3940
e: enquiries@workingpartnersltd.co.uk

Write4Kids.com (US)
www.write4kids.com

Writers' & Artists' Yearbook
A & C Black
36 Soho Square
London W1D 3QY
t: 020 7758 0200

Writers' Circles
www.writers-circles.com
39 Lincoln Way
Harlington
Bedfordshire LU5 6NG
t: 01525 873197
e: diana@writers-circles.com
Directory of writers' circles, courses and workshops. Free listings.

Writers' Guild of Great Britain
www.writers.org.uk/guild
15 Britannia Street
London WC1X 9JN
t: 020 7833 0777
f: 020 7833 4777
e: admin@writersguild.org.uk

Index

advances, *80, 94–5, 175*
age, *262*
agents, *2, 3, 5, 13–16*
    choosing, *22–4, 33–5*
    first meeting, *74–7*
Amazon, *177, 195–6, 221, 240–2*
auctions, *10–11*
author questionnaires, *186–7, 190*
Authors' Licensing and Collecting Society (ALCS), *91, 256–7*
Authors Registry, *91, 256–7*

backlists, *4*
barcodes, *104, 137*
binding, *127, 154*
blogging, *195, 199–202*
blurb, *149–50*
boilerplate agreements, *100*
book fairs, *18–19, 242*
book packagers, *12–13, 109–13*
Books in Print, *105*
bookshops, *204–8, 228–32*

Cataloguing in Publication (CIP), *105*
classifications, *102*
contracts, *92–100*
copy editing, *120–1, 145–6*
copyright, *88–91, 140, 178*
costs, *142–3*

cover design, *147–50*
covering letters, *40–3*

deadlines, *80, 118–19*
design, *125, 146–54*
digital rights management (DRM), *178*
discipline, *258–9*
discounting, *141, 220–1, 222, 229*
distribution, *128, 232–4*

earning money, *252–5*
ebooks and epublishing, *170–6*
editors, *9–10, 77–8, 119–24, 129*
end matter, *124, 152*

feedback, *69–70, 77, 121–3*
front matter, *124, 151*
frontlists, *4*

genres, *19–21*

illustrations, *94, 118, 153–4*
imprints, *2–3*
Independent Publishers Guild, *242–3*
indexes, *125, 146*
ISBN, *103–4, 137–8, 140*

libel, *100*
libraries, *105–6, 240*
literary consultants, *71–4*
literary festivals, *18, 68, 208–9*

moral rights, *91*

negotiation, *79, 87, 98–9*
networking, *68–9*
Nielsen BookData, *104–5, 236*

online sales, *221, 240–2*

payments, *80, 223–4, 225*
permissions, *94, 100–1*
plagiarism, *101–2*
presentation, *49–51, 117–18*
pricing, *141–3, 179–80, 226*
print on demand (POD), *156, 158–61, 176, 235*
printing, *127, 154–6*
production, *126–8*
promotional material, *187–9*
proofreading, *52, 124–5, 144, 152*
pseudonyms, *107–8*
Public Lending Right, *106–7*
publicity, *182–4*
    bookshops, *204–8*
    media, *189–204*
    self-publishing, *161–3*
publishing houses, *2–3, 5–12*
    choosing, *22–4, 33–5*
    offers from, *78–85*
    production, *119–29, 184–5*

readings, *70, 206, 210–11*
records, *224–5*
rejection, *61–6*
remaindering, *96, 243*
research, *16–18, 34*
rights, *80, 88, 96–7, 160*
    electronic, *175–6, 179*
    selling, *80, 129*
royalties, *95–6, 175, 255–6*

sales, *2, 128–9, 220–43*
Scribd, *173–4*
self-publishing, *136–69, 176–7*
    distribution, *236–8*
    sales, *223–5, 229–30, 232, 236–8*
social networking sites, *202–4*
Society of Authors, *257*
submissions, *35–53, 59–61*
supermarkets, *221, 228–30*
support network, *261–2*
synopsis, *44–9*

taxation, *254–5*
timing, *24–5, 116–17, 227–8*
titles, *42*
tools, *260–1*
typesetting, *127, 156–7*

vanity publishing, *157–8, 175*
versatility, *258*

websites, *195, 197–9*
wholesalers, *221, 234–8*
word count, *108*
writer's block, *259–60*
Writer's Guild, *257*
writing skills, *31, 66–7, 67*